The Coming Crisis
in Israel

2080

The MIT Press
Cambridge, Massachusetts, and London, England

The Coming Crisis
in Israel

Private Faith and Public Policy

Norman L. Zucker
with the assistance of
Naomi Flink Zucker

This book was set in Linotype Baskerville,
printed on Nashoba Eggshell,
and bound in Interlaken AVI-539 Matte
by The Colonial Press Inc.
in the United States of America.

Photographs for Chapters 1, 3, 4, 5, 10, 11, and 13 are reprinted
by courtesy of the Government Press Office,
State of Israel; those in Chapters 2, 6, 7, 8, 9, and 12,
by courtesy of the Embassy of Israel, Washington, D.C.

Library of Congress Cataloging in Publication Data

Zucker, Norman L
The coming crisis in Israel.

Bibliography: p.
1. Israel—Religion. 2. Judaism—Israel.
3. Religion and state—Israel. I. Title.
BM390.Z8   296.3′87′7095694   73–987
ISBN 0–262–24018–1

To Sara Deborah
and
George Samuel

בָּרוּךְ אַתָּה, יי, הַמַּבְדִּיל בֵּין קֹדֶשׁ לְחֹל.

Blessed art Thou, O Lord,
who hast made a distinction between
the sacred and the profane.

From the *Havdalah* prayer recited at the conclusion of Sabbaths and festivals.

Acknowledgments

Since 1958 when I first visited Israel and began thinking about this book, I have discussed it with many people, all of whom gave graciously and generously of their time and their thoughts. With each visit to Israel I accumulated more intellectual obligations, and to name all the Israelis who helped me, in one way or another, would be an impossible task. However, I want to thank specifically the following Israelis: High Court Justice Haim H. Cohn, Professor Menachem Elon, Rabbi Shlomo Goren, Professor Norman Greenwald, Yehuda Haffner, Professor Menachem Haran, Maurice A. Jaffe, Professor Isaiah Leibowitz, former Minister of Justice Dr. Pinchas Rosen, Minister of Religious Affairs Dr. Zerah Warhaftig, and Dr. Uri Yadin.

I am indebted to my friends Professors Martin Birnbach, the late Edward McNall Burns, and Allen Schick, and Rabbi Melvin Granatstein for reading and criticizing various sections of the manuscript. The late Dr. Nelson Glueck shared his views with me, and Dr. Max Gruenewald provided encouraging assistance at a crucial juncture.

The usual author's exculpation clause holds: no one named should be held responsible for the views, errors, or omissions of the book. In fact, many will vigorously disassociate themselves from some, if not all, of my conclusions. I hope on balance, however, that my presentation is scholarly and fair.

It is also a pleasure to acknowledge the financial assistance given to me by Tufts University Research Council, the Gustav Wurzweiler Foundation, Inc., the Penrose Fund of the American Philosophical Society, and the University of Rhode Island Research Committee. My research assistants, Barbara Pollack and Roberta Silverman Milman, faithfully filed notes and clippings, and Stephen Katzen helped in tracking down a variety of fugitive references. Mrs. Stella Briere, Mrs. E. Howard Nichols, and Mrs. Elaine P. Taylor uncomplainingly translated my crabbed manuscript into typescript.

This book, in many ways, is a joint effort, and the phrase "with the assistance of" tries to indicate just that. Without my wife's help this book never would have been completed.

Norman L. Zucker
Kingston, Rhode Island

The Coming Crisis
in Israel

1
Theopolitics
in Israel

The State of Israel is poised atop a delicate balance of concessions made to the secularists and the religious as the demands of each threaten to topple the government. At the extreme of the religious position are those Orthodox who see in the establishment of a Jewish state an opportunity to re-create a nation based upon, and entirely faithful to, Jewish law and tradition. The opposite standpoint is taken by those secularists who argue that Israel is no more than the homeland of a people having common historic roots. Were these two views representative of the majority of Jews in Israel, a Kulturkampf would long since have been inevitable. But for most Israelis—and for most Diaspora Jews, for whom the problem also assumes some urgency—neither a theocratic state nor a totally secular one is possible. The ethos of the new nation is derived from the theology as well as the history of Judaism.

These attitudes may be seen in the political arena, where nearly the entire range of Israeli opinion, from militantly Orthodox to militantly secularist and including the flexible moderates, is represented. It is there that the Orthodox, organized in political parties, have engaged in theopolitics, the attempt to establish a Torah state by means of legislation. Israel's electoral system of proportional representation and her history of ideological doctrinairism have encouraged multipartyism, which, in turn, has required government by coalition. Thus far no coalition government could be formed without the country's largest and most prestigious political party, Mapai. And Mapai, for practical political reasons, could not put together a viable coalition

Blowing the shofar in an army camp.

without including the National Religious Party (NRP). The NRP and two smaller ultra-Orthodox parties are dedicated to building Israel in their image of a Torah state, and they work to achieve their goal through the passage of legislation that incorporates Orthodox norms. Mapai and the Mapai-led Israel Labor Party have surrendered to some of the demands of the religious parties because they do not totally reject religious values, nor do they desire a totally secular state.

Amid the exercise of political threats and compromises, Israel has not been able to define completely her relationship to Judaic norms. Israel has no comprehensive written constitution because the Constituent Assembly could not agree on how Judaic law would mesh with the new nation's organic legislation. "Who is a Jew?" has become a question with different secular and religious answers. Through pressures for the enactment of specific piecemeal legislation, however, the religious parties have succeeded in achieving certain of their goals. The Orthodox rabbinate enjoys a virtual monopoly of Jewish religious authority and is established in the state. Certain Judaic norms have been incorporated into the legal system. Civil marriage and divorce do not exist in Israel, and the state maintains a system of rabbinical courts. Religious schools are part of the state educational structure, and Orthodox religious practices dealing with such matters as the Sabbath and dietary rules are observed in state facilities.

But all of these acts have been at best accommodations, not solutions, leaving both militant secularists and ultra-Orthodox hostile and dissatisfied. Religious-secular rela-

3

tions, normally tense, sporadically erupt in violence, and tensions at times have required cabinet decisions and resort to the courts.

In the absence of a final religion-state definition, religious issues constantly assume political overtones and character. These issues are not "private" matters affecting only the rabbinate and the observant, they are of primary public concern because they involve claims of legitimacy that are dependent on the state for action and enforcement. The nonreligious and the non-Jewish Israeli are affected too, and the issue of religion in a free society is raised.

It is paradoxical that the Jews, who through centuries of dispersion wanted their private faith to be free of the restrictions of public policy, now face the problem of how Judaism can flourish within the framework of a sovereign democratic Jewish state. With the establishment of the State of Israel a dilemma emerged: Ought Judaism assert a claim upon the secular authority, thereby obtaining nonreligious sanction for essentially religious activities? In short, what are to be the relations between the secular authority—the Israeli body politic—and Judaism, the soul that survived in Jews throughout history?

2
The
Restoration
of Zion

From the Roman destruction of the Second Jewish Commonwealth until the creation of the State of Israel, the Third Jewish Commonwealth, the Jewish people were without a geographic home, placed beyond the immediate problem of religion and a Jewish state. Judaism, however, remained an ethnic religion. The Dispersion nourished a theology that interwove religious and national threads. With the Babylonian exile of the First Commonwealth had come the nucleus of a Jewish community outside the Holy Land and a religiously inspired desire to return. "By the waters of Babylon we sat down," lamented the psalmist, "we wept when we remembered Zion." This attachment to Zion grew, to the extent that the destruction of the Temple by the Romans during the Second Commonwealth has been commemorated ever since in Jewish ritual. Palestine continued as a center of Jewish culture until the third century C.E. (Common Era). But as Palestine declined, creative, cultural, and religious life continued to flourish in the academies supported by the now large Babylonian Jewish community. It was there that the core of traditional Jewish learning and practice expanded. Centering on the Torah, amplified in the Talmud and Midrash, and ritualized in the first *siddur* (daily prayerbook), a heritage common to all Jews in the Dispersion was initiated and adopted.

Over the centuries the Dispersion created various Jewish communal clusters that developed into three major geographic branches: (1) the Ashkenazim—the Jews of middle and northern Europe; (2) the Sephardim—the Jews of Portugal, Spain, and parts of the Mediterranean basin; (3) the Orientals—various eastern communities such as the Yem-

Inauguration of Israel's first president, Chaim Weizmann.

enites, the Iraqis, and the Bene Israel of India. Although the three branches developed sociological and physical differences, as well as some ritualistic and liturgical differentiation, they were of the same unifying root. All continued to yearn for the Land of Israel. Belief in the restoration of Zion became a principal of Jewish religious devotions. Prayers for the rebuilding of Jerusalem found place in the three daily services, in the grace recited after meals, and in the marriage and burial ceremonies. Services for both the festival of Passover and the fast of the Day of Atonement conclude with the hope: "Next year in Jerusalem." Whether in frigid, temperate, or torrid zones, the observant Jew practiced a ritual that was rooted in the agricultural and climatic conditions of Israel. He prayed for rain even in the midst of the monsoon and, living in an urban culture, celebrated the harvest season, thus perpetuating, even in exile, religious unity inspired by a theological commitment to the national homeland. Those Jews who dwelled in the Diaspora conformed, where necessary, convenient, or permitted, to the official local secular code but simultaneously maintained a societal order structured by the Torah and expanded by the rabbis in the commentaries.

The concepts of exile (*galut*) and redemption and return to Zion (*geulah*) were essential throughout the Dispersion. Together the exile and delivery themes memorialized glories of past nationhood, reconciled the Jew to his circumstances, and foretold an elusive golden future when there would be "the end of the days" and the Children of Israel would dwell in their rightful land. The ideals of redemption and return to Zion, as expressed in the messianic prophecy, however, have created some practical problems.

Many Jews in the past suffered economic and emotional upsets when they flocked to false messiahs (Solomon Molcho, David Reuveni, and most famous of all, Shabbetai Tzevi), who failed to lead them to the Promised Land.

More realistic than messianic redemption, though no less religiously inspired, was the concept of Judaic self-redemption, which, although of limited influence, was a bridge to later religious Zionism and an overture to organized political Zionism. Self-redemption built on the traditional yearning for return, as well as the vigorous spirit of European nationalism of the early nineteenth century, and looked for its attainment less to heavenly means than to earthly schemes. The foremost exponents of the self-redemption movement were Sephardic Rabbi Yehudah Alkalai (1798–1878) of Serbia and Ashkenazic Rabbi Tzevi Hirsch Kalischer (1795–1874) of Posen, a province in western Poland.

A rabbi's son, Alkalai was born in Sarajevo but spent his boyhood in Jerusalem, where he came under the influence of the kabbalists. In his writings, however, he departed radically from the traditional pious belief that the Messiah would come by miraculous acts of Divine grace, and he proposed, as a preamble to the redemption, the creation of Jewish settlements in the Holy Land. Alkalai argued that it would be possible to purchase Palestine from the Turks, as in Biblical times Abraham had bought Machpelah from Ephron, the Hittite. To this end, Alkalai advocated, among other things, calling a "Great Assembly" and the creation of a national fund for land purchase.

Like Alkalai, Kalischer was both a pietist and a modernist. As early as 1836, he had written to the Berlin branch of the Rothschild banking family explaining that "the beginning of the Redemption will come through natural causes by human effort and by the will of the governments to gather the scattered of Israel into the Holy Land." [1] He attempted to translate his beliefs into working deeds by getting a group to purchase land for colonization near Jaffa, and later he was instrumental in persuading the Alliance Israélite Universelle (an organization created in France in 1860 and dedicated to the protection of Jewish rights) to found an agricultural school in Jaffa.

Somewhat akin intellectually to the spiritually centered Rabbis Alkalai and Kalischer was their German contemporary Moses Hess (1812–1875), who led a highly unorthodox religious and political life. Hess was the first Zionist philosopher to be "completely a man of the nineteenth century." Active in ideological politics and the German revolution of 1848 (where his activities earned him the death sentence), he collaborated for a time with Karl Marx and Friedrich Engels. But Hess's collaboration with the founders of "scientific socialism" ended when he stressed ethical socialism rather than materialistic determinism. In *Rome and Jerusalem,* his classic work on Jewish nationalism, he expounded in idealistic, if impractical terms, his conception of the restoration of Zion and the historic civilizing mission of a dynamic Israel. But the Judaic self-redemption expressions of Alkalai, Kalischer, and Hess, while important, are considered to be "proto-Zionist" rather than Zionist since, as Ben Halpern has noted, they "gave rise to no movement of historic consequence, leading continuously to the establishment of Israel." [2]

While the self-redemption movement was a reflection of and a reaction to the emergent nationalism of the nine-

11

teenth century which in its wake brought western Jewish emancipation, it was also, in some ways, a response to recurring anti-Semitism. By the eighteenth century, in western Europe, the brutal, systematic, and violent persecutions of the Jews had been replaced by less violent and more humane discrimination. This softer attitude was also reflected in official national policy, following the lead of the United States, where it had become the policy of the government to give "to bigotry no sanction, to persecution no assistance." [3] After American Jews, in 1787, were given the same rights, privileges, and immunities as all other citizens, France followed, in 1790, with an official emancipation of its Jewish citizens. Similar official acts occurred somewhat later in Italy (1870) and Germany (1871), and in Great Britain the last formal disabilities were removed in 1890.[4]

The emancipation—the removal of civic, political, and economic restrictions imposed on Jews—brought about the gradual assimilation of western European Jewry into the various bodies politic. And with it, operative religious law became no longer subject to rigid communal enforcement. The emancipated Jew in western Europe had a choice. He could choose to abide by either secular practice or religious law or, in the vast majority of cases, evolve according to his own conscience and personality an accommodation of the two. But, important as they were, government pronouncements of legal freedom and civic equality did not erase the noxious substance of anti-Jewish feeling.

In eastern Europe, where the vast majority of European Jews lived, conditions were oppressive. In 1794, just when legal emancipation was dawning for western Jewry, Czarina Catherine of Russia promulgated a ukase establishing a

"Pale of Settlement." Some years before, as a legacy of the first Polish partition, Russia suddenly had acquired a large Jewish population (Jews not having been permitted to live in Russia since the reign of Ivan IV). Creating the Pale— roughly the area of the former Polish Kingdom—and restricting Jews to it, was Catherine's solution of "the Jewish problem." Subsequent partitions of Poland enlarged Mother Russia's territory, but, unhappily for the official court, it also enlarged the Jewish population. Repression was intensified under Alexander I and compounded under the brutal reactionary Nicholas I, who imposed on Jews a twenty-five-year period of military conscription. The living death of conscription was reduced to six years under Alexander II, and for a short time it seemed possible that Russian Jews were to have their legal disabilities removed and that they were to be accorded the emancipation then being enjoyed by Jews in the west. The warm humanity of the thaw, however, was soon followed by cold reaction. After Alexander II's assassination in 1881, hardship and bloody persecution, reminiscent of the fury and wantonness of the Middle Ages, revisited European Jewry. All-encompassing legal disabilities were imposed by the infamous May Laws, which were issued as "Temporary Rules," but it was well known throughout all the realms of the czar that there was nothing quite so permanent as temporary legislation affecting the Jews, and the May Laws remained in harsh effect until in March 1917 the Revolution forceably uprooted them.[5]

The extreme czarist repression produced an understandable trauma and, more important, a political Zionist response. By the 1880s the limits of the marginal existence of *shtetl* life had been breached by the growth of *Haskalah*. Shtetl life, religion-centered and oriented toward other-worldly values—scholarship or, more frequently, scholasticism and minute analysis of talmudic tomes—was superimposed on a backward agricultural economy. The omnipresent deprivation has been symbolized by Tevye the dairyman, Sholem Aleichem's folk everyman, who could say without rancor: "I was, with God's help, a poor man." [6] This kind of simplistic piety and resignation, however, crumbled with the rise and spread of Haskalah.

The Haskalah, or Jewish Enlightenment, originated in western Europe in the eighteenth century and spread from there to eastern Europe. It was a movement that deemphasized and downgraded the prevalent preoccupation with the Talmud and allied studies; it stressed instead the importance of practical knowledge, the need for secular study, and the appreciation of secular culture. It was hospitable to ideologies challenging the status quo and antithetical to the inner-directed and self-sustaining European religious communities. The confluence of Haskalah with the realization, in the pogroms of 1881, that eastern Jewry could not hope for the emancipation realized in the west gave impetus to a variety of responses, among them the movement for Jewish nationalism.[7]

Among those shocked by the pogroms was Dr. Leo Pinsker (1821–1891), a man who had tasted the delights of the temporary emancipation, even having been honored by Czar Nicholas I for his medical services in the Crimean War. Pinsker, completely russified and comfortable in secular circles, articulated the emotional crisis of the pogroms in his famous pamphlet *Auto-Emancipation* (1882), which

Arthur Hertzberg has characterized as "the first great statement of the torment of the Jew driven to assert his own
nationalism because the wider world had rejected him." [8]

After the publication of *Auto-Emancipation,* Pinsker,
not content merely to expound a rationale for Zionism, became involved in its organizational aspects. When various
Zionist groups formally convened as the Lovers of Zion
(*Choveve Zion*) in a founding conference in Kattowitz, Upper Silesia, Pinsker was elected president. The short-term
practical results of the founding of the Lovers of Zion, however, were limited. They were plagued by financial difficulties and blocked ultimately by the inhospitable position of
the Turkish government that ruled Palestine. Moreover, in
a foreshadowing of Zionist ideological schisms to follow,
the movement was divided between the modernists and the
Orthodox. (Pinsker, like Herzl later, was not committed to
the proposition that a Jewish state could be established only
in the Land of Israel; it was the physical establishment, not
the location, that was important. To the Orthodox, however, this was the apogee of heresy.)

The Lovers of Zion, nonetheless, were significant as fore-
runners of the political Zionism associated with Theodor
Herzl and the twentieth century, and as an ideological and
organizational bridge between the Jews of western Europe,
disillusioned by the emancipation, and the acutely suffer-
ing Jews of eastern Europe. Along with the BILU settlers,
they began the Jewish repopulation of the Holy Land.[9]
From 1882 to 1903 some 25,000 newcomers, mostly Russian
and Romanian Jews escaping from pogroms and other persecutions, arrived in Palestine and became the First Aliyah.
Aliyah (pl. *aliyot*), means "immigration." But one can un-

15

derstand the ethos of aliyah and its relevance to twentieth-century religious, political, and cultural Zionism only through its literal meaning, "ascent." In classic terminology one spoke of ascending to Jerusalem and Zion. It had both a physical and a spiritual or idealistic meaning. Even today, the dual connotation remains; those who emigrate from Israel are called pejoratively *yordim,* "descenders" (*yored,* singl., literally one who goes down).[10]

The First Aliyah, and all subsequent aliyot, provided the human resources requisite for statehood, although throughout the Dispersion there had always been a small nucleus of Jews who made their homes in the Holy Land. Jerusalem, Hebron, Safed, and Tiberias, the four cities having a special significance, had always sustained, if not by natural increase then by immigration of the pious or persecuted, some Jewish settlement. By the beginning of the First Aliyah, Jews in Palestine numbered approximately 24,000.[11] Except for some western Jews who in the 1870s had established an agricultural school and an agricultural colony, the Jewish population was pious, poor, and provincial. Out of touch with modern learning, spiritually inner-directed, they eked out a precarious subsistence as petty tradesmen and artisans. Without the constant inflow of charity from abroad it is doubtful that their continued existence would have been possible.

This small Jewish population constituting the "Old" *Yishuv* (settlement) was more than doubled in the twenty-one years of the First Aliyah. During this Aliyah, Petach Tikva, the agricultural colony founded in 1878, was revived and new agricultural colonies established. Without the largess of Baron Edmond de Rothschild, these attempts

at colonization would have failed; but Rothschild philan-
thropy in itself could not have sustained large-scale immigration to Palestine. Before the First Aliya terminated, new
ideological and organizational impetus for Jewish return
had been provided by Theodor Herzl and the World Zionist Organization.

Theodor Herzl (1860–1904), the founder of modern political Zionism, was born in Budapest and, while still in his
teens, moved with his family to Vienna. He received his
doctorate in jurisprudence from the University of Vienna
but never seriously practiced law; instead he devoted himself to writing, and in 1892 he became the Paris correspond-
ent for Vienna's most important newspaper, the *Neue Freie
Presse*. Despite his early exposure to Jewish nationalism by
his grandfather, a friend of Alkalai, the young Herzl was
not particularly interested in matters affecting European
Jewry until he arrived in Paris, where Edouard Drumont,
author of the noxious and widely circulated *La France
Juive,* was publishing an anti-Semitic newspaper. Some two
years later, he wrote a play, *The New Ghetto,* in which he
made the point that, although legal equality had been proclaimed, the liabilities and burdens of the invisible ghetto
lingered. It remained, however, for the events of the Dreyfus Affair to propel him into an activist policy of political
Zionism.

It should be remembered that the Dreyfus case was more
than a public exercise in anti-Semitism. The Dreyfus Affair
rocked French political life because it was associated with
the monarchist-republican and clerical-anticlerical conflicts.
Involved in the fraudulent charge that Captain Alfred
Dreyfus had sold military secrets to Germany was an at-

tempt to discredit the Republic. Dreyfus was championed by the republicans and the anticlericals, as well as by such liberal literary figures as Emile Zola and Anatole France. Later, in 1905, Dreyfus would be cleared of all guilt, restored to the army, promoted to the rank of major, and decorated with the Legion of Honor, but by then Herzl was already dead, and the movement that he had launched now had organization and direction.

In May 1895, during the early stages of the Dreyfus Affair, Herzl secured an interview with Baron Maurice de Hirsch, who was then engaged in a philanthropically inspired scheme of Jewish colonization of Argentina. Herzl discussed with the Baron plans for calling a congress of Jewish notables to deal with the question of migration to a sovereign Jewish state. De Hirsch and other wealthy Jews whom Herzl approached were unreceptive, but Dr. Max Nordau, the eminent publicist, encouraged him. In February 1896, Herzl, in *The Jewish State* (*Der Judenstaat*), proposed the creation of a Jewish state as a practical corrective to anti-Semitism. Herzl worked feverishly to implement his thesis. He founded *The World* (*Die Welt*) in order to publicize his objectives and was instrumental in convening the First Zionist Congress in August 1897 at Basle, Switzerland. The Congress adopted an anthem, "Hatikvah" (Hope), a flag, and a program and then gave them practical force by creating the World Zionist Organization, electing Herzl its first president. The Basle Program, the first official expression of political Zionism, had for its final goal the creation of a publicly recognized and legally secured Jewish homeland in Palestine. Today, in Israel Herzl's portrait hangs in a place of honor in the Knesset, "Hatikvah" is the national anthem, and the blue and white banner designed for the First Congress by David Wolffsohn, a Cologne merchant, is the national flag.

The articulation of a Zionist program and the creation of the World Zionist Organization simultaneously unleashed Jewish anti-Zionist feelings that, even after the establishment of the State of Israel, are still present. Many Orthodox European Jews were suspicious of some of the Zionist leaders because of their nonobservance of tradition and ceremonies and hostile because of their activities violating the Orthodox conception of messianic deliverance and restoration. Other opposition stressed the idea that since the Dispersion the Jews had been a purely religious community, and that the creation of a nation would be unwise. In America, the year 1898 that saw the establishment of the American Federation of Zionists also saw the Conference of American Rabbis announce its disapprobation of the Zionist movement because, in the words of one of the delegates, "America was the Jews' Jerusalem and Washington their Zion." [12] Other opponents argued that Zionism stimulated anti-Semitism, or that in time historical progress would dispel anti-Semitism. Still others, following the lead of Achad Ha-Am (Asher Ginsberg), felt that the revival of a secular Jewish culture through the medium of Hebrew was an absolute prerequisite to the establishment of a Jewish national home.

But despite opposition from without and internal dissension, political Zionism under Herzl's direction gained momentum. Before Herzl's death in 1904, five more world congresses were held, and the Jewish Colonial Trust and the Anglo-Palestine Company were established as ancillaries to the World Zionist Organization.

Initially, Herzl planned to secure from the Ottoman Sultan in Constantinople a special charter authorizing autonomous Jewish colonization in Palestine. In pursuit of this end Herzl attempted high-level diplomatic negotiation. First he obtained an interview with Kaiser Wilhelm II of Germany in the hope of having him persuade the Sultan, his friend and ally, to consider the chartered company proposal. When nothing came of this, Herzl tried direct negotiation with the Sultan, but this too proved fruitless. Now discouraged, Herzl again shifted his tactics and attempted to cultivate Britain, in the illusory hope that she could and would exert some beneficial pressure on Turkey. While in England Herzl made contact with Joseph Chamberlain, then British Colonial Secretary, and unwittingly precipitated the first great crisis of Herzlian political Zionism.

In the summer of 1903, prior to the opening of the Sixth Zionist Congress in Basle, Chamberlain suggested to Herzl that land in the British East Africa Protectorate (a portion of present-day Kenya) might serve as territory for a Jewish state.[13] The recent Kishinev pogrom convinced a reluctant Herzl that the offer by the British Foreign Office should be placed before the Congress. At the opening session of the Congress Max Nordau, in presenting the East Africa proposal to the delegates, termed it a *Nachtasyl,* a night haven, a halfway refuge on the road to the Holy Land. Although some of the delegates felt that any basis for security was better than none, the East Africa proposal for all practical purposes was defeated when the east European delegates,

among them young Chaim Weizmann, walked out in protest to emphasize their belief that a Jewish homeland could
be established only in the Holy Land. The East Africa
offer was organizationally disruptive. At the next Zionist
Congress, held in 1905, the East Africa matter was again
raised and rejected. A few delegates who, under the leadership of British novelist Israel Zangwill, maintained that
harsh reality dictated that areas other than Palestine could
be suitable for colonization, seceded from the Congress and
formed the Jewish Territorial Organization. The territori-
alists endured a series of disappointments and with the
coming of World War I quietly faded into oblivion. During this time the World Zionist Organization, now led by
David Wolffsohn, Herzl's successor, continued its quest for
a charter and actively supported the Second Aliyah.

The Second Aliyah (1904–1914) brought to Palestine
some 40,000 Jewish immigrants, most of them fleeing from
the cataclysmic social upheaval and repressive reaction that
characterized eastern Europe in the decade prior to World
War I. These newcomers were numerically insignificant in
relation to those migrating Jews who sought their zion outside Zion.[14] (Some two and a half million Jews fled west-
ward, and of these nearly two million settled in the United
States during the years of the First and Second Aliyot.)
Nonetheless, it was the pioneers of the Second Aliyah, reenforced by those of the Third Aliyah, who forged the
dominant prestate ethos that still, if only in the abstract, is
important in the maturing Israeli nationalism.

Associated with the Second Aliyah were some of Israel's
most famous national heroes, Aharon David Gordon, Berl
Katzenelson, Yitzchak Ben-Zvi, and David Ben-Gurion,

21

who embodied the labor Zionist values of self-sacrifice, renunciation, equalitarianism, and collective purpose.[15] Their ideals of manual labor and return to the soil, they believed, could be realized best in agricultural settlements and collectives.

The Second Aliyah also brought into being trade unions and sundry mutual aid societies. The nuclei of present-day labor and religious parties were formed, and party organization and alignments became operative. Hebrew emerged from its restricted use in prayer and study and began to develop as a modern vernacular. But in 1914 the Yishuv was pulled into the vortex of spreading hostilities, bringing the Second Aliyah to a close. Now there began another era of post-Herzlian diplomatic Zionism.

The World Zionist Organization, with its members residing in both the neutral and warring countries, soon found it necessary to revise its organization and its prewar policies. The Zionist executive, located in Berlin, and the field offices in Jaffa and Constantinople found communication with the Zionists in the Allied countries inadequate. The attempt to circumvent this anomalous situation by establishing a "neutral" office in Copenhagen was unsuccessful. The essential continuity of the Zionist movement was in the Allied countries. In America, Louis Dembitz Brandeis, soon to begin his illustrious if controversial membership on the Supreme Court, became president of the Provisional Executive Committee for General Zionist Affairs, and in England Chaim Weizmann began to play a central role in Zionist activities.

The Yishuv was also affected by the war. Not yet self-supporting, it suffered extensive hardships. Economically, the war curtailed exports and, just as importantly, eliminated financial assistance from overseas. Politically, the Turkish authorities, never particularly solicitous of the Palestinian Jewish population, and now fearing Jewish sympathy for the British, began a policy of repression. Those who refused to serve in the Turkish Army were either imprisoned or deported. Among the deportees were subsequent Israeli leaders, Ben-Gurion and Ben-Zvi, who continued their Zionist activities outside the Ottoman Empire. Others, led by the fiery Vladimir Jabotinsky, carried supplies for the British at Gallipoli under the now humorous, but descriptive name, Zion Mule Corps. When the Corps was disbanded in 1916, the ex-muleteers formed the nucleus of the Jewish Legion and participated in General Allenby's campaign that drove the Turks out of Palestine. It was within this wartime milieu, particularly because of Turkey's adherence to the Central Powers, that new political opportunities for Zionism and Arab nationalism were generated.

The entry of Turkey into World War I on the side of the Central Powers raised the question of the future status of Palestine. During the war, in response to Zionist pressure and as a means of protecting British interests in the Middle East, British Foreign Secretary Arthur James Balfour issued an official statement:

His Majesty's Government view with favor the establishment in Palestine of a national home for the Jewish people, and will use their best endeavors to facilitate the achievement of this object, it being clearly understood that nothing shall be done which may prejudice the civil and religious rights of existing non-Jewish communities in Palestine, or the rights and political status enjoyed by Jews in any other country.

With the termination of hostilities, Palestine became a Mandate of Great Britain.

From the beginning, even before the Mandate became official, there was acrimonious dispute among the British, the Jews, and the Arabs, each group having its own set of objectives. Their diverse goals—British imperial interests and conflicting Zionist and Arab nationalisms—were to cause even more bitterness in time, finally to explode in the wake of World War II. According to the terms of the Mandate, which gave recognition to "the historical connection of the Jewish people with Palestine and to the grounds for reconstituting their national home in that country," Britain, as the mandatory, was responsible for implementing the Balfour Declaration. The concept of the establishment of a Jewish national home, long the raison d'être of political Zionism, had now attained international sanction through the agency of the League of Nations. And even the United States, a non-League nation, endorsed the policy of a Jewish national home. But while the Balfour Declaration and the Mandate obligated Britain to honor Zionist nationalism, the same documents contained promises to the Arabs. The Balfour Declaration's stipulation that "nothing shall be done which may prejudice the civil and religious rights of existing non-Jewish communities in Palestine" was reiterated in the Mandate, which affirmed that "the rights and positions of other sections of the population are not prejudiced." [16]

The Churchill White Paper of 1922, named after the then colonial secretary Winston Churchill, attempted to define British policy and reconcile Jewish and Arab claims. However, the Churchill Memorandum began to erode the promise of a national homeland contained in the Balfour Declaration. While it stated that "the Jewish people are in Palestine as of right and not on sufferance," it also retrenched by pointing out that it was not contemplated "that Palestine as a whole should be converted into a Jewish National Home, but that such a home should be founded in Palestine." To fulfill this policy "the Jewish community in Palestine should be able to increase its numbers by immigration subject to the economic capacity of the country to absorb new arrivals" and "an increasing measure of self-government may be contemplated." [17]

Contrary to intention, however, the Memorandum's key principles of increasing Jewish immigration and self-government provided the basis for continuing conflict during the Mandate. The introduction of the concept of immigration subject to the country's economic absorptive capacity was an incursion into the Balfour Declaration, which had imposed only the provision that the civil and religious rights of the existing non-Jewish community should not be prejudiced. But the Zionist Organization was not, at the time, particularly concerned about economic absorptive capacity. Dr. Weizmann commented that "each Jew coming to Palestine brought some economic absorptive capacity with him in his valise." [18]

Jewish national aspirations in the Holy Land were in sharp conflict with Arab national drives. Those Jews who had settled in Palestine prior to the First Aliyah had oc-

25

cupied an inferior economic status. The "Old Settlement" of pietists was numerically insignificant, economically stagnant, and preoccupied with religious concerns; consequently they did not pose a threat that would disturb or challenge the customary society. This, however, was not true of the *chalutzim* (agricultural pioneers) who had come to build the land that Herzl had described in his prophetic *Altneuland* (Old-New Land).

The Third Aliyah (1918/19–1923/24), composed mainly of Jews fleeing the turmoil of the early years of the Russian Revolution, restored the Yishuv to its prewar population of 100,000 and further expanded the labor-Zionist program. With this Aliyah came many of the people who constituted the power elite during the Mandate and the first two decades of the state: among them, Golda Meir, Dov Yoseph, and Abba Khoushi. The progress made by the labor-Zionists of the Second and Third Aliyot stemmed from their idealistic philosophy, as summarized by the concept of *chalutziut* (pioneering spirit). The story of the chalutzim who fed their cattle while they themselves starved, because the cattle were not, after all, Zionists, is perhaps apocryphal but expresses this spirit. Not all immigrants, however, had such accommodatingly elastic stomachs, nor were they all willing to endure the hardships attendant upon the creation of a new society.

If idealism waned when confronted with reality in the middle 1920s, immigration did not. The Fourth Aliyah (1924–1926) brought in well over 60,000 people who fled eastern Europe, but were unable to migrate to the United States because of the severe immigration restrictions of the National Origins Act. These new Palestinians, particularly those who fled Polish anti-Semitism, gravitated to the cities of Tel Aviv, then only fifteen years old, Haifa, and Jerusalem, intensifying the depression that was then beginning. With economic recovery came additional immigration. By 1931, there were approximately 174,000 Jews in Palestine, nearly 17 percent of the total population of slightly more than a million. It was this population influx, with its nationalist aspirations and the pressures to westernize and modernize that it placed on the traditional Middle Eastern social structure, that contributed to the agitation and political turmoil of the Mandate.[19]

Under High Commissioner Samuel (1920–1925) and his capable successor, Lord Plumer (1925–1928), relative calm prevailed in Palestine, and the Yishuv was considerably strengthened by the Third and Fourth Aliyot. But the quiet concealed growing Arab hostility toward the Jews, occasioned by "the disappointment of Arab political and national aspirations and fear for the economic future." Beginning in 1928, Arab riots were renewed. In response to the disturbances, Britain appointed a Commission of Inquiry, the Shaw Commission.[20]

The Shaw Commission's report to Parliament, in March 1930, deemphasized the Mandate's requirements for the encouragement of a Jewish National Home, stating baldly "that in the matter of immigration there has been a serious departure . . . from the doctrine . . . that immigration should be regulated by the economic capacity of Palestine to absorb new arrivals." Not only did the Commission call for stringent regulation of immigration, but it also called for an investigation of land policy. The Land Report of Sir John Hope-Simpson, a monument to expert incom-

27

petence, concluded that, until further development had occurred, "there is no room for a single additional settler."
That June the Mandates Commission of the League of Nations took issue with the trend of British mandatory policy.
Britain, however, ignored the Commission and issued in
October a "definitive" policy statement in the 1930 White
Paper. The Lord Passfield (Sidney Webb) White Paper,
despite Prime Minister Ramsay MacDonald's attempts to
qualify it in response to Zionist objections, basically reiterated the recommendations of the Shaw Commission and
the Hope-Simpson Land Report. Some years later, the Peel
Report, commenting on the 1930 policy, noted that it "betrayed a marked insensitiveness to Jewish feelings." [21]

But policy statements notwithstanding, during the period 1930–1936 Palestine enjoyed a period of unprecedented growth and Jewish immigration continued—the
Fifth Aliyah (1932–1939) had begun. In the seven years
preceding World War II, the wave of immigration brought
in nearly 225,000 people. The new *olim* (immigrants) had
flowed in largely from eastern Europe and to a lesser extent
from Oriental countries. And now, spurred by Hitler's
rabid anti-Jewish policies, large numbers of German and
central European Jews joined the migration. Unlike the
eastern Europeans and Orientals, most of the escapees from
Nazi persecution were highly educated and many had considerable capital. It was these people of the Fifth Aliyah
who gave to the Yishuv a powerful developmental impetus
and a decidedly European character and outlook.[22]

Arab reaction to this population influx was understandably antagonistic. In an attempt to appease the Arabs the
mandatory government introduced an ordinance restricting

the sale of land and created a new Statistical Bureau to check estimates of absorptive capacity. Nonetheless, in that same year, 1936, Arab riots broke out against both the British and the Jews. As in the past, the British appointed a commission to investigate. The report of the Peel Commission was published in 1937. In a radical departure from previous commission reports and the League's Mandate policy, the Peel Report declared that the Mandate had become unworkable: Arab and Jew could not cooperate; their nationalist drives were irreconcilable. The only solution was a tripartite partition: a Jewish state (comprising the northeastern part of Palestine and the narrow Mediterranean coastal plain as far south as Tel Aviv), a Protectorate or Mandate for the Holy Places (beginning at Jaffa and widening to include Jerusalem and Bethlehem), and an Arab state (which would include the rest of Palestine and be incorporated into the area ruled by Emir Abdullah and known as Transjordan). Nothing, however, came of the partition proposal. The Zionists, upset about the reduction in land area, were unenthusiastic; the Arabs refused to entertain the possibility of land reduction and were intractable; and the Mandates Commission, sensing the League's imminent demise, was ambivalent and noncommital.[23]

In Palestine conditions remained unsettled, and Arab violence, bordering on open rebellion, continued. In a complete political somersault, the Woodhead Partition Commission announced in October 1938 that partition was impractical, and a month later another White Paper, proceeding from and reaffirming this assumption, proposed a conference to be attended by the Zionists, representatives of the Palestine Arabs, and, in an innovation, representatives of the neighboring Arab countries. The London conference was really not a conference; the Arabs refused to sit with the Zionists, and consequently separate Anglo-Arab and Anglo-Jewish meetings were held. The result of the abortive meetings was Britain's unilateral issuance of the notorious MacDonald White Paper of May 1939.[24]

The Chamberlain government, oblivious to the aggressive stirrings of Nazism, declared its intention of establishing in Palestine, if it appeared to His Majesty's Government that circumstances would not require its postponement, an independent state within ten years. After this promise with its built-in abrogation clause, the White Paper went on to define future immigration and land policy. Subject to the criterion of economic absorptive capacity, over the next five years only 75,000 immigrants would be admitted, after which no further Jewish immigration was to be permitted except in the unlikely event that the Palestine Arabs would acquiesce in it. Illegal immigration was to be prevented, and Arab land sales to Jews were to be subject to High Commission approval. The White Paper was a "Palestine Munich." In an attempt to safeguard imperial interests Britain had half appeased the Arabs, completely alienated the Jews, and abandoned her basic obligations under the Mandate. Ostensibly issued as an alternative policy to partition (the Peel Report), the White Paper, in Winston Churchill's words attempted to create "one more precarious Oriental ghetto." [25]

The White Paper aroused a furore. In Parliament, where opposition was strong, it secured approval by a relatively small majority. And when it was submitted to the League's Permanent Mandates Commission, a majority found it not in accord with the provisions of the Mandate. When war erupted in September 1939, David Ben-Gurion, then chairman of the Jewish Agency, summarized Zionist policy: "We shall fight the war as if there were no White Paper, and the White Paper as if there were no war." [26] Since the League did not meet because of the outbreak of war, and as the Mandatory Commission had found the White Paper to be a definite modification of the Mandate, the Zionists had a reasonable legal position for refusing to accept, and attempting to circumvent, the new immigration restrictions. This legal rationale was buttressed by an appeal to a higher moral law.

"The story of Palestine from May 1939 to the end of the war," Arthur Koestler has noted in a superb simplification, "is essentially the story of Jews trying to save their skins, and of the efforts of the Mandatory Power to prevent this through an immigration blockade maintained by force and diplomatic pressure." [27] Flight was the only alternative to slaughter for the Nazi-persecuted Jews, and Britain blocked flight. At the outbreak of war Britain decreed that no one from Germany or German-occupied Poland, except the small number who had valid prewar entry visas, could enter Palestine. (The ostensible logic in excluding refugees from "enemy occupied territory" was to prevent the infiltration of enemy agents.) As the German armies progressed through Europe, succeeding countries became, according to the definition of the Immigration Ordinance of 1939, "enemy occupied territory" from which no Jew was permitted to enter Palestine. In the face of these regulations, attempts at "illegal immigration" increased. In retaliation, Britain suspended all immigration for two decisive half-year pe-

31

riods: October 1939 to March 1940 and for a similar period in 1940 to 1941.

On September 1, 1939, the day Hitler began the invasion of Poland, the British killed the first two refugees who were trying to enter Palestine "illegally." With the doors to Palestine closed, "over the Mediterranean and Black Seas unclean and unseaworthy little cargo boats crept from port to port or tossed about on the open waters, waiting in vain for permission to discharge their crowded human cargoes. Hunger, thirst, disease and unspeakable living conditions reigned on those floating coffins." [28] When permission to land never came, the seeds of anti-British Jewish terrorism were sown. During the war terrorist activities were carried out only by the miniscule Stern Gang, which, after the war, was joined by the Irgun Tzevai Leumi (National Military Organization). The rebel groups argued that the Mandatory had violated its trust and consequently was an illegitimate foreign occupying force. But aside from these deviations, during and after the war discipline and restraint prevailed in the Yishuv. Palestinian Jews cooperated with Britain in fighting the war, though they defied the ban on illegal immigration. And as Hitler's "Final Solution to the Jewish Problem" took effect, an ever-expanding Zionist impulse for the establishment of a national home hardened and took on renewed urgency and force.

When World War II ended, the immigration issue again became paramount. In a genocide unparalleled in human history six million Jews had perished. And when the remnants of European Jewry emerged from hiding, or more frequently from concentration camps, they found that they had no place to return or to go to; they were Displaced

Persons. But all the horrors of Auschwitz, Bergen-Belsen, Buchenwald, Dachau, Maidanek, Mathausen, Treblinka, and Theresienstadt, or the fact that the Arabs had actively supported the Axis, could not persuade the British government to abandon the 1939 White Paper. In response to this callousness, under the sponsorship of the Sternists and the Irgun, militant terrorism erupted in Palestine; large-scale clandestine immigration was organized. Britain forceably repressed the unauthorized immigration and detained intercepted "illegals" in concentration camps on Cyprus. American attempts to ameliorate the plight of the DPs resulted, first, in the establishment of the 1946 Anglo-American Committee of Inquiry, and then the Morrison-Grady plan which proposed to divide Palestine into a British zone and autonomous Jewish and Arab provinces. But nothing came of these labors, and the civil war in Palestine escalated with bloody ferocity. British intransigence, however, could not halt the dynamic forces set free in the wake of the war. In February of 1947, after the unsuccessful London Conference, the British government, no longer able to cope with the Palestine problem, decided to turn the Mandate over to the League's successor, the United Nations.

A special session of the General Assembly was called, and after prolonged debate an eleven-nation investigative committee, the United Nations Special Committee on Palestine (UNSCOP), was established. After investigation, UNSCOP unanimously recommended the termination of the Mandate but disagreed on the post-Mandatory formula for government. The majority recommended political partition with aspects of economic integration, while the minority recommended a federal state. Debate on these proposals took place against a background of cold war power politics. The Arabs were adamant and rejected both sets of proposals; nonetheless, the General Assembly, on November 29, 1947, adopted the partition plan and established a United Nations Palestine Commission to supervise the creation of the new "Jewish and Arab states." The announcement of partition triggered an Arab general strike throughout Palestine, and signaled the impending full-scale Arab-Jewish conflict. The cooperation of the Mandatory at this point could have eased the transition greatly and reduced bloodshed. Instead, His Majesty's Government announced that the Mandate would terminate on May 15, 1948, but that the Government would not assist the UN because its proposed solution was not acceptable to both parties. This morally bankrupt action, taken in the hope of strengthening Britain's interests, was an invitation to violence and chaos in the Holy Land.

Conditions in Palestine deteriorated rapidly. Britain pursued a policy of favoritism to the Arabs, and open clashes between Jews and Arabs, and Jews and Britons, became more frequent. The turmoil occasioned the reconsideration by the General Assembly, in April 1948, of the partition plan. But while debate was going on, the Jewish Agency for Palestine informed the United Nations that the "Jewish State," authorized by the partition plan, would be proclaimed the moment the Mandate terminated. At a meeting of the Provisional State Council held in the Tel Aviv Museum on Friday afternoon, May 14, 1948, David Ben-Gurion read a Proclamation of Independence.[29]

3
The
Institutions
of Theopolitics

After David Ben-Gurion read the Proclamation of Independence, Rabbi Yehudah Leib Maimon, who was to become Israel's first minister of religious affairs, arose and in a voice choked with emotion intoned the ancient *she-he-heyanu*, the benediction that gives thanks to the Almighty "who hast kept us in life, and preserved us, and enabled us to reach this season." [1] The Proclamation was then signed by the members of the People's Council, which thereupon became the new parliamentary authority, the Provisional Council of State.

The Provisional Council carried over into the new nation the pattern of politics that had developed during the Yishuv. The Yishuv, the community of Jews in Palestine prior to the founding of the state, was an autonomous parapolitical structure. Significantly, the Yishuv was democratically organized. This is an interesting phenomenon insofar as the immigrant "Founding Fathers" came from the repressive societies of Russia, Poland, or Romania and were to a large extent untouched by the Western democratic political tradition. But the Jewish settlement of the Holy Land was composed primarily of Zionist and/or religiously committed immigrants who brought with them a unique legacy: for more than twenty-five centuries throughout the Diaspora, the Jews had maintained autonomous communities, albeit with varying degrees of independence and authority. In eastern Europe the *Kehillah* (pl. *Kehillot*) was the organized Jewish community, a socioreligious organization from which a variety of forms of elective and representative government emerged.[2]

In the more than quarter century of the mandatory re-

An election campaign rally of the Torah Religious Front.

38

gime, the Yishuv had gained valuable experience in democratic procedures and self-rule. The many political parties learned the necessity of working together. A core of political elite and potential civil servants gained experience and training. Economic progress was made as a growing number of settlements reclaimed the soil and a few industries were begun. A basic educational system was established that fostered an intense nationalism, and institutions of higher learning were founded. The Histadrut, the all-encompassing federation of trade unions that sponsors cultural, educational, medical, commercial, industrial, and publishing activities, became a powerful and stabilizing influence that combined idealism with practical efficiency. An underground militia was formed, its members were trained, and it acquired the rudiments of military equipment. And the population now laid claim to a prime requisite of nationhood—a common language. On May 14, 1948, there were over 650,000 Jews—a tenfold multiplication of the number there were in 1920—of whom well over half a million spoke Hebrew as their first language. In short, democratic traditions and institutions, along with a feeling of national identity, had had a chance to take root.

The structure of government that ultimately emerged was the product of many interrelated forces: Diaspora and Yishuv experiences, the ideological and social movement nature of the parties, the dominance of positions of power and leadership by Europeans, especially those from central and eastern Europe, and the force of certain personalities. Taken altogether, these factors resulted in the creation of an essentially ceremonial presidency, a strong prime minister and cabinet, and a parliament (Knesset) elected by proportional representation and operating in relation to a disciplined multiparty system.

Each of the three presidents of Israel—Chaim Weizmann, Yitzchak Ben-Zvi, and Shneour Zalman Shazar—has personified the thrust of the Zionist movement. Their lives and their careers have paralleled and are analogous with the experiences of the other political activists who dominated Israeli national life through the first two decades of statehood. All three presidents were born not in Israel but in east European shtetls. All received the traditional religious education (so that if they were not themselves religious, they understood and had a feeling for Orthodoxy) and then went on to complete their education in secular universities. All three distinguished themselves not only as Zionists but as men of broad intellectual achievement.

The symbolic attributes of the office of the presidency may increase in time, but it is highly unlikely that there will be an accretion of actual executive function and power. More than two decades of precedent and the prime minister–parliamentary structure will act to prevent this.

Formal political power resides in the Knesset, which theoretically has unlimited legislative scope. Growing out of the Knesset as a major institution of power is the executive (the prime minister and the cabinet). The cabinet is the government. In practice, the cabinet, under the leadership of the prime minister, controls and directs Knesset sway. A cabinet may be ended not only by Knesset repudiation or expiration, but it also may dissolve itself in any of three ways: (1) if the prime minister resigns or dies; (2) by agreement among the coalition partners; (3) when one or more of the coalition parties rejects cabinet policy, departs from the government, and in a Knesset vote deprives the government of a majority.

The electoral mechanism that emerged from the Provisional Council was similar to that of the Jewish Community government under the Mandate and was based on a rigid proportional representation system that enabled the minor parties to share power. A 120-member unicameral national assembly (Knesset), elected from the country at large (that is, a single national constituency), was created. Any party polling 1 percent of the countrywide vote was entitled to membership in the Knesset.

The parties stem from the colonization and pioneering associations of the prestate era. These chalutzic movements, particularly the Zionist labor ones, imbibed from the revolutionary ferment of eastern Europe certain premises: the party, the movement, and the cause were vehicles in a historical process; and the ideological purity of the movement must be protected and fostered. The doctrinaire aspect of Israeli party politics was, and is, reinforced on the practical level by a host of party activities. Party adherence went, and still goes, beyond the act of registering electoral support. Affiliated with political parties are newspapers, youth groups, athletic associations, recreational, cultural, and educational activities, banks, insurance companies, housing projects, collective and cooperative settlements, and comprehensive health and social welfare services and institutions.

Multipartyism, which had been the dominant feature of prestate politics, was perpetuated now with the founding of the state by the doctrinaire quality of the parties and their ability to gain Knesset representation by polling 1 percent of the vote. The plethora of parties has lined up on two parallel left-right axes: a secular axis and a religious one. For the elections to the first Knesset in 1949, the left to right ideological lineup of the major secular parties was Communists, Mapam, Mapai, Progressives, General Zionists, and Herut.

Beginning on the extreme left is the Communist party known as Maki, from the initials of its Hebrew name. From the beginning Maki was characterized by conflicts, since the party attempted to involve both Jews and Arabs. Until the UN Partition Resolution in November 1947, it followed the USSR's official policy on Palestine: Zionism was attacked as a form of "bourgeois nationalism" and a "tool of British imperialism." Only from the time of the UN Partition Resolution to the beginning of the First Knesset in 1949 did the Israel Communist party support Jewish aspirations for national independence. The clear trend of Maki's development since 1949 has been toward the arabization of the party. This policy reached its logical conclusion with the 1965 Sixth Knesset elections, when the party split to form two wings, Jewish and Arab. The Communists are completely outside the mainstream of Israeli politics. They were included in the Provisional Council of State, but they have never participated in any of the governing coalitions.[3]

Standing to the right of the Communist party is Mapam (United Worker's party). Mapam believes in a vigorous socialist planned economy and working-class collectivism. It is antireligious, vocally supports Jewish-Arab friendship, and advocates a foreign policy of nonalignment with either of the world blocs and neutralization of the Middle East.[4]

To the right of Mapam for the first two elections was Mapai (Israel Worker's party). Mapai, founded in 1929 when labor Zionism had already become a mass movement, resulted from a series of amalgamations of Palestinian labor groups. Its founding platform expressed the prevailing ethos: "The Palestine Labor Movement is united by the historic aim of devotion to the rebirth of the Jewish nation in Palestine as a free laboring people, rooted in all branches of the agricultural and industrial economy and independently developing its Hebrew culture . . . to build a society based on labor, equality, and liberty." [5] Mapai quickly became a central factor in the life of the Yishuv, and its history and the names of its leaders—Yitzchak Ben-Zvi, Berl Katzenelson, David Remez, Chaim Arlosoroff, Moshe Sharett, Abba Eban, Levi Eshkol, Dov Yoseph, Pinchas Lavon, Golda Meir, and David Ben-Gurion, to name but a few—have become almost synonymous with the state itself.

As the most powerful party before Independence, Mapai provided leadership and direction for the Jewish quasi government, managed much of the Zionist international diplomacy, and controlled the Histadrut and the Jewish Agency. Since then, Mapai has remained Israel's most powerful party. In every government it has been the party around which the coalition has been built. Mapai has dominated the Israeli political scene for two reasons: first, because its leaders have personified one of Israel's central ideals, chalutziut, and second, because of its nondoctrinaire pragmatic ideology and pluralist nature. Mapai's political posture is slightly left of center on the secular political spectrum. While it favors a secular state, it is not hostile to many historic and religious aspects of Judaism. Mapai's economic program pays lip service to the "socialist ideals which are the basis of its existence," but as the leading party responsible for the direction of Israel's growth it has permitted the development of private enterprise while it advocates gradual democratic planning of the economy.[6] This broad interweaving of democratic socialism with Zionist principles has appealed to all levels and occupations in the economy and to a large extent accounts for Mapai's strength.

To the right of Mapai, approximately in the center, were the Progressives, who favored a liberal but nonsocialist attitude toward labor and social welfare. Next were the General Zionists, who were more capitalistic in outlook than the Progressives. And lastly, Herut (Freedom), the most rightist, emphasized free initiative and the encouragement of private enterprise without restrictive controls. Herut, also, has always been highly nationalistic and has advocated that Israel's borders should be the country's "historic boundaries." [7]

Since the first election a process of fusion and faction has occurred. Mapam's unwillingness to criticize the Soviet Union's anti-Semitic policies and military aid to Egypt brought about a schism within the party after the 1951 election. The result of the split was the re-formation of Achdut ha-Avodah (Labor Unity) which took an ideological stance to the right of Mapam and to the left of Mapai. Achdut ha-Avodah remained as a separate party for the 1955, 1959, and 1961 Knesset elections.[8] Prior to the 1965 election Achdut ha-Avodah joined with Mapai in an alignment. (An alignment is an arrangement in which the parties agree to retain their organizational autonomy while coordinating their electoral and parliamentary activities.) At the same time David Ben-Gurion, a former premier and longtime Mapai leader, broke away from Mapai. Ben-Gurion and his dissident followers formed a new Knesset faction known as Rafi, from the initials of its Hebrew name, Reshimat Poale Israel (Israel Labor List). Rafi's main point of departure from Mapai was electoral reform. Rafi wanted to abandon the list system of proportional representation for a constituency system. Other differences involved personalities, styles, and contending aspirations for political power.[9] After the Six-Day War, Rafi merged with the Mapai–Achdut ha-Avodah Alignment, and the three factions adopted the name Israel Labor Party. Ben-Gurion and a small coterie of his supporters, however, unlike the other Rafi members, still refused to unite with Mapai, and they became a Knesset party known as the State List. Now, aside from the State List, it only remained for Mapam to join the Israel Labor Party to complete the electoral consolidation of the secular left. This finally came about in 1969, when Mapam joined the Israel Labor Party in an alignment.

The electoral unity of the secular left has deflected considerable political friction from the national party arena to intraparty conflict. The constituent factions of the Israel Labor Party still have their own discrete ideologies, supporters, and organizational apparatus. The ideological disagreements and partisan jealousies that existed among the four parties before unification have not and will not magically disappear.

The history of fusion and faction that has characterized the parties of the secular left also has occurred on the secular right. The Progressives and General Zionists united as the Liberals for the fifth Knesset election in 1961. But it was an uneasy marriage, and in the spring of 1965 most of the General Zionists joined forces with Herut to form a new bloc known as Gahal. Many of the former Progressives, however, objected, preferred to retain their ideological purity, and set up the Independent Liberal party. The Independent Liberals sought to project themselves as political centrists. They opposed equally the leftward alignment, which they contended was flirting with extremist socialism, and the Gahal bloc, which they felt was too rigidly rightist.

Paralleling the secular political spectrum is the religious spectrum whose parties consider their mission to be not in the realm of politics but in the realm of spiritual leadership. The presence of religious parties on the Israeli political scene has resulted in a pattern of party politics which can be termed theopolitics. Theopolitics is the attempt to attain theological ends by means of political activity.

In 1949 four religious parties contested the first election under the rubric of the United Religious Front (URF). Despite their electoral unity, the constituent parties of the bloc—Mizrachi, Ha-Poel ha-Mizrachi, Agudat Israel, and Poale Agudat Israel—held somewhat divergent religious and political philosophies and have had different historical antecedents. Mizrachi (while the Hebrew word *mizrachi* translates into English as "eastern," the name actually stands for a combination of two Hebrew words, *Merkaz* and *Ruhani,* which mean "Spiritual Center") was founded by European Jews in 1902 to infuse the spirit of Orthodoxy into the Zionist movement. According to its own literature, Mizrachi

is that party in Zionism which strives for the upbuilding of the Jewish National Home . . . on the basis of Israel's religious traditions in the belief that The Land of Israel was not intended to be merely a dwelling place of the Jewish people but also the abode of the Jewish spirit. The party's synthesis of its philosophy is well indicated in its slogan: The land of Israel for the people of Israel on the basis of the Torah of Israel.[10]

Organized as a political party in Palestine in 1918, Mizrachi is composed mainly of urban, middle-class, Orthodox Jews who are primarily concerned that Israel be built and governed according to the traditional teachings of the Orthodox rabbinate. Its economic program is to the right of center in that it opposes socialism, collectivism, and labor domination and supports private enterprise and economic laissez-faire. Primarily because of these conservative economic attitudes, a group of industrial workers and farmers split away from the parent Mizrachi in 1922 and formed Ha-Poel ha-Mizrachi party (Mizrachi or Spiritual Center Workers' party). Taking as its slogan "Religious Law and Labor," Ha-Poel ha-Mizrachi advocates a program that integrates religious Orthodoxy, socialism, and Zionism. Labor-oriented Ha-Poel ha-Mizrachi established Orthodox collective farms and cooperatives in an attempt to counteract similar activities on the part of the secular Zionists.

More intransigently Orthodox than the Mizrachi groups are the Agudah parties. Agudat Israel (Union of Israel) was founded in Europe in 1912 and is the organizational

47

home of those ultra-Orthodox who are willing to participate in the Israeli political process. Agudat Israel believes that

the aim of the party is to enable the Jewish people throughout the world to live according to the principles and practical precepts of the Torah, eternally in force for the public life of the Jewish people, and directing the life of the individual as far as it is concerned with the former.[11]

Agudat Israel opposed Zionism and the Mizrachi movement. During the Mandate Agudat Israel did not participate in the organizational life of the Yishuv but, with the establishment of the state, agreed to participate. Agudat Israel mainly conceived of national reconstruction as the building of *yeshivot* (theological seminaries).

Poale Agudat Israel (Workers of the Union of Israel) is the labor wing of Agudat Israel. It was founded in Warsaw in 1922 with the object of counteracting the antireligious and non-Orthodox sentiments and practices among the workers. In 1934 Poale Agudah began to establish rural villages in Palestine on the principle that the Messiah would come only if His Chosen People merited redemption in the Holy Land. The political aim of the Poale Agudat Israel, like that of its parent body, "is the transformation of the State of Israel into the Torah State which bases its constitution, legislation, and the manner of life of its residents on the written Torah and tradition." [12] The essential difference between the parent body and its labor wing is that the parent stresses relations of man to God and concentrates its attention on the study of the religious literature so as to prepare for God's redemption, while the worker party's approach is more activist; God's intention will be realized by human exertion.

In all of the elections the proportionate strength of the religious voters has remained firm and significant. Given the division of the party system, the religious vote has emerged as an important and enduring bloc. No government can alienate the religious or ignore their views; to do so would run the risk of gravely disrupting the body politic. Running together as the United Religious Front in the first election, the four religious parties won 16 Knesset seats. For the second election, the parties disagreed among themselves as to the apportionment of each constituent party's seats in the Knesset and campaigned separately. Mizrachi won 2 seats, Ha-Poel ha-Mizrachi 8 seats, Agudat Israel 3 seats, and Poale Agudat Israel 2 seats. Some unification took place for the third election in 1955, but the religious parties were still divided in philosophy and electoral support. Contending that the Mizrachi parties were lukewarm in their advocacy of a Torah State, Agudat Israel and Poale Agudat Israel combined for the election as the Torah Religious Front (TRF) and won 5 Knesset seats. The more moderate Orthodox groups, Mizrachi and Ha-Poel ha-Mizrachi, combined to form the National Religious Party and won 11 Knesset seats. This party pattern remained for the 1959 elections, when the NRP received 12 Knesset seats and the Torah Religious Front 6 Knesset seats. The Torah Religious Front, however, soon splintered. Agudat Israel and Poale Agudat Israel disagreed over the question of joining the coalition. For the next three elections, Agudat Israel and Poale Agudat Israel each ran separate lists. Both parties maintained a stable strength, winning 4 and 2 Knesset seats, respectively, in the elections of 1961, 1965, and 1969. In contrast to the ultra-Orthodox Agudah parties, the moderate Mizrachi factions achieved a firm union as the National Religious Party. The NRP won 12 Knesset seats in 1961, 11 in 1965, and 12 in 1969.[13]

In addition to the religious parties, mention must also be made of a theologically fundamentalist group of only a few hundred families, the Natore Karta (Guardians of the City). The Natore Karta's purist interpretation of the totality of God asserts that Jews must accept unquestioningly their fate on earth and must not try to change their condition or interfere with Divine Will. Divine Providence will, in its own time, ultimately send the Messiah. Any attempts at the establishment of a secular government, accordingly, are sinful. During the Mandate the Natore Karta, like Agudat Israel, pursued an anti-Zionist policy and went their own way. When the State of Israel was established, they refused to recognize it and dismissed it, stating: "We openly declare that we do not recognize the regime of blasphemers; we do not accept their authority, and we do not bow to their rule. We are in no way bound by their laws and directives." [14] Members of the Natore Karta still do not recognize the existence of Israel, and on election days they lobby at polling stations in an attempt to persuade people not to vote. The Natore Karta by its very presence adds to the religious-secular polarization. Just as the National Religious Party is restricted from diluting its Orthodoxy by the fear that the Agudah parties will accuse it of not fighting sufficiently hard for a Torah state, so too are the Agudah parties afraid of being considered lax by the Natore Karta.

The strength of the religious parties lies not so much in their absolute numbers but in their position of critical leverage. The 1949 election returns signaled the beginning of a pattern; it was clear that a Knesset coalition was a necessity and that Mapai as the largest party in the country would be the cornerstone of any government. Although Mapai had a substantial lead over all the other parties, it still needed another 15 Knesset votes to command a parliamentary majority. A workable coalition had to be constructed. The arithmetic of coalition building is simple, but Israeli politics complicates the addition. A coalition with either the secular left or the secular right presented arithmetic alternatives but political impossibilities. The ideological differences were too great to be bridged. None of the remaining secular parties had sufficient strength alone to sustain a majority alongside Mapai, and bringing two of them together with Mapai still could not give Mapai a sound coalition base. David Ben-Gurion, therefore, was forced to form a coalition with the United Religious Front.

In exchange for the coalition participation of the United Religious Front, Mapai agreed to maintain and extend the religious status quo agreement. (This agreement which had been arrived at after hard bargaining in the summer of 1947 took the form of a letter to the ultra-Orthodox Agudat Israel from the Executive of the Jewish Agency and was signed by David Ben-Gurion, the Executive's chairman, J. L. Fishman as representative of the Mizrachi, and Yitzchak Gruenbaum on behalf of the General Zionists. The letter indicated a willingness to accede to the religious camps' desires "in regard to marriage, the Sabbath, education, and the dietary laws in the Jewish State when it is established in our own days" but also pointed out "that it is not the intention to establish a theocratic state." The status quo agreement allayed the fears of the religious camps and was instrumental in securing the political cooperation of the Agudists in the Provisional Council of Government.) But the desire of the religious parties to see the establishment of a "Torah state"—their very raison d'être—made it impossible for them to remain content with the status quo. The religious parties now demanded, as a condition of joining the coalition, that restrictions be placed on the importation of nonkosher meat. Ben-Gurion was willing to placate the United Religious Front in this and what he considered other small matters in return for the vital assurance of coalition stability. Accordingly, the army and other public institutions were to use only kosher food, and transportation services run by the state (the airline and intercity passenger trains) were to observe the Sabbath.[15]

The gains made by the religious parties as a condition of joining the first coalition government were the first fruits of theopolitics. During the ensuing years theopolitics flourished in the fertile ground of coalition politics. All long-term Israeli cabinets to date have been coalitions centering around Mapai and have included the National Religious Party. Mapai policy normally (emergency situations obviously negate the "politics as usual" conditions) has excluded the extremes of the secular political spectrum, the Communists on the far left, and Herut (now part of Gahal) on the far right.[16]

Mapai has, therefore, turned to the religious spectrum for its principal continuing ally. The beneficiary of this situation has been the National Religious Party with its centrist economic policies, which are generally acceptable to either side of the secular parties that might potentially join the coalition. The NRP is additionally attractive as a permanent coalition satellite because it is the most moderate of the religious parties in its theological demands and because it is the only party that could conceivably be induced to enter a coalition on the right that would exclude Mapai. These factors have made the NRP's political influence considerably greater than its raw voting strength. Mapai in the past has usually been willing to accept the demands of the NRP and the other religious parties in order to maintain Mapai hegemony and achieve government stability. As a result, political stability has rested on a delicate balance of secularist and religious viewpoints, achieved through the techniques of concession, compromise, and deliberate ambiguity.

Further legislation has been achieved through the conjunction of feelings of Jewish nationalism with the workings of theopolitics. Illustrative of this is the Pork Prohibition Law. After the elections of 1961 Mapai needed support from the religious parties in order to build a cabinet. In exchange for the votes of the National Religious Party and Poale Agudat Israel, Mapai acquiesced in the passage of a national pork prohibition law. (Pig flesh is food prohibited to Jews by religious dietary laws.) Originally the religious parties wanted a sweeping measure that would prohibit the raising and sale of pigs throughout the country. But Ben-Gurion insisted in precoalition negotiations that pig breeding be allowed in certain areas inhabited mainly by Christians. The law, as passed, prohibits the breeding, keeping (except for research and zoological purposes), or killing for food of pigs in any part of Israel, save

53

in those areas specified by law (Nazareth and some smaller localities where Arab Christians form a majority). Stiff penalties for violation of the law were specified.

Those who argued in favor of the bill did so for religious and/or nationalistic reasons. Tyrants, from the period of the First Temple in Jerusalem to the Russian czars, have used pigs to degrade and subjugate the Jews. Arguing that it was more than the scriptural admonition "And the swine . . . of their flesh ye shall not eat . . . they are unclean to you," one Knesset member summed up the pig's role in Jewish history. Alluding to the tyrant Antiochus Epiphanes, who attempted to enforce worship of Greek gods in Jerusalem in the second century B.C.E. (before the Common Era), she said:

Perhaps, if he or one of his soldiers had thought of forcing Jews to eat camel meat in order to subjugate them, the camel would occupy a place in the national consciousness of the Jewish people. But it happened with the pig.

Another recalled bitterly that as a child he had been persecuted by other children who tried to smear pork fat on his lips. For many then, the rationale for passing the antipig act was primarily nationalistic. Only the pig was singled out for legislative exorcism: other nonkosher animals had no legislation restricting them passed, or even thought of. The pig was the only offender.

Those parties which opposed the bill, Mapam, Achdut ha-Avodah, and the Communists, argued that legislation enforcing an ancient dietary law that was ignored by a significant segment of the population would constitute religious compulsion. It was well known that many Israelis ignored the dietary laws. Pig production, despite the fact that it was banned by local ordinances in many parts of the country, was a thriving business (nearly 5000 tons of pork were marketed in the year before the ban went into effect). Appeals to freedom of dietary choice were reenforced by more mundane pleas to heed the pocketbook. It was argued that the pig was one of the cheapest meat products and to deny people the opportunity to purchase pig products acted to limit their purchase of meat.[17]

The passage of the antipig law was heralded by the religious elements as a significant step in moving Israel toward the goal of a Torah state. Israel's religious image was being maintained. The Diaspora Jew now could look to Israel and see a national affirmation of a hallowed principle of religious law. The Israeli secularist who found his dietary inclinations circumscribed was told that he was not being forced to observe the dietary laws, and the restriction on the purchase of pig products was not really such a terrible hardship, especially in the face of the benefit to the national consensus. But the fact remains that, aside from a minor concession to the non-Jewish minority, the state, irrespective of the rationale, had legislated in favor of the Orthodox at the expense of the secularist.

In the first through the seventh elections the electorate more than tripled, but the basic ideological distribution of voters remained relatively stable. Fundamental change has been occurring, but very slowly. The most significant organizational change has been the formation of the Israel Labor Party. But the factions connected with the omnibus party, Mapam in particular, while less than formerly, still cherish and nourish their doctrinaire attitudes.[18] The Israel Labor Party, and the other parties as well, soon will have to go through a painful crisis of succession. This is inevitable. The passing of the veteran leadership, largely of east European origin, and the assumption of leadership by those who have lived most of their young lives in Israel will be major inputs of the future.

As long as the wide-based Israel Labor Party holds together it will present a formidable challenge to the parties of the secular right. Yet it is doubtful that the secular right will, in the immediate future, succeed in coalescing to form a wide-based nonsocialist bloc. The small Independent Liberal party takes its title word seriously; expediency might dictate making common cause with Gahal, but the pull of uncompromised ideological integrity remains strong. Further complicating the possibility of a strong unified rightist party is the fact that within Gahal the differences between the Liberals and Herutists remain strong. And then too, there is the presence of the Herut secessionist faction, the Free Center. It should also be pointed out that even in the unlikely possibility that the rightist members of the Knesset could band together, unless there was a major departure from the voting patterns established in the first seven elections, a rightist party by itself or even a rightist party in combination with all the religious parties could not command the absolute parliamentary majority necessary to form a government. Accordingly, assuming the continuation of past electoral behavior patterns, the future set and direction of Israeli politics will revolve around the stability and strength of the Israel Labor Party.[19]

The religious segment of the electorate has remained relatively stable as the electorate has grown. It has fluctuated from a low of 15 seats in 1951 to highs of 18 seats in 1959,

1961, and 1969. It is highly unlikely that there will be a serious erosion in the strength of the religious voters. While not an immediate possibility, the potential for a united religious bloc (similar to the one that existed for the elections of the First Knesset) cannot be completely dismissed. The old leadership of the Agudah parties is dying out, and the younger adherents of ultra-Orthodoxy, albeit zealous in their religious devotion, are learning to accommodate their traditionalism to a modernizing Israel. Admittedly there are considerable areas of disagreement between the moderates of the NRP and the ultra-Orthodox Agudists; but they are essentially disagreements on matters of degree, interpretation, emphasis, and observance. On core issues, the moderate-Orthodox and the ultra-Orthodox share large areas of ideological congruence. Should the religious parties ever be excluded from a national government, always a possibility should the Israel Labor Party ever attain a viable majority, the religious parties would still have considerable strength on the local level.

If the Israel Labor Party achieves sufficient strength to govern alone, coalition government and the bargaining and compromise that have characterized Israeli politics over the last two decades would be eliminated. The dominant party, as never before, would be independent of the religious parties, and the established course of concessions to the Orthodox in exchange for their support, concessions that bring Israel closer to the religious parties' concept of a Torah state, would be abandoned. While the immediate result might be a termination of new preferments given to Orthodox Judaism by the state, it is extremely unlikely that any concessions already given to the Orthodox would be rescinded substantially or modified.

Postulating a situation in which a secular majority composed the government and controlled the Knesset, the religion-state arrangements that have become institutionalized, nonetheless, would not be radically disturbed, for a number of compelling pragmatic reasons: (1) As long as the Arab-Israel conflict is unresolved and defense and security requirements remain paramount, no Israeli government would be so foolhardy as to introduce the extremely divisive issue of tampering with the religious status quo. (2) Israel is still developing and remains in need of the support of Diaspora Jewry. Any attempts at rearrangement of Orthodox Judaism's preferred position might alienate sources of Orthodox support and/or religiously inspired immigration. (3) Much of Israeli nationalism builds on biblical and religious roots and is a response to historic persecution. So while many Israeli secularists might resist Orthodox restrictions imposed on the nonreligious, there remains a widespread and deep-rooted attachment to Judaism which is an integral part of the Israeli civic consciousness. The yoke of religion may chafe the militant minority, but for the great majority of the non-Orthodox the yoke rests—by virtue of selective acceptance—lightly. (4) It should be emphasized that it would be a mistake to assume that the majority of tradition-oriented or Orthodox Jews vote only for one of the three religious parties. A much larger proportion of the Israeli electorate is religiously oriented than that which votes for the religious parties. In a pioneering study, Aaron Antonovsky of the Israeli Institute for Applied Social Research analyzed various attitudes toward religion. One of his interview questions was "Should the government see to it that public life be conducted in accord with Jewish tradition?" Of the respondents, 23 percent felt that the government should "definitely" enforce religious tradition in community life. An additional 20 percent replied that such regulation would "probably" be wise.[20] Another indication that a feeling for Orthodoxy infuses the adherents of some of the secular parties is that 29 percent of Israel's parents send their children to religious state schools, and about 7 percent more send their children to the recognized independent schools of the Agudat Israel. In short, religious sentiments are more widespread than "straight" electoral patterns show. Religious Jews, obviously, also vote for some secular parties. (5) The history of Israeli party politics is a record of faction and fusion, and, although there may exist a wide-based secular labor party, there is always the possibility of history repeating itself and factionalization again occurring. Given the possibility that party splintering might take place, the need for coalition rule would again arise; consequently, few party leaders would be willing deliberately to reduce areas of potential party support. (6) Since many aspects of religious affairs are controlled by the municipalities, no matter what happens on the national level, theopolitics will continue to operate undiminished on the local level.

Other aspects of the future of Israeli politics are also subject to speculation. It will remain for the sabra generation, once it comes to power, to face the new challenges presented to the old institutions and to resolve the core issue of Israeli society: Is Israel to be a secular or a religious state? [21]

4
The Conflict
over
the Constitution

It is significant that, although the Constituent Assembly was able to agree on and establish the operative framework of the Israeli body politic, it could not agree on a comprehensive written constitution. The Israeli legislators were unable to draw up a constitution primarily for fear of touching off a Kulturkampf, a fear that still exists. In many respects the deliberations over a written constitution were a microcosm of the religion-state problem and a foretaste of the religious issues that would agitate Israeli political life.

The drafting of a constitution was undertaken before the state was established. Immediately after the adoption of the UN Resolution of November 29, 1947, the executive of the Jewish Agency considered the matter of a constitution. The task of preparing a draft constitution was given to the Agency's political secretary, Dr. Yehuda Leo Kohn, an expert on constitutional law.[1]

In drafting the constitution Kohn was influenced by several factors: the UN Resolution, the Yishuv's multi-party political structure, the failure of parliamentary democracy in much of Europe between the two world wars, and Kohn's own traditional Judaism. Kohn's words are instructive:

. . . the case of Israel is *sui generis*. It is a new state, as new in its way as the political community which the Pilgrim Fathers set up in America; but Israel is not a new country and the Jewish people is certainly a people with a history. If its constitution is to command the enduring loyalty of its citizens and the respect of Jews throughout the world, it must be rooted in the spiritual tradition which constitutes

Outside a polling station in the Mea Shearim quarter of Jerusalem.

the timeless heritage of the whole House of Israel. That tradition is of very specific and significant character. Its spiritual basis is the monotheistic conception of God—invisible, omnipotent, one and indivisible, an embodiment of absolute justice, the Ruler of the universe, the Father of man. The projection of that conception in the moral sphere is an austere code aiming at the sanctification of matter by the creative force of the spirit. Its ultimate goal is the establishment of the Messianic Kingdom, embodying a rule of universal justice freely acknowledged by all the children of men. From its early beginnings, Judaism has aimed not merely at individual perfection, but also at the shaping of a social order. It is concerned not only with the salvation of the soul but also with the political community in which that soul has its roots and being. The great figures of our spiritual tradition were definitely hewn in a political frame. They aspired to the evolution of "a kingdom of priests and a holy people," ruled not by kings or priests-kings, as was the practice all over the ancient East, but by the Deity alone —perhaps the boldest effort ever conceived of shaping reality in the image of the absolute. Judaism is a design for molding the life of a community in accordance with the dictates of a higher order: kindness to the poor, but justice to be accorded equally to the rich and the poor; the sanctity of the Sabbath, but no less so the holiness of the working day; freedom of contract, but, above that, the greater freedom of the Sabbatical and the Jubilee Years which restore liberty to the slave and give back to the poor man his lost heritage —such are its characteristic prescriptions. Returning to active political life after centuries of Dispersion and disintegration, the citizens of Israel are faced again by that timeless challenge. The State of Israel is being rebuilt under modern conditions. It cannot but adopt the institutional forms and civic conceptions by which alone the mass life of a modern political community can be organized. But if these forms and conceptions are to have more than a transient meaning, they must strike roots in the deeper recesses of the soul of the people. It is not by abstract declarations

63

but by the infusion of the Hebrew spiritual tradition into its functional framework that the constitution of Israel can alone be rendered Jewish, can alone be rendered safe.[2]

The draft constitution consisted of a preamble and nine chapters. The preamble gave "thanks to Almighty God for having delivered us from the burden of exile and brought us back to our ancient land" and expressed the resolve "to rebuild our Commonwealth in accordance with the ideals of peace and righteousness of the Prophets of Israel." The first chapter dealt with general principles such as the name of the state and the design of the state as "the National Home of the Jewish People with the right of all Jews to immigrate." The second chapter dealt with fundamental rights and had provisions to safeguard the freedom of conscience and of religious worship. The Jewish Sabbath and holy days were to be "days of rest and spiritual elevation," recognized as such in the laws of the country. (The holy days of other religious denominations were accorded equal treatment.) In the fifth chapter the judicial structure was outlined. There was to be a series of courts culminating in a Supreme Court with the power of judicial review of legislation. In addition, the religious courts of the Jewish, Moslem, and Christian communities would exercise jurisdiction in matters of personal status. The eighth chapter dealt with the reception of the existing legal system and stipulated that "future legislation in Israel shall be guided by the basic principles of Jewish Law." [3]

The debate in the Provisional Council over the specifics of the draft and over the entire question of whether or not a written constitution should be adopted was highly emotional. This was understandable, for at stake were basic values and symbols, the structuring of practical political and economic power, and the determination of a secular versus religious conception of Israeli nationality.

The debate was not conducted on party lines—certain basic positions were taken by the parties, but their members expressed mixed opinions. Certain issues continually cropped up, particularly those relevant to the central question: To what extent should the constitution of a Jewish state be of a specifically Jewish character? During the Provisional Government the parties had an opportunity to present their views officially to a special committee of the State Council.

Mapam argued that the preamble of Dr. Kohn's draft had too strong a religious cast. They also felt that Jews, as well as Christians and Moslems, should be assured freedom of conscience, and to that end, civil marriage should be allowed for those who did not want any religious solemnization. Mapam, however, with its Zionist leanings, had no objection to the ordaining of religious festivals as national holidays. The moderate religious groups, Mizrachi and Ha-Poel ha-Mizrachi, argued that in a Jewish state Hebrew should be the only official language and that the president must be a Jew. At the extreme of the religious viewpoint, Agudat Israel argued that it would be adequate to declare: "Israel's Torah is her constitution." There was no need for a constitution because the Torah includes not only precepts for man's spiritual guidance but also social directives. Furthermore, they argued for an absolute prohibition against conscription of women.

Some of the Orthodox had qualms about the extent of participation, and even the legitimacy of participating, in

65

a secular Jewish state. The Natore Karta sect, the most
fanatical of all the ultra-Orthodox, refused to recognize the
existence of the state because it had not been established
by the Messiah. Noncooperation and nonrecognition were
the watchwords. The Natore Kartaites would not even concern themselves with such irrelevancies as a constitution.[4]

Other religious Jews were in a quandary: they readily
admitted the desirability in a modern society of certain
provisions, particularly female equality and the abolition
of the death penalty, but they could not reconcile these
provisions with traditional Jewish law. The draft constitution granted absolute equality to women, but Jewish law
clearly sets them apart. Maimonides could be quoted:
"Women are not placed in kingship . . . and similarly regarding all offices in Israel, only men are appointed to
them." The draft constitution also prohibited capital pun-
ishment, but religious law, albeit under extraordinarily
strict procedural safeguards, nonetheless recognized the
right of organized society to impose the death penalty for
a variety of reasons. No one argued that these ancient penalties were appropriate, but the issue remained: If they were
incorporated in the constitution but were not followed,
would this not be an inconsistent action?[5]

The debate during the Provisional Government period
produced few surprises and was taken up again during the
First Knesset. Taking a strong secular stand, the Communists and Mapam argued bitterly against any attempt to
give permanence to the religious courts. The chairman of
the Constitution, Legislation, and Juridical Committee, at
one point remarked insightfully:

The main point of the question is the Religious Bloc's fear of the Constitution that we will approve. Because without a Constitution you can always make particular demands, whether they be or not be fulfilled. In view, however, of the ratio of power in the Knesset and in the country, the Religious Bloc fears that the Constitution will be a secular one.

The extreme Orthodox were intransigent. The intensity of their feeling comes through in their words:

We will see in a secular Constitution an attempt to give up our holy Torah, for which generations sacrificed their life. . . . Against this we will fight, against this we will rise with all our strength, soul, and might, without compromises and without concessions.

The laws of the Torah are pledged to the people of Israel, and this is the reason why we will fight against every approved law that is counter to the laws of the Torah with all our strength, and will see in it compulsion of our religious conscience.

The aim of the religious Jewry is that only the laws of the Torah shall be decisive in all realms of life of the State.

The Agudat Israel party, having for decades opposed Zionist statehood, now that they were in the Knesset became the most vocal exponent of the spiritual uniqueness of the new state. Laws that were not imbued with the spirit of the Torah were suspect. A representative of Agudat Israel, in an emotional moment, declared: "Any Constitution created by man can have no place in Israel." [6]

The apparently irreconcilable constitutional controversy contributed to national acrimony. Energies were being deflected from the pressing tasks of national survival. Prime Minister Ben-Gurion's Mapai-led coalition government depended on the cooperation of the United Religious Front. Ben-Gurion, who had favored a written constitution during the 1948 Provisional Government, now felt that its adoption should be postponed. Zerah Warhaftig, a chief spokesman for the moderates in the United Religious Front, who earlier had seen no conflict between his religious opinions and the possibility of a written constitution, now yielded to the pressure of the more extreme rabbinic leaders of the Agudat Israel. In fear of losing supporters, the moderate religionists now took the position that a written constitution was undesirable at that time. Israel's constitution was to be a bridge between the Jewish past and the Jewish future and must reflect the singular Jewish *Volksgeist*. Further, the Ingathering of Exiles was not complete—the constitution should reflect the will not of a few but of all. Unable to get their particular version of a "Torah Constitution," the religious factions united in their unyielding opposition to a written constitution.[7]

Arguing most strongly against the Orthodox position, interestingly enough, were Mapam on the left and nationalist Herut on the right. Between the Orthodox and their opponents were a few Mapai and General Zionist party members, as well as Progressives who, in general, favored a written constitution but did not want to offend the Orthodox and precipitate a Kulturkampf.

To buttress their various opinions, a number of arguments were presented. Those opposing the adoption of a written constitution argued that conditions were unsettled: war was raging on the borders and there was little prospect of a viable peace with Israel's Arab neighbors, thousands of immigrants were pouring in every month, and a host of basic economic and administrative problems of pressing urgency were still pending. Let conditions stabilize somewhat before turning to the task of writing a constitution. A written constitution in the first years of a new state was not an imperative; a case in point was the United States. Furthermore, a democratic nation did not need to have a constitution; England was an example of this. Conversely, nations that had a written constitution were not necessarily democratic. These arguments were countered by the views that a formal constitution would enhance the authority of the state, strenghten its political frame, define and guarantee fundamental rights, and serve as an important influence in politically educating the newcomers and the young.

But arguments for and against the *need* for a written document were ancillary to the fact that there was no consensus on the *content* of a constitution. For the Agudists only a Torah Constitution was acceptable. Militant and aggressive in their beliefs, and having a history of separatism in the Yishuv era, the Agudists would tolerate no dilution of their conception of Orthodoxy. They insisted that if there had to be a written constitution, the Torah should be paramount. Judaism and its rituals should determine individual behavior. The government itself must observe the rituals and be enjoined from committing any offense against Jewish law.

The Mizrachi factions were more flexible and more willing to accommodate to the exigencies of a modern society. They avoided the claim that the law of the Torah was the only legitimate law. The moderates, for example, were willing to accept greater legal equality between the sexes. The differences between the religious camps prompted cynics to say that there must be two Torahs.[8]

Aside from the fact that the religious minorities could accept only their own specific versions of the Jewish ideal, there were many practical problems arising out of the concept of a "Torah Constitution." Judaism does not have a political philosophy dealing with the modern democratic nation-state. Talmudic law originated in the Holy Land and developed in the Diaspora, where the Jews had little need to concern themselves with the ordering of a body politic. Consequently, political concepts such as constitutional limitation, checks and balances, separation of powers, the rule of law, presidential or parliamentary structure are rudimentary in Talmudic law.

The central question of the role of religion in a modern Jewish state deadlocked the Knesset. Any resolution of the issue offensive to either secularists or the religionists would be no resolution, for a Kulturkampf was certain to follow. To resolve this dilemma, a member of the Progressive party, on June 13, 1950, introduced a compromise resolution:

> The First Knesset directs the Constitution, Law and Justice Committee to prepare a draft Constitution for the State. The Constitution shall be constructed article by article in such a manner that each shall in itself constitute a fundamental law.
> Each article shall be brought before the Knesset as the Committee completes its work, and all the articles together shall comprise the State Constitution.

The proposal was approved: Mapai, the Progressives, the Sephardim, and the Wizo faction supported it; Mapam, the General Zionists, Herut, and the Fighters (former Sternist faction) voted against it; and the United Religious Front abstained as a group to emphasize that they could not vote for a measure which did not guarantee basing the constitution on Orthodox doctrine.[9]

The adoption of the compromise resolution terminated the debate. The principle that a written constitution should be adopted was accepted, balanced by the potent hedge that the document would be neither imminent nor comprehensive. For the time being, fundamental laws were to be adopted individually.

The Basic Laws envisioned by the 1950 resolution were slow in coming. A decade passed before the first Basic Law was enacted in February 1958. Entitled "Basic Law: The Knesset," it consolidated legislation previously adopted concerning, primarily, the election and functions of the Knesset. Three other Basic Laws have been adopted: one dealing with the state's lands; another relating to the office of the president; and a third dealing with the government as the state's executive authority. A number of constitutional law specialists have expressed disappointment over the present status of the constitution. They feel that it is doubtful if the Basic Laws dealing with state lands and the presidency are of constitutionally superior standing, and, conversely, they feel that various laws enacted under the rubric of ordinary legislation are inherently superior laws and are constitutional without the title of Basic Law. For some, the creation of a constitution by installments has been a disappointing experience.[10] There are important areas, civil liberties in particular, that have no established guidelines. But certain salient facts remain. Despite the considerable criticism of the existing constitutional system, it functions successfully. Furthermore, the very same issues that restrained the constitution makers during the Provisional Government and the First Knesset and postponed the completion of a codified constitution are present today. Despite more than twenty years of statehood, a change in the population matrix, and the rapid increase in the number of sabras (native Israelis) born after the attainment of statehood, Israel is no closer to a final religion-state definition than it was when the issue first came to the fore. The partisan polemics surrounding religious-political issues are no less strident, the passions no less fiery, and the righteousness of the militant secularists and religionists not at all diminished with the passage of time.

The result of the compromise was the continuation of coalition politics. The definition of the basic religion-state relationship was postponed to be resolved in the future through the political process. In the words of Chief Rabbi Yitzchak Ha-Levi Herzog, a "synthesis of democracy and theocracy" was possible.[11] Pragmatism had won over ideology. Only the Natore Karta had neither gained nor lost. In the avoidance of a Kulturkampf, state and religion had been neither wedded nor divorced. A secular state had been established; but, given the presence of the religious parties, and the open-endedness of the compromise, "private" religious questions would continue to be "public" in character.

5
The Establishment
of the
Orthodox Rabbinate

CHAPTER 5

One of the major successes of theopolitics has been the institutionalization of the Orthodox rabbinate within the state. The Orthodox rabbinate in Israel has been established as a monopoly—neither Reform nor Conservative rabbinic ordinations are recognized—and it is, in part, supported by the state. This monopoly and state support, in conjunction with the coercive tactics of the religious parties in the Knesset, has given the Orthodox rabbinate a good deal of power. It uses this power to further the observance of Orthodox norms, often violating the civil rights of the nonobservant Israeli.

The Orthodox rabbinate has arrived at its present preferred status by stages. The generalized principles that govern the rabbinate and the public order were developed during the Ottoman empire, carried over in their basic patterns by the British mandatory regime, and are now being modified by Israeli legislation. Under the Turks the millet system recognized special courts for the Jewish and Christian communities. These courts were under the direct control and supervision of the respective religious leaders, who had their powers and jurisdictions clearly delineated in royal charters (firmans) issued by the sultan. The Jewish court was under the Chakham Bashi, the equivalent of a chief rabbi. In theory the Chakham Bashi was the representative of all the Jews of the empire, but in practice the rabbis elected or appointed by the local communities in the cities of Jerusalem, Hebron, Safed, Tiberias, and Jaffa–Tel Aviv were recognized as representatives to the provincial governor. Jewish Community regulations prescribed the elec-

Chief Rabbi Yitzchak Nissim and Rabbi Yaakov Toledano, minister of religious affairs.

toral composition of its members, and it was an accepted tradition that the Chakham Bashi be a Sephardi.

After the British drove the Turks out of Palestine, the religious courts continued without major change. As the position of Chakham Bashi was vacant, Sir Herbert Samuel, the first high commissioner, appointed a commission to make proposals for establishing a supreme religious authority. The committee recognized the influx of Ashkenazic Jews, who by now outnumbered the Sephardim, and proposed a joint Chief Rabbinate and Chief Rabbinical Council to be selected by a special assembly. In February 1921 the assembly elected Rabbi Avraham Y. Kook as Ashkenazic chief rabbi and Rabbi Yaakov Meir as Sephardic chief rabbi. A hierarchical court structure—local rabbinical tribunals, an appellate court, and the Joint Supreme Court in Jerusalem—was established. These rabbinical courts were given exclusive jurisdiction in matters of marriage, divorce, alimony, confirmation of wills, and jurisdiction in any other matter of personal status (for example, maintenance, guardianship, legitimation, adoption of minors, and so on) where the parties to the action gave their consent. The Natore Karta and the Agudat Israel objected to this arrangement and vehemently insisted on their own separate rabbinical authorities. These objections were ultimately recognized by the Religious Communities Organization Ordinance, which provided for the overall secular and religious framework of the Jewish Community in Palestine while permitting any Jew to opt out of the Community.[1]

With the termination of the Mandate the secular institutions of the Jewish Community were replaced by new governmental machinery appropriate to a sovereign state. The religious institutions continued to exist and were, with some modifications through a variety of Knesset acts, over a period of time incorporated into the body politic. In addition, a Ministry of Religious Affairs was created to deal with both the Jewish and non-Jewish communities, although in actual practice the Ministry's major work is primarily with Orthodox Jewish concerns.

All the state's religious institutions are interrelated, although there is a functional administrative separation. The Chief Rabbinate and the Chief Rabbinical Council (a group of senior rabbis) control Jewish religious authority and decide on the interpretation of Jewish law (halakhah), and in the process are vested with legal and administrative state powers. It is the Chief Rabbinate through its secretariat which supervises and certifies rabbinical ordination, certifies rabbis to teach in religious state schools, controls the training of religious judges, the licensing and performance of religious scribes and circumcisers, and enforces some of the dietary regulations; for example, the rabbinate certifies that imported meat and locally produced foodstuffs are kosher.

The Ministry of Religious Affairs, as a natural result of theopolitics, has become the fief of the religious parties (primarily the NRP). It works closely with the established rabbinate and actively promotes Orthodox Judaism. The Ministry is responsible to the Knesset for the general administration of the rabbinical courts and holy places and for the supervision of dietary regulations in government institutions and public places. It also supervises the production and export of ritual articles. Working with the rabbinate and the local religious councils, the Ministry helps

78

finance talmudic academies (yeshivot) with general funding and capitation grants to needy students and contributes money toward the building and maintaining of synagogues. Furthermore, as a recent *Government Yearbook* notes, "Any local applicant, individual or institutional, gets religious books and ritual appurtenances gratis or at token cost from the Ministry, and publication of religious writings is subsidized." The Ministry supports a public council that, by information and propaganda, seeks to combat desecration of the Sabbath. There are also a committee to develop the sanctity of Mount Zion and a fund to counter conversionist activity among impoverished Jews. The Ministry through its Divisions maintains contact with the Diaspora, disseminates religious information, carries out research, and acts as a coordinator of religious events and ceremonies.[2]

The local religious councils and the religious committees in the smaller localities, as their names imply, deal on the local level with a variety of public services of a religious nature. They maintain ritual baths, supervise ritual slaughter, issue certificates of kashrut (dietary fitness), and register marriages and divorces, all of these being functions for which they receive fees. Fees alone, however, cannot support the councils' functions, and financing is provided by the state, which contributes one-third, and the local authorities, which contribute two-thirds, to the basic budgets.[3]

The minister of religious affairs, a secular political official, also plays an important role, which may have far-reaching political and theological overtones, in the ordinary administration of his office and in the elective process by which the two chief rabbis and the Chief Rabbinical Council are constituted. A neutral or hostile minister, technically a possibility if a strong secularist antireligious government ever achieves a solid power base, could attempt either to neutralize or to hamper state support to the rabbinate. To date, however, the Ministry has acted to enhance the power of the Orthodox, particularly since 1961, when Dr. Zerah Warhaftig of the National Religious Party, an able exponent of his party's principles and objectives, became minister of religious affairs. As to the minister's role in guiding the theological direction of the organized state rabbinate, a cursory history of the Chief Rabbinate–Chief Rabbinical Council elections is illustrative.

As noted previously, in 1921 a special assembly elected the Ashkenazic and Sephardic chief rabbis. When Avraham Kook, the Ashkenazic chief rabbi, died in 1935, an electoral assembly chose Dr. Yitzchak Ha-Levy Herzog to succeed him and reelected the incumbent Sephardic Chief Rabbi Meir. The electoral assembly convened again, four years later, after the death of Rabbi Meir and elected Rabbi Ben-Zion Ouziel Sephardic chief rabbi. The death of Rabbi Ouziel in 1953 created the first vacancy for the office of a chief rabbi since the establishment of the state.[4]

The tradition of reelecting the incumbent chief rabbi—in this instance, Ashkenazic Rabbi Herzog—was upheld, and his office was filled without a contest. But at the same time a bitter contest over the vacant Sephardic chief rabbi's seat developed between Rabbi Yitzchak Nissim, who was identified with the National Religious Party, and Rabbi Yaakov Toledano, who was a nonparty man. Rabbi Nissim won the election. Rabbi Toledano retired to his private pursuits but returned to the public scene in 1958 when

Prime Minister Ben-Gurion, in an attempt to break the growing power of the politicized Orthodox, appointed him minister of religious affairs. The basis for future party and personal clashes had now been laid. Under the election regulations of the rabbinate, new elections had to be held in 1960, but the orderly application of the regulations was disturbed by events. Before the 1960 elections were held, Ashkenazic Chief Rabbi Herzog died, thereby giving Minister Toledano an opportunity to change the rules without violating the tradition of reelecting an incumbent. In drawing up the 1960 election rules, Rabbi Toledano stipulated that a candidate for the office of chief rabbi must be an Israeli citizen and under seventy years of age. (Rabbi Nissim, the incumbent Sephardic chief rabbi, was not affected by the new rules, but these restrictions appeared to be an attempt to rig the elections against the two major Ashkenazic candidates affiliated with the NRP, Rabbi Joseph Soloveichik of the United States, and Rabbi Issar Y. Unterman, who exceeded the age limitation, in favor of Rabbi Shlomo Goren, a nonparty man.) After considerable discussion, Minister Toledano withdrew his objection to non-Israeli candidates but stood firm on the age limitation. Toledano argued, with some merit, that since a chief rabbi is head of the religious courts, and the law requires a religious judge (*day-yan*) to retire at seventy-five, a man in his seventies could not complete his five-year tenure without violating the law.[5] The Chief Rabbinical Council refused to accept this argument and declined to appoint anyone to the election committee. This refusal to appoint their share of the electoral committee was followed by an even more adroit political move. The Chief Rabbinical Council proclaimed a boycott of the rabbinical elections and called upon the observant to decline to be nominated to the electoral college that was to choose the two chief rabbis and the six other rabbis who would comprise the new Chief Rabbinical Council. With the issue deadlocked, rabbinate elections were not held as scheduled.

The Chief Rabbinate, that is, Rabbi Nissim and the Council, were operating in contravention of their tenure limitation. The rationale for the continued operation of the Chief Rabbinate under questionable legal standing, it was reported, was to make the Mapai-led government bear the responsibility for whatever inconvenience the public might experience because of the government's refusal to extend the sitting rabbinate's tenure. The tactic of continued operation forced the government to correct the anomalous situation by special Knesset legislation that legalized the rump Chief Rabbinate. Prolonged attempts to break the impasse between Rabbi Toledano, who was supported by Ben-Gurion, and the Chief Rabbinical Council, which was headed by Rabbi Nissim and supported by the NRP, came to naught. In 1961 Rabbi Toledano died, and after the elections of that year Mapai, as a necessity of coalition bargaining, conceded the post of minister of religious affairs to the National Religious Party. Nonetheless, it was not until 1964 that elections for the Chief Rabbinate were held.[6]

The rabbinical elections of that year were widely considered to be a contest between the Orthodox traditionalists supported, in the main, by the National Religious Party, and the more liberal or flexible Orthodox elements that had the encouragement of Mapai. Rabbi Goren, then forty-seven, a widely respected scholar and colorful senior chaplain of the Israeli defense forces, ran for the office of Ashkenazic chief rabbi against Issar Y. Unterman, then approaching seventy-eight. Expressing the views of the "modernists" Rabbi Goren stated: "The Rabbinate so far has not awakened to the fact that there is a Jewish State, and that halakhah must be brought up to date to make the State viable." [7] Rabbi Goren long before the election had urged the reestablishment of a Sanhedrin (grand religious council) to interpret and resolve issues of Jewish life in view of scientific and technological change and the establishment of a Jewish state.[8] The "flexible" Orthodox oppose, along with the traditional Orthodox, deviations from biblical and talmudic law, but they emphasize the need for flexibility. The "modernists" made a good showing, but the strict traditionalists retained control. Unterman defeated Goren by three votes for the position of Ashkenazic chief rabbi. The incumbent Sephardic chief rabbi, Nissim, was returned to office by a substantial margin, but, significantly, the candidacy of an incumbent had been challenged. With the Ashkenazic post now occupied for the first time in six years, a plenary Chief Rabbinate was now in office.[9]

Unterman was installed as chief rabbi in a colorful ceremony that underscored the official ties between the Orthodox rabbinate and the state. The president, prime minister, president of the Supreme Court, cabinet ministers, Knesset members, and a host of other dignitaries viewed the proceedings. The new chief rabbi indicated in his inaugural address his intention of taking a strong stand against missionary activity and expressed the hope that he and the Sephardic chief rabbi would succeed in uniting Jewry.[10]

This expression of unity, however, was but a pious hope. The fanfare and speeches could not conceal the substantive issues arising out of the unsettled authority of the Chief Rabbinate. It could not be forgotten that the Chief Rabbinate and the Chief Rabbinical Council, although religious institutions, were considered public bodies because secular law regulated the way they were financed and constituted and were, as such, subject to judicial control of the secular High Court of Justice, even in some matters of religious rulings.

Pointedly absent from the inauguration ceremonies were those among the devout who did not recognize the authority of the Chief Rabbinate: the adherents of Agudat Israel who have their own final authority, a council of Torah sages, the Natore Kartaites, and others who follow their own leaders. Among the Orthodox who accept the authority of the established rabbinate, there were many who were disenchanted by the delays and distressed by the acrimony and politicking that accompanied the establishment of the election machinery. They wondered if the political interplay between secular Mapai and the religious parties in the coalition was in the best interests of the rabbinate. There was present, they reasoned, the deplorable possibility that the rabbinate could become subject to official pressure and influence. They feared for the independence and prestige of the rabbinate. Others among the Orthodox pointed out that religious leaders should establish their authority by virtue of their own personal qualities and the general consent of the faithful, without any need for formal electoral procedure based on secular legislation. Every ordained rabbi is equal in spiritual authority to all other rabbis.

Rabbinical luminaries had, in the past, established their reputations and enjoyed the widespread respect and honor of their followers without such procedures. Piety, scholarship, justice, kindness, and wisdom could not be guaranteed or ensured by an election. And finally, there were those who questioned the advisability of or need for a dual Chief Rabbinate. They argued that the differences between the Ashkenazim and the Sephardim, although sociological —and at that the "Sephardic" classification was imprecise! —were not theological. For a lengthy period prior to the elections the Rabbinate had functioned with only one Chief Rabbi. There was but one Torah and one halakhah.

Under Unterman and Nissim the Chief Rabbinate declined in prestige. The Askenazic Chief Rabbi frequently was at odds with the Sephardic Chief Rabbi. It appeared that both rabbis were devoting more energy to preserving prerogative and form than to adjusting halakhah to the realities of a Jewish state. Little spirituality emanated from the Chief Rabbinate. As their term drew to a close in 1969, all the previous issues that roiled the rabbinate were resurrected. The advanced age of the incumbents—Rabbi Unterman was in his eighties and Rabbi Nissim in his seventies—again suggested that an upper age limit be set. Also, the philosophical and personality clashes between the two men only reinforced those critics who argued against a dual Chief Rabbinate. The cabinet, in fact, at one point discussed and dismissed the possibility of writing into the rabbinical elections law a ten-year limit to the dual Chief Rabbinate. However, after much bickering between the Alignment and the National Religious Party over the composition of the electoral college, and after several extensions of the Chief Rabbinate's allotted term, elections for the office of Ashkenazic and Sephardic Chief Rabbis and the Chief Rabbinical Council were held in October 1972. As in the previous election, Rabbi Goren, who had retired from the military chaplaincy to become Tel Aviv's Ashkenazic Chief Rabbi, challenged Rabbi Unterman. Rabbi Nissim was challenged by the highly regarded Sephardic Chief Rabbi of Tel Aviv, Ovadia Yosef. In a precedent-breaking election the elderly incumbents were defeated by Goren and Yosef, both in their fifties. Moreover, some of the more conservative members of the outgoing Chief Rabbinical Council were defeated for reelection.

Rabbis Goren and Yosef probably will direct some of their efforts to the adaptation of halakhah to the needs of Israeli society. But it remains to be seen if respect and regard can be restored for the institution of the Chief Rabbinate. The Chief Rabbinate is now solidly built into the Israeli political system. It enjoys institutional preferment and state support. Its very presence in the Holy Land automatically cloaks it with tremendous potential for prestige and spiritual leadership. To date, however, its potential for spiritual leadership remains unfulfilled. The Orthodox Rabbinate, by concentrating on consolidating its position, has diminished its spiritual standing and has caused rifts with the Reform and Conservative branches of Judaism.

6
Reform
and
Conservative
Judaism in
Israel

While the ultra-Orthodox do not accept the jurisdiction of
the state Chief Rabbinate, the Chief Rabbinate and the
Ministry of Religious Affairs in their turn have refused officially to recognize Judaism's Reform wing and have an
uneasy relationship with the Conservative branch. The
Orthodox argue that Conservative and Reform Judaism
were responses to Judaism's minority status in a Christian
setting and that they therefore have no place in a Jewish
state.

The mere thought of a vigorous Conservative movement
in Israel has made the Orthodox establishment decidedly
unhappy, and while the record is replete with instances of
disagreement and derogation of Conservative rights and
privileges (particularly in the areas of marriage and divorce), the Orthodox-Conservative relationship is in no
way as embittered and polarized as the Orthodox-Reform
relationship. This is so because to some extent the Conservatives have a wider area of theological agreement with the
Orthodox; unlike the Reform Jews, who reject the authority of halakhah, most Conservatives affirm the halakhah
subject to interpretation but do not go as far as the Orthodox, who maintain the totality of the divine authority of
halakhah in its biblical and rabbinic expressions. Then,
too, until recently Conservative Judaism was not overly
concerned with the organized propagation of its philosophy
in Israel. However, at its annual convention in 1968, the
Rabbinical Assembly, the international association of Conservative rabbis, announced its desire to broaden non-Orthodox Judaism in Israel. In calling for "an alternative

The rabbis of different communities seated on a dais beside the case
containing the Scrolls of the Law.

Jewish religious expression" in Israel, Rabbi Ralph Simon, vice-president of the Assembly, opined that "At the present time the average Israeli is unhappy with the established Orthodox tradition. He cannot satisfy his spiritual needs with the rigid fundamentalism that is characteristic of Israeli Orthodoxy." [1] This challenge is certain to be resisted strongly by the Orthodox. The challenge by the Reform Jewish movement, in contrast to the recent stirrings of the Conservatives, began some time ago.

Reform Judaism in Israel (or Progressive Judaism, as it is generally referred to outside the United States) has met with hostility, vituperation, and obstacles. When Dr. Nelson Glueck, the famous archaelogist and president of the Reform movement's Hebrew Union College–Jewish Institute of Religion, announced plans for a biblical and archaeological school in Jerusalem and mentioned that the college would hold Reform services, Rabbi Unterman, then chief rabbi of Tel Aviv, declared: "We shall fight against it. . . . It is not a question of a place of worship but of making a niche for a new interpretation which misrepresents Judaism. Reform Judaism started in Germany 150 years ago. It started in the United States a century ago. . . . It has never reached Israel. There is no place for it here." [2] The school, however, with its synagogue, was ultimately built and put into operation. Rabbi Unterman's fears were not dispelled when, at the school's inauguration, Dr. Glueck told the assembled notables:

. . . We think of this School as a meeting place where its staff and its guests will assemble together with Israelis for the creative exchange of philosophic ideas, for the purpose of engaging in religious discussion and prayer and for the

91

purpose of achieving for ourselves and others in Israel complete freedom of religious expression and practice in all of its forms and phases.

The Synagogue will occupy a central place in the total concept of our School . . . prepared to serve American and Israeli visitors who feel attracted to it and who may undertake to create forms of worship growing out of the modernity of present-day Israel but rooted in the fundamental principles of our religious past.[3]

But rhetoric alone cannot create congregations. Getting a toehold in Israel has proved difficult for Conservative and Reform alike. In a celebrated instance in 1962, township officials refused to permit a Reform group in Kfar Shmaryahu, one of Tel Aviv's northern suburbs, to hold Reform services in a public hall occasionally used by the Orthodox for their services. The Reform group appealed to the secular courts. The lawyer for the local council argued that, although the local council had made the facility available for Orthodox religious services, they were nonetheless justified in refusing to allow public property to be used for purposes that offended the majority of the community. Failure to give permission for the use of the room did not keep the Reform Jews, the council's lawyer argued, from exercising what he called their "pseudo-religion." [4] The Supreme Court, however, felt differently and made it clear that a municipality may not discriminate against one religious group in favor of another in providing public facilities.

Some four years later, a Reform congregation attempted to rent a hall in a building owned by the B'nai B'rith, the worldwide Jewish service organization. An agreement to rent the hall was canceled, allegedly for fear that the Orthodox rabbinate would revoke the building's certificate of dietary fitness. Since the maintenance of the building was based on the rental of its hall and catering facilities, the loss of the certificate of kashrut would mean that for all practical purposes the catering would stop and the hall not be used: the loss of kashrut approval would have serious economic implications. The local B'nai B'rith district's refusal to rent the hall to the Reform group was rationalized as being in line with "significant social forces which were necessarily influencing factors." Eventually, after a howl of protest was raised, the world executive of B'nai B'rith instructed its Israel district to make its rooms available to the Reform congregation. During the contretemps over the hall it was reported that Dr. Warhaftig, the minister of religious affairs, had said that he would be prepared to regard Reform Judaism as a sect and to treat it as a minority like Islam and Christianity.[5] Reform Jews however, do not think of themselves as a separate sect but as a legitimate interpretation of Judaism and considered the minister's remarks gratuitous. To quiet the furore, the Eshkol cabinet was forced to take the undignified step of verbally reaffirming the religious freedom in Israel guaranteed by the Proclamation of Independence.

Today the battle of the halls is largely resolved. Organized Reform Judaism in Israel consists of seven congregations with a combined membership of around 2000. Evaluating the condition of Israel's Reform movement, Mendel Kohansky, a perceptive observer of the Israeli scene, has written:

The results of a decade of intensive work by a group of dedicated young Reform rabbis do not indicate that the movement has struck roots in Israeli soil, despite the sympathy and moral support of a large part of the population. (A recent public opinion poll sponsored by the *Jewish Chronicle* of London showed that 41% of the public favored recognition of Progressive rabbis, 26% were against, and 33% had never heard of the movement.) The paradox is that this sympathy and moral support come from the liberal-minded, Western-oriented circles in Israeli life which are firmly rooted in secularism or agnosticism. Few of those who will at any time be willing to sign a petition or even speak for the Progressives are interested in attending a Progressive service themselves. Also, many of those who give moral support to the movement do so out of *negative* feelings—i.e., abhorrence of official religion with its restrictive power.[6]

In 1965 the handful of congregations of Progressive Judaism (there were then six) held their first national conference. It was a quiet meeting in a public school, and few took note of the Progressives' concern for what they considered to be the need for a religious alternative.

Progressive Judaism, however, received considerably more attention some years later when, in 1968, the World Union of Progressive Judaism held its International Convention in Jerusalem. An uproar ensued when the convention committee announced its intention of holding prayer services at the Western Wall, in the Reform manner with men and women praying together.[7] Warhaftig, as minister of religious affairs and responsible for the supervision of the Wall, announced he would not permit such a service. Speaking for the Orthodox he angrily announced: "it is an incontrovertible law that men and women must not pray together at the Wall." The issue reached the Knesset floor, where the debate was tumultuous. In an effort at compromise, Warhaftig agreed to refer the matter to the House Committee on Internal Affairs. Chief Rabbi Unterman appeared before the committee to speak against mixed prayer, and the committee upheld the minister's ban. The religious press used the occasion to deprecate the Reform movement, and one paper, the Agudat Israel daily *Ha-Mo-diyah,* called the Reform Jews "traitors to their people, their land, and their God" and suggested vituperatively that they "build a wall near one of their temples and go there to pray with their wives and mistresses." [8] The Orthodox threatened to block the alleged desecrators' access to the Wall, and the situation appeared to be at an impasse with a very real likelihood of violence. On the morning of the scheduled prayer session the Progressives announced the cancellation of their service at the Wall. The incident prompted the *Jerusalem Post* to comment:

A *Kulturkampf* over the Western Wall had loomed large last week, when the World Council for Progressive Judaism asked permission to hold mixed family-style worship at the Western Wall and encountered fierce resistance from the Chief Rabbinate, the Religious Affairs Ministry and Jerusalem's orthodox citizens. The Cabinet didn't want to decide, so it appointed a Ministers' Committee. The Ministers hummed [*sic*] and hawed. With nobody wanting to take responsibility, the baby was left in Premier Eshkol's lap. As the black-garbed yeshiva students thronged the Western Wall plaza thirsting for martyrdom, the Premier persuaded the Reform leaders to yield, postpone their mixed prayer and win kudos for tolerance.[9]

For twenty years the devout had been denied access to their holiest site because of Arab hostility, and their cries of outrage were genuine. Under the jurisdiction of the

Ministry of Religious Affairs, Christians and Moslems are allowed to visit their holy places in an atmosphere of respect and courtesy. But in the Jewish state, Reform Jews, male and female, together, may not pray in violation of Orthodox practice forbidding mixed worship. Indeed a commentary on established Orthodoxy's influence, pressure, and power.

7
The
Legal
System

The very character of Israel's evolving legal system has been enmeshed in theopolitics in an attempt to answer the root question: What is the role of Jewish law in a Jewish state? The demand that Jewish law (halakhah) serve as a basis for the Israeli legal system, although primarily asserted by the religious, to a large extent also is supported by the nonreligious. Observant Jews believe that halakhah derives from suprahuman authority and is totally binding. Incorporation of halakhah into the Israeli legal system is an intermediate stage in their effort to make the State of Israel an Orthodox Jewish state. Many of the nonobservant, on the other hand, consider Jewish law a vital part of their cultural heritage and a means of emphasizing the historical continuity of the Jewish people with the Land of Israel.[1]

The attempt to incorporate halakhah into the legal system is related to the overall movement to create a corpus of indigenous Israeli law. After the creation of the state, the Provisional Council of State enacted a reception statute that incorporated into the laws of Israel a vast body of jurisprudence which was operative at the time of independence. As a part of this operative legal system there were components of French law, Ottoman law, English law, and the religious law of the resident recognized communities. The decision of the Provisional Council to carry over the prevailing legal system was the only practical one at the time. However, the diversity and complexity of the often conflicting legal philosophies, along with the desire to have a legal system responsive to the needs of the new Jewish polity, spurred the movement for a grand design for a modern, comprehensive, system of Israeli law. But, much like the

A rabbinical court of appeals in session.

constitution, and for many of the same reasons, the Israeli legal system is evolving piecemeal. Progress in the replacement of the extant foreign elements, while considerable, is occurring slowly, and at present the legal system is far from homogeneous.

The confluence of the religious and nationalistic ideological streams has had practical results. There has been the enactment, where relevant, of Jewish content into the legal system. The Ministry of Justice maintains an adviser on Jewish law who actively tries to incorporate, where possible, principles of Jewish law into all draft legislation submitted to the Knesset. Jewish content has been incorporated into some statutes. Jewish law occupies a prominent place in the curriculum of the School of Law of the Hebrew University, and there is an Institute for the Research of Jewish Law. And as one might well expect, Jewish religious law occupies an important place in the studies of Bar-Ilan University, an Orthodox-sponsored institution. The present situation has been delineated by Menachem Elon, one of Israel's leading authorities on Jewish law.

. . . Jewish Law has been a considerable source of legislation by the Knesset and . . . resort or reference to it was a matter of some regularity in the various legislative processes. How far it has formed the basis of such legislation varies from subject to subject. In criminal and public law it does so to a limited extent. In civil law its contribution is greater and in family and succession law considerable. We do not infer the fact that a given law is based upon Jewish principles merely because its content embodies such principles but also because the different elements that operate in the legislative field—the Government and its representatives and the Knesset and its members—emphasize specifically in the Explanatory Notes to Bills and in the course of debate in the Knesset that the source of an enactment falls within Jewish Law. Although in point of law the statements made in the Explanatory Notes and in the Knesset are not binding upon the courts in construing any particular Law, in point of jurisprudential and historical truth such statements indicate the source from which it is drawn, and it is to be presumed that the courts are fully conscious of the fact when they interpret that Law. . . .

There are, however, many other Laws which do not rest on Jewish Law. There are various reasons for this. One of them certainly is the degree of preparedness of Jewish Law on a particular topic but our investigations have shown that this reason is far from being decisive. At times provisions contrary to Jewish Law have been enacted in the clear knowledge and acknowledgement that the Knesset is not prepared to accommodate itself to one or other given principle.[2]

Halakhic law has many marvelous aspects: it is adaptable, flexible, and most importantly, humanitarian. It is no accident that the Hebrew terms for "justice" (*tzedek*) and "charity" (*tzedakah*) are derived from a common root. But these positive aspects are counterbalanced by very substantial negative aspects. Halakhah in many respects is inadequate to the needs of a modern technological society. This is so because, paradoxically, with the emancipation of Western Jewry, the judicial activity of rabbinic courts declined. With this decline in activity during a period of rapid change, halakhah developed substantive lacunae, a circumstance that cannot be tolerated in a viable legal system. There are also important philosophical problems associated with attempts at any large-scale or total incorporation of halakhah into the Israeli legal system.[3]

Insofar as halakhah is considered to be divinely inspired, if it is incorporated into the legal system by Knesset action, thereby undergoing a secular process, a number of logical contradictions present themselves. Can halakhah retain its inspired origin when effected by the coercive power of a secular legislature, especially a legislature composed of non-Jews and Jews who do not accept Orthodox norms? Do not the very mechanics of incorporating halakhah through the political process into the legal system and its coexistence with man-made legislation involve secularization of divine law? The very act of selective reception is a denial of the sanctity of halakhah, which must be accepted in its totality. Can halakhah ever be reconciled with a secularly based Jewish state? For the Orthodox purist, the answer is simple and direct: the divinity of halakhah cannot be compromised, its primacy cannot be denied. Its incorporation into the Israeli body politic as a shared selective element is a purely political activity having no relevance to theology. Halakhah as an expression of theology will prevail only when the State of Israel becomes a truly Jewish Torah state effectuated through God's divine intervention in the form of messianic redemption.[4]

This position of theological purism, however, is not shared by most of the religious population. The objections raised by the theological purists are bypassed by most of the religious population, who place a religious interpretation upon the creation of the state. The historical reality of the State of Israel and all its secular apparatus can be explained by them as "a beginning of redemption." Man must work toward a perfect Torah state, and the vehicle for such work is theopolitics. Selective incorporation of halakhah as expressed in rabbinic interpretation is a small step in the right direction.

Theopolitics also has brought about a situation in which the secular state maintains, as part of its legal system, a religious court system.[5] Rabbinical courts have exclusive jurisdiction primarily in matters of marriage and divorce and in other limited matters of personal status, notably certain aspects of alimony and maintenance. But it is the secular authorities who must impose penal sanctions when a person refuses to comply with a rabbinical court ruling.[6] In other areas of personal status rabbinical courts enjoy concurrent jurisdiction with civil courts, but only by option of all the litigants. However, there has been circumscription by the Knesset of religious law (frequently over the objections of the religious parties). This circumscription has taken place in particular in areas where religious law is anachronistic. For example, the Marriage Age Law, the Women's Equal Rights Law, the Guardianship Law, the Succession (inheritance) Law, and so on, all are secular incursions that in some manner restrict traditional religious law.[7] The Women's Equal Rights Law was opposed by the extreme Orthodox and not by the moderate Orthodox. It gave men and women "equal status with regard to any legal proceeding" and overruled some religious laws that discriminated against women (various aspects of property relations, guardianship, and inheritance), requiring that religious tribunals follow civil courts in these matters.

When the Dayyanim Law, which deals with the qualifications, appointments, independence, tenure, and other administrative aspects of rabbinical judges, was passed by the Knesset in 1955, there was violent debate surrounding it. The debate centered on the proviso that the rabbinical judges (*dayyanim*), before taking their seats, had to swear allegiance to the State of Israel only and not to the laws of the state. (Judges in civil courts are required to swear allegiance to the laws of the State of Israel.) In arguing successfully against an amendment to the Dayyanim Law which would have required dayyanim to pledge allegiance to the laws of the state, a representative of Agudat Israel summarized the feelings of many of the religious when he stated that, where a law of the state conflicted with a religious law, the dayyan must follow the religious law.[8]

The bifurcation of jurisdiction between the rabbinical and civil court systems has created a situation of unceasing friction. The rabbinical courts believe their authority, under the halakhah, to be extensive. The civil courts, which retain residuary jurisdiction in all matters, view the rabbinical courts as a special judicial system with limited powers defined by law. In interpreting the laws defining the jurisdiction of the rabbinical courts, the civil courts have tended to narrow the jurisdiction of the rabbinical courts by means of strict interpretation of the law. The result has been that whenever there has been a conflict between the religious and civil courts, the secular view has prevailed.[9] The supremacy of the secular system over the religious system is certain to continue and grow. This is so because the underlying legitimacy of the religious courts comes not from the voluntary acceptance of halakhah, which would preclude secular inhibition, but from their establishment as part of the secular legal system.

8
Marriage
and
Divorce

CHAPTER 8

One important area in which Jewish law has prevailed in the legal system is that of marriage and divorce. The Marriage and Divorce (Rabbinical Courts Jurisdiction) Law of 1953 prohibited civil marriage and gave complete and exclusive jurisdiction over Jewish marriage and divorce to the Orthodox rabbinical courts. The main change brought about by the Marriage and Divorce Law was that it enlarged the rabbinate's jurisdiction, now giving it authority over all Israeli Jews, whereas previously, rabbinical authority had been restricted to persons listed in the official register of the Jewish community. Voting on the Marriage and Divorce Law was tied in with voting on the National Service Law. (The ultra-Orthodox were opposed to the National Service Law because they felt it violated their conception of female purity.) Both bills were brought before the Knesset for the final reading as a single package. The rabbinate was extremely anxious to see the Marriage and Divorce bill passed, so much so that the Chief Rabbinate, in a politically adroit move, issued a statement reaffirming opposition to the national service bill but counseling the religious parties in the coalition to avoid a crisis. This permitted the Mizrachi to vote for the national service bill, thus assuring the passage of the Marriage and Divorce bill.

The decision to eliminate civil marriage and divorce, particularly since it was so crucial to the formation of the Israeli national image and was central to the religion-state problem, provoked widespread debate.[1] Not only adherents of the religious parties were in favor of exclusive Orthodox rabbinical control over marriage and divorce; substantial

A member of the Bene Israel with her child.

108

support came from a large cross section of the population. Those favoring exclusive rabbinical jurisdiction advanced a number of religious, nationalistic, and pragmatic arguments. Proponents of the law stressed the desirability of safeguarding the unity of the Jewish people. If civil marriage and divorce were permitted in Israel, it would only emphasize the differences between religious and nonreligious Jews. Also many Orthodox would be chary about intermarrying with the progeny of Jewish couples married in civil ceremonies. While halakhically unsound, the feeling that such a forbidden marriage would taint the innocent children of such a union, nonetheless, would create distinct differences between Jews who observed religious norms and those who did not. Thus, for example: a divorce granted by a civil court might be regarded as valid by the husband, but the wife might consider herself obliged not to remarry until she received a religious divorce. According to the halakhah, a child of the second marriage of a woman whose first marriage had been dissolved only by civil divorce would be considered illegitimate and could not marry a Jew.

Another argument advanced was that since marriages between Jews and non-Jews are not possible under religious law, civil marriage would encourage marriages out of the faith. These mixed marriages were of vital concern because the continuity of the Jewish community itself would be jeopardized. If Israel, which should reflect the very ethos of Judaism, should sanction civil marriage and divorce, it would appear to be sanctioning intermarriage. A noxious precedent for the Diaspora would be established. This would lead to a further increase in mixed marriages throughout the Diaspora. In Israel itself, many nonreligious or secular-oriented Israelis would see nothing inappropriate in marrying a non-Jew who would become an Israeli citizen, thereby affirming allegiance to Jewish nationality and peoplehood but not to Judaism as a religion. In time this would compound the chasm between the religious and the nonreligious, creating cleavages in Israeli society which would be unbridgeable. Israel would be rigidly divided into a population of two nonintermarrying groups.

And finally, although conceding that there were some religious prohibitions that might cause distress in individual cases, nonetheless, a few sacrifices were necessary for the greater good. Isolated situations of hardship were a small price to pay for the continued unity and survival of the Jewish people. It was the strict observance of religious marriage that had preserved the Jewish family and assured Jewish survival throughout the millennia.

The opponents of the law retorted that the unity of the Jewish people was more fiction than fact. There were sharp divisions, both in Israel and the Diaspora, between the Orthodox and the non-Orthodox. Giving monopolistic control of marriage and divorce to the Orthodox rabbinate would be certain to sharpen the fractionalization within Jewry. Civil marriage would not create as great a gap in Israeli society as suggested, because the religious segment of the population tended to segregate itself voluntarily, and besides, there was no halakhic prohibition against remarrying the Jewish children of a civil union. The religious were inflating the potential problem. As to marriages out of the faith, this they acknowledged to be of serious concern, but such marriages were not caused by the presence of civil marriage. They were, instead, symptomatic of disenchantment with Judaism. A return to Judaism had to be inspired not by coercion but by conviction.

The presence of civil marriage in Israel would not contribute materially to national disunity. Jews married in civil ceremonies, surrounded by a Jewish culture, would remain Jewish. The formality of a religious ceremony would not tend to make them any more Jewish. In the matter of civil marriage fostering interfaith marriages, the Israeli example would not be very significant for the Diaspora, and in Israel the children of a mixed marriage would adjust to the Jewish majority and opt for Judaism.

Indeed, Israel was not like all other nations; it was a Jewish state, and as such it was incumbent upon it to be a democratic, not a theocentric, state. The essence of Judaism was voluntary acceptance of religious beliefs. The abandonment of civil marriage and divorce was an antidemocratic step; it violated the religious freedom of all those non-Orthodox Jews who might choose not to adhere to the Orthodox formulas for marriage and divorce. And certainly, it violated the civil liberties of those of its citizens who might not want to regulate their lives by any religious norms, much less Orthodox religious norms. A democratic state surely must maintain freedom from religion as well as freedom for religion.

Furthermore, the hardships caused by the prohibitions and injunctions of religious law, since they were archaic and unrelated to contemporary life-styles, should not apply to the entire population but only to those who voluntarily agreed to abide by religious precepts. These hardships were

111

not as isolated as suggested. Nor should the few have their rights abridged simply because they were in the minority. Of specific relevance were problems associated with *cohanim, agunah*, and *chalitzah*.

Religious law stipulates that a descendant of a priestly family—(*cohen,* cohanim (pl.): Hebrew for priest)—may not marry certain categories of women: namely, a harlot, a woman born of an illicit priestly marriage (*helallah*), a proselyte, a divorcee, or a woman who has received chalitzah. As there are a large number of priestly descendants (Cohen is a common Jewish family name and has a wide range of variants; for example, Cahan, Cohan, Kagan, Kohn, and so forth), the ancient prohibition against a cohen marrying a divorcee has considerable contemporary significance. Quixotically, under Jewish law the prohibition of the marriage of a cohen to a divorcee or a woman who has received chalitzah is only ab initio, and, once celebrated, the marriage takes effect. There are notable examples of a cohen leaving Israel to get married to a divorcee in a civil ceremony and then returning.[2]

The term agunah applies to a woman whose husband's death is suspected but not proved. Thus, women whose husbands have deserted them or disappeared might be doomed to a twilight zone of "legal marriage without benefit of husband." In the absence of satisfactory proof of the husband's death, the agunah who wishes to establish a new relationship with a man has no religious alternatives. She may secure a civil divorce and remarry outside Israel, or she may enter into a common-law marriage without benefit of rabbinical sanction. In either case, she is considered by Jewish law to be an adultress, and any children of such a union would be considered illegitimate (*mamzerim*).[3] Although since early talmudic days the rabbis have attempted to relax the usual rigidity of the laws of evidence, creating a presumption in favor of the husbandless wife, the problem of the agunah remains one of the most serious facing rabbinic jurisprudence.

According to a biblical injunction in Deuteronomy (25: 5–10), when a married man dies childless, his brother must marry the widow so as to preserve the deceased's name. This custom of levirate marriage declined by talmudic times through the use of a biblical provision for its evasion, chalitzah. Although levirate marriage is no longer required under rabbinic law, a childless widow cannot remarry until she receives a "release" from the brother of the deceased. The ceremony whereby the brother defaults and the widow is "released" is chalitzah (Hebrew for "taking off"). In chalitzah, the widow removes a shoe of the levir, recites the relevant biblical verses, and further indicates (generally by spitting on the ground in front of him) her contempt and rebuke for his failure to honor his duty to perpetuate the name of his brother. Since the childless widow cannot remarry unless she receives chalitzah, if the brother-in-law is inaccessible or refuses to perform the rite of chalitzah, hardship may arise. There is also another possibility of hardship, but for the brother-in-law. Under the Rabbinical Courts Jurisdiction (Marriage and Divorce) Law, a recalcitrant brother who refuses to give chalitzah to the widow when so ordered by a rabbinical court is liable to imprisonment. (However, imprisonment cannot take place until the attorney general applies to a secular district court to enforce this penalty.) The possibility could arise then that a brother-in-law, who as a matter of principle, refuses to participate in an ancient religious rite because of a strongly held secular conviction, would be compelled to languish in prison.[4]

In addition to the secularists, who want the right of civil marriage and divorce as a matter of principle (this issue is raised continually by the militant secularists), strict Orthodox control of marriage and divorce has created particular problems for newcomers to Israel. Thus, immigrants who wish to be married in Israel must prove to the Orthodox rabbinate that they are Jewish or else undergo conversion. This has created strains with the Conservative and Reform wings of Judaism because the Orthodox frequently are reluctant to accept "proof of Jewishness" from Conservative rabbis. Reform Jews are automatically suspect because some reform rabbis are willing to marry a Jew to a Gentile. The matter of divorce in the relationships between the Orthodox rabbinate and the other wings of Jewry is even more complex. As a general rule Reform Jews do not bother with a religious divorce, although a Reform Jew who wanted a religious divorce could get one from a rabbi qualified to grant it. In the eyes of the Orthodox, Reform Jewry is populated with divorced persons who remarried on the basis of civil divorce only. These people (according to halakhah) are living in adultery and consequently their children are illegitimate and are disqualified from marrying a Jew.[5]

The leaders of Conservative Jewry, along with the Israeli Chief Rabbinate and the Ministry of Religious Affairs, are agreed in principle that not all rabbis, Orthodox rabbis included, are qualified to grant a divorce. Despite this agreement in principle, friction has arisen because, at times,

Conservative bills of divorce have not been honored in Israel. In 1963, in protest over the Israeli rabbinate's refusal to recognize the validity of certain divorce documents granted by its central rabbinical court, the Conservative movement's Rabbinical Assembly canceled a meeting scheduled to be held in Israel. And sometime later, former Israeli Attorney-General Gideon Hausner was engaged by the Rabbinical Assembly of America to explore the possibility of taking legal steps to compel the Israeli rabbinate to recognize halakhically valid divorces granted by Conservative rabbis.

Orthodox rabbinic scrutiny has presented problems for the children of immigrants—when the newcomer wishes to marry, he must prove to the satisfaction of the rabbinate that his mother was Jewish. In the case of a large number of immigrants (particularly those who immigrated from Soviet Russia or Iron Curtain countries, and survivors of the Holocaust) where the father was Jewish and the mother Gentile, a generalized pattern has emerged. In those cases where the mother was not converted, or where her conversion was motivated by reasons other than religious conviction, the children, although raised as Jews, are required to undergo formal conversions.[6] Although this practice is general, as long as it affected individuals, it attracted only sporadic public attention. In what was, however, perhaps the most dramatic instance of Orthodox rabbinic control creating difficulties for immigrants to Israel, the entire Bene Israel community was involved.

The Bene Israel (Sons of Israel) are members of a Jewish group that came to Israel from India. Their origin is uncertain, but according to Bene Israel tradition their progenitors were shipwrecked off the western coast of India in ancient times—the date most frequently given is 175 B.C.E. For many centuries the descendants of the shipwrecked few held themselves distinct from their Hindu neighbors, continuing to practice certain forms of Judaism, although they had no rabbis and were without any contact with the rest of Jewry. Their isolation was eventually broken, though the exact date when this occurred is uncertain. It is generally agreed, however, that by the middle of the nineteenth century there was well-established contact with Iraqui Jews who were traders. Theodor Herzl recognized the Bene Israel as Jews and invited representatives of the Bene Israel community to participate in the First Zionist Congress held in Basle in 1897. The Bene Israel, however, refused Herzl's invitation, replying: "Jews in India are an Orthodox community and look upon the fulfillment of the restoration of a Jewish Kingdom by the Divine Hand." [7] An answer mirroring the stand taken by Europe's anti-Zionist *Protestrabbiner*. Nonetheless, by the middle of the 1960s well over 7000 of the community's approximately 28,000 members had emigrated to Israel.

Even while the Bene Israel were still in India, doubts had been raised as to whether they might marry other Jews. The Bene Israel community had no rabbis and no recognized rabbinical courts; accordingly, the extent and strictness of their observance of rabbinical family law was a matter of grave concern. These doubts were resolved in various rabbinical responsa, but each responsum related only to individual cases, and decisions both prohibiting and permitting marriage were rendered. With large numbers of Bene Israel in Israel, many rabbis were faced with determining the eligibility of an individual Bene Israelite to marry. Various rabbis gave divergent judgments. In order to introduce some uniformity, Chief Rabbi Nissim in 1957 appointed a study commission of halakhic authorities to review the situation. After an exhaustive investigation, in October 1961, the Supreme Rabbinical Council issued the following decision:

> There are no doubts concerning the Judaism of the Bene Israel; from the earliest period they were bound closely to and maintained relationship with the seed of Israel. But because they were cut off for an extended period from the centers of Torah, there arose Halakhic concern over the manner and laws of the marriage and divorce practices that prevailed among them. . . . The Council has decided that there is no basis for forbidding marriages of the Bene Israel and therefore marriage with them is permitted.[8]

The overall ambiguity created by the varying responsa was put to rest. The Bene Israel were now placed squarely on equal footing with all other Jews. In a solemn ceremony, two leaders of the Bene Israel received a copy of the Supreme Rabbinical Court's decision. All that was now needed was the administrative formality of Chief Rabbi Nissim circulating the decision to the country's rabbis and formulating directives for the marriage registrars.

It was at this juncture that an extremist ultra-Orthodox minority voiced dissent. "We will rouse all Torah scholars abroad against the Chief Rabbinate's ruling allowing marriage between Jews and members of the Bene Israel community," Rabbi Yeshayahu Scheinberger of the Natore Karta warned. The dissident minority within the country and in the Diaspora announced their firm opposition to the ruling. Agudat Israel, at best reluctant to accept any authority of the Chief Rabbinate, also flatly rejected the ruling. In order to appease the ultra-Orthodox minority, Chief Rabbi Nissim issued implementary directives; the screaming minority was quieted, but the spirit of the original decision was violated. While marriage between two members of the Bene Israel community, according to the directives, creates no difficulty, when one of the couple contemplating marriage is not a Bene Israelite, it is incumbent on the registering rabbi

1. To search and investigate whether the mother or grandmother, and as far back as possible to trace the lineage of the prospective bride or groom of the Bene Israel community, was a Jewess or whether she came from a family into which intermingling with non-Jews or proselytes had occurred.

2. To search and investigate whether the parents or the grandparents, as far back as is possible to trace the lineage, of the person seeking a marriage, were married after a divorce or whether there was in the family a kinship marriage such as is forbidden by Jewish law.

The rabbi registering marriages being certain there are no doubts concerning the cautions listed above, he shall marry the couple.

There being an area of doubt regarding any of the cautions listed above, the rabbi registering marriages is to refer the matter to the district *Bet Din* (rabbinical court). The *Bet Din* will judge the case and determine whether the marriage is permitted in principle or not and if permitted, if proselytization or immersion (in a ritual bath) are required, or not.[9]

The Bene Israel who only a few months earlier had felt themselves accepted, now, understandably, felt stigmatized. They reacted immediately. Their Actions Committee began a campaign to redress what they believed to be a serious grievance. Letters and telegrams were sent to Israeli leaders, and the matter simmered for months. When occasional difficulties occurred over the registering of a few Bene Israel marriages, considerable publicity was given to them. In actual fact, however, most rabbis were willing to officiate at "mixed" marriages, that is, a Bene Israel member to another Jew. The problem was not so much a practical one as an emotional one. This was especially so after the minister of religious affairs and the Sephardic chief rabbi worked out a modus vivendi whereby local rabbis who were reluctant to register "mixed marriages" were circumvented, leaving the task to rabbis who could do so without violating their convictions. Members of the Bene Israel group, nonetheless remained dissatisfied, feeling that the qualifying directives categorically diminished their status as Israeli Jews. This dissatisfaction erupted violently in the summer of 1964.

In an attempt to compel the Chief Rabbinate to rescind the qualifying directives, about twenty-five Bene Israel families staged a sit-down strike outside the Jewish Agency headquarters in Jerusalem. Soon the strike was underscored by demonstrations in which 2000 Bene Israel and their supporters marched. During the demonstration a few demonstrators burned an effigy of Chief Rabbi Nissim. As the strike continued, the cabinet discussed the religious status of the Bene Israel and sufficient signatures of Knesset members were collected to summon the recessed Knesset back into session. In a countermove, hundreds of rabbis gathered at Hechal Shlomo (the seat of the Chief Rabbinate) and heard Rabbi Unterman proclaim the Rabbinate's defiance of any attempt by a secular authority to impose its will in matters of halakhah. The Knesset met in special session and easily passed a resolution calling upon the Chief Rabbinate to remove the causes of any feeling of discrimination among the Bene Israel. The opposition parties—Herut, Liberals, Mapam, and the Communists—abstained because they considered the resolution too weak. The resolution was based on a cabinet decision to which all parties in the coalition government subscribed. Premier Levi Eshkol in presenting it, pointed out that a large segment of the public was no longer able to accept the discrimination of the directives, and thus the matter was a public problem; then, for balance, he expressed sharp criticism of the "irresponsible and objectionable aspects" of the demonstration, an obvious reference to the burning of an effigy of Rabbi Nissim. The resolution, as passed, affirmed the Knesset's view of the Bene Israel as "Jews in all respects, without qualification and with the same rights as all other Jews, including matters of personal status." [10]

The Rabbinate, now on the defensive, and heeding behind-the-scenes pressure, announced its intention of deleting from its directives specific references to the Bene Israel. Satisfied, the Bene Israel strikers returned to their homes. Shortly thereafter, new directives were issued in which the words "Bene Israel" were deleted. The reformulated marriage directives, in a face-saving compromise, contained a general injunction to investigate any case in which any doubt arose as to family status.

The Bene Israel issue should have been a purely religious matter, but it turned into a divisive secular-religious confrontation that eroded the standing of the Chief Rabbinate. In first bowing to the militant ultra-Orthodox and then retreating in the face of cabinet and Knesset action, the

Chief Rabbinate proved itself susceptible to political pressure, thereby creating a situation in which its decisions appeared to be based on considerations other than the pure interpretation of halakhah. If the secular arm of the state could interfere in one instance, then there is present the potential for future interference. Unless the rabbinate begins to demonstrate more flexibility in its interpretation of halakhah, taking into account present human and social needs, the issue of exclusive rabbinical control of marriage and divorce will remain as a constant irritant exacerbating secular-Orthodox relationships.

9
The
Educational
System

Public education in Israel mirrors the divergent philosophies of the secular and religious camps that regard control of education as the key to perpetuating their ideologies.[1] The educational system, therefore, is a prize in many political maneuvers as the religious parties try to enhance their position in it.

The Israeli educational system, like the country's other important institutions, had its basis in the prestate years. The earliest schools maintained by the Yishuv were religious in nature and were concentrated in the Holy Cities of Jerusalem, Hebron, Safed, and Tiberias. They were supported almost exclusively by funds donated by Diaspora Jews. Beginning in the second half of the nineteenth century, schools teaching secular as well as religious subjects were established under European sponsorship. When the Laemmel School, the first school in which secular subjects were taught, was established in Jerusalem in 1856, some of the ultra-Orthodox were enraged at this "modernistic" deviation. Before the school opened its doors, they blew a shofar at the Wailing Wall and issued a ban of excommunication against any parent who had the temerity to enroll his son in such a heretical institution.[2] But the ultra-Orthodox pietists could not stem the encroachment of secular-oriented schools, which proliferated with the coming of the immigrants of the First Aliyah. These newcomers were motivated by nationalistic Zionist ideals and enrolled their children in the secular schools that were sponsored by Jewish international and national organizations. When the British took over Palestine from the Turks, there existed a network of Jewish schools both secular and religious.

An Orthodox child.

The British permitted the resident communities to maintain their own school systems. The Jewish Community received little financial support from the Palestine government but enjoyed virtual autonomy in the operation of a Jewish national school system. Responsibility for the Jewish national school system was assumed by the Zionist Organization in 1918. This responsibility was transferred to the Jewish Agency in 1929. And finally, in 1932 the Vaad Leumi (National Council) of the organized Jewish Community in Palestine assumed general responsibility for the administration of the school system. In all instances, however, the final, legal responsibility for education rested in the Palestine government.

The Mandate's policy of laissez-faire created a climate of benign neglect which permitted the growth of the Jewish educational system. This growth reflected the intense ideological pluralism and doctrinaire character associated with the Yishuv. Jewish education came to be divided into three trends: general, religious, and labor. Each trend represented a definite ideological and political orientation.[3] By 1932 the Vaad Leumi exercised central administrative supervision over the three trends, which were represented equally. The trends, which differed sharply from each other in scholastic atmosphere and long-range educational goals, had in common only minimal curricula: each trend enjoying wide independence in drawing up its curricula and syllabi and appointing teachers and inspectors.

The schools of the general trend reflected the ideology of the General Zionists. They emphasized an uncompromising nationalist-Zionist orientation. In these schools study of the Bible, Hebrew literature and language, and other

Jewish-oriented subjects were geared to a national revival movement and taught along with subjects of a standard secular curriculum. Religious training and ritual observance were considered best left to the home and synagogue. The schools of the religious trend were affiliated with the Mizrachi movement and aimed at molding pious, observant Jews. The Mizrachi schools emphasized religion-centered subjects (Torah, Talmud, Mishnah) and practiced a lifestyle centering around worship and religious rites. Adequate secular instruction was also given, but it was supplementary to the primary religious offerings. All instructors in the religious trend were expected to be Orthodox. The schools of the labor trend were affiliated with the Histadrut (the federation of trade unions). They aimed at inculcating labor Zionist values of egalitarianism, chalutziut, and the dignity of manual labor. Social sciences, along with skill development in industrial and agricultural subjects, predominated in their curriculum. Religious subjects received less attention than at either general or religious schools; nonetheless, Bible and some religious subjects were studied, if only from historical and literary viewpoints.

In addition to the three recognized trends, there existed the schools of the ultra-Orthodox Agudat Israel who, as previously noted, refused to participate in the Jewish Community. The Agudat Israel schools, along with a scattering of other unaffiliated ultra-Orthodox schools, were totally committed to a pietistic life. These schools concentrated almost exclusively on religious subjects.

During the Mandate, the Jewish national school system grew tenfold and developed into a viable professional educational system appropriate to a new state. The system included preschool kindergartens, elementary and secondary schools, vocational training schools, special schools for handicapped children, and teacher-training academies. Of special significance was the fact that it was a complete system of *Hebrew* education, not that the use of Hebrew carried over into general social discourse as a vernacular language. Although school attendance was not compulsory, most Jewish children received at least an elementary school education. On the primary level, the three trends enjoyed approximate parity. On the level of secondary education, the general trend was clearly dominant. Only the nascent institutions of higher learning, the Hebrew University and the Haifa Technion, being outside the immediate scope of the organs of Jewish self-government, were free of the ideological compartmentalization imposed by the trends.[4]

Despite the progress of the Jewish school networks, the educational system of the Yishuv had a number of serious defects. A basic flaw stemmed from the very trends themselves. While agreeing on a common objective of building a secure Jewish national home, the trends differed so substantially in their social, economic, and political outlooks that the educational process by its very nature emphasized and perpetuated the existing differences in the resident population. The trend educational system, allied to competing ideological-doctrinaire political movements, became an adjunct of raw politics. In addition, the system suffered from chronic financial difficulties and serious administrative flaws. The trend system of decentralized administration inhibited fixing responsibility, created a situation of haphazard, uncoordinated, and ofttimes conflicting educational priorities, was wasteful in its duplication, and thwarted long-range planning. When the state came into being, one of its challenges was to build on the strengths and remedy the weaknesses of the educational system inherited from the Mandate period.[5]

During the period of the Provisional Government (May 1948 to March 1949), the Department of Education of the Vaad Leumi, now under the supervision of a cabinet committee, transformed the Jewish national school system into the state school system. There were no substantial changes in the administrative structure, but the Agudat Israel schools now were recognized as a fourth trend, since the Agudat Israel party had, with the establishment of the state, abandoned its policy of separatism and joined the coalition. A number of ultra-Orthodox schools remained independent, but the Arab schools now came under the jurisdiction of the new state system. After the elections to the First Knesset a Ministry of Education and Culture was established. Its first minister was Zalman Shazar, who was to become Israel's third president.

Under Shazar's guidance a Compulsory Education Law was passed by the Knesset in September 1949. The law provided for free and compulsory (education under the Mandate was neither free nor compulsory) primary education for all children from five to thirteen years inclusive.[6] The law also took cognizance of certain sociopolitical realities and contained an escape clause under which the minister could allow children to attend one of the nonrecognized educational institutions specified in a ministerial directive. This, of course, legally recognized "nonrecognized" schools. The intent of the escape proviso was to avoid conflict with the Natore Karta and other Orthodox extremists, who refused to acknowledge the Jewish state and would not include secular subjects in their courses of study.[7] The law also left intact the four existing trends: general, labor, Mizrachi religious, and Agudat Israel religious. While many secularists believed the curricula of the religious schools to be inadequate and, for pragmatic nationalistic reasons, wanted the broadest possible educational scope for all segments of the population, nevertheless, they realized that giving the Agudat Israel trend parity and avoiding outright conflict with the other extremist religious elements was a necessary political compromise. Nonetheless, religious-political issues continued to arise within the educational system.

The first of these conflicts dealt with the education of children in immigrant camps. In 1949, 239,076 immigrants entered the country. The influx of new citizens was important not only because of its absolute numbers but also because of its ethnic and age composition. Of the 1949 immigrants, nearly half came from Asia and Africa, were traditional in religious outlook, and had large families with many children of school age. (Of these, some 50,000, practically the entire Jewish community of Yemen, had been airlifted to Israel by Operation Magic Carpet.)[8] The European immigrants tended to be less Orthodox, more politically sophisticated, and have fewer children of school age. It was widely believed at that time that the Asian and African segment of the population was the key to electoral power within the not-too-distant future; consequently, the education of their children, particularly those coming from Yemen, Libya, and Morocco, became a political issue.

In February 1950 the three ministers representing the

United Religious Front (URF) began a boycott of cabinet meetings. The boycott stemmed from the Orthodox bloc's demand for control of the education of children in immigrant camps, children who, in the main, came from religious families. The religious groups charged that nonreligious camp officials were forcing immigrant parents to enroll their children in secular schools. The Orthodox were particularly concerned about the schooling of Yemenite children.

Plucked from medieval isolation in South Arabia, the Yemenites were Orthodox and completely innocent of party politics and the contending appeals of socialism and free enterprise. For the Yemenite, school and religion had never been separated. These simple, pious people, the Orthodox factions argued, should not be subjected to a bewildering choice of school trends. The boycott lasted only a few days and an uneasy compromise was achieved.

The compromise provided that the four recognized trends of the education law—general, labor, Mizrachi, and Agudat Israel—would not apply to the immigrant camps. Instead, the minister of education was to run the schools in the camps, offering both religious and nonreligious instruction. The Yemenites, however, were not to have any option. Yemenite children automatically would be assigned to a state-run religious school. It was a straitened arrangement doomed to failure, for under it the religious and the nonreligious elements each hoped to attract the larger enrollment. Both Mapai and the United Religious Front were unhappy about the compromise. The URF continually charged that a nonreligious education was being forced on children who had come from strictly observant homes. To some extent these charges were substantiated by the findings of a Knesset investigating committee headed by Yitzchak Ben-Zvi.[9]

An immediate cabinet crisis was averted, but in late 1950 a new cabinet crisis loomed as a result of demands made by the religious parties that a newly created ministry be headed by one of their members. Ben-Gurion refused to accede to this demand and resigned.[10] In the negotiations that followed, the religious parties made some slight gains, among them, a separate division for religious schools in the Ministry of Education to be headed by a member of a religious party. The second cabinet was confirmed by the Knesset on November 1, 1950. The reconstituted coalition cabinet, however, lasted only a few months and came down over the still-smoldering issue of education in immigrant camps and transitional settlements (*maabarot*, pl., *maabarah*, sing.).

The immigrant camps were short-term reception centers. The maabarot, on the other hand, were semipermanent transitional settlements in which the newcomers through work and welfare projects began the process of assimilation into Israeli society. Mapai was unwilling to surrender to the religious control of education in the maabarot. The URF was equally opposed to surrendering to the secularists.

The situation was further exacerbated when Mapai's minister of education and culture, David Remez, proposed that in the maabarot the Yemenite children would not be enrolled automatically into religious schools but that the regular choice of educational trends would apply. In an attempt to appeal to the religious sensibilities of the new immigrants Mapai had organized a religious subdivision of the labor-trend schools. The URF threatened to bolt the coalition, arguing that the socialist-labor movement, Johnnies-come-lately to the teaching of religion, should leave religious education to those who had always shown a concern for it in the past: Mizrachi and Agudah. Mapai remained firm. As a conciliatory gesture, however, they offered to create a special cabinet committee composed of the prime minister, the minister of education, and one of the United Religious Front ministers to supervise religious schools in the maabarot. The URF rejected this proposal, believing that it was not really a concession at all, since Mapai would outvote the URF. As the rift widened between Mapai and the Orthodox, the General Zionists, who had long urged the abolition of what they considered the divisive trend system, and seeing a chance to embarrass Ben-Gurion, introduced a motion of censure over the government's handling of the immigrant education issue. The URF broke with the coalition, and its votes for the censure motion enabled it to be carried. Ben-Gurion, apparently feeling that the time was now ripe to break with the Orthodox, decided to treat the censure motion as a vote of no confidence. In a surprise move (censure motions do not require cabinet resignation), Ben-Gurion announced the entire cabinet's resignation.[11]

The conflicts over the assignment of immigrant children to the various trends convinced many, particularly Prime Minister Ben-Gurion, that the trends system was divisive and threatened national unity. In the campaign for the Second Knesset only the most unyielding doctrinaire parties, the Communists, Mapam, and the Torah Religious Front

(Agudat Israel and Poale Agudat Israel) wanted to retain the trends without any major modification. Those in favor of the existing system put forth the argument that the trends best enabled members of a democratic community to select by free choice the kind of education they wanted for their children. The National Religious Party (Mizrachi factions) wanted "state education with two autonomous and coequal directions, one of which would be religious." [12] The Mizrachi hoped by this approach to eliminate its competition—the Agudat Israel trend and the religious sub-trend of labor—and achieve dominance in religious education. The secular center and right parties—Progressives, General Zionists, and Herut—wanted to replace the trends with a unified system of state education that would include an option for parents who wanted a religious education for their children. The position taken by these parties was not a major departure from their previously held opinions and was in line with their overall political ideology. Mapai, in a dramatic shift, also came out for the abolition of the trends and a unified national system.

Mapai's about-face, which was not approved by the entire party, was in response to several developments that had occurred since independence. In the first place, the top leadership of the party sincerely believed that since the state had come into being the trends had outlived their usefulness. Also, it was in Mapai's self-interest to recognize some new realities and make the most of them. The relative strength of the trends had shifted in labor's favor. In a unified system of state education there was no danger that the labor trend would be swamped by the general trend. Just the opposite would occur: labor-trend values, specifically Mapai's version of socialist Zionism, would emerge as dominant. The mass of new immigrants would then be exposed to Mapai's influence at the expense of the other parties. As the trends were currently cast, the chief beneficiaries were the most rigidly doctrinaire parties. Mapai as the keystone party responsible for the operation of the government could not enjoy the luxury of rigidity. Moreover, being the power center in the coalition, Mapai could control the Ministry of Education, a consideration of no small significance.

The results of the 1951 elections paved the way for the passage of a law restructuring the educational system. But because of inertia, opposition, and the delays involved in working out compromise provisions acceptable to the coalition parties, it was not until August 1953 that the State Education Law was passed. At the time of the abolition of the existing trends, the distribution of student enrollment was[13]

Trend	Percent of Total Enrollment
Labor	44.2
General	26.5
Mizrachi	17.8
Agudah	7.8
Nontrend	3.7

The new law changed the old nomenclature and these relative relationships somewhat. The system of four recognized trends was replaced by "state education," "religious state education," and nonofficial "recognized" educational institutions. All partisan political activity was prohibited. However, the traditional ideals of the labor trend were incorporated in the official aims of state education. In articulating the philosophy that was to be common to all schools the law was most definite. Article 2 states the following:

> The object of State education is to base elementary education in the State on the values of Jewish culture and the achievements of science, on love of the homeland and loyalty to the State and the Jewish people, on practice in agricultural work and handicraft, on *chalutzic* (pioneer) training, and on striving for a society built on freedom, equality, tolerance, mutual assistance and love of mankind.[14]

To implement this goal, the minister of education and culture was given the power to amalgamate and reorganize schools. He also was empowered to determine basic curricula and adopt supplementary programs. (This effectively put him in control of secular elementary education.) In exercising his powers, however, he is legally required to consult an Education Committee on matters relating to state education and a Council for Religious State Education on matters relating to religious state education.

The former labor and general trends merged and became state education. Mapai, in control of the Ministry of Education, was protected. The religious schools in labor's subtrend merged with the Mizrachi trend and became religious state education. Religious state education according to the law means "State education, with the distinction that its institutions are religious as to their way of life, curriculum, teachers and inspectors." The Agudat Israel, as uncompromising as ever, opted to preserve its autonomy and

135

assumed the status of a nonofficial "recognized" school system. In short, while the new law provided an opportunity for numerous reforms and improvements, the functional-philosophic differentiation of the trend system was not eliminated, only reduced slightly. For all practical purposes only one trend was eliminated, three operative trends remain: labor superimposed on the general, the Mizrachi now operating under the rubric of state religious education, and the Agudat Israel school network as a "recognized" system. Theopolitics had succeeded in building religion into the state's educational structure.

While education has been freed of flagrant political partisanship, politics remains a major factor in educational considerations. Mapai influences state education, while religious state education is under the sway of the National Religious Party.[15] The minister of education usually has had two deputies, one a Knesset member who, like the minister, is a member of Mapai, and the other affiliated with the NRP.[16]

The ultra-Orthodox values of Agudat Israel are perpetuated in their independently recognized schools. Although the State Education Law authorized the minister of education to impose a "basic curriculum" on recognized nonofficial schools, the minister's control over Agudat Israel's schools, at best, is negligible. "The curriculum approved for Agudat Israel primary schools," Aharon F. Kleinberger, Professor of Comparative Education at the Hebrew University, has observed, "provides for a greater number of weekly periods to be devoted to traditional religious studies (Bible, Talmud, liturgy) and for a smaller number to be devoted to modern secular subjects (arithmetic, nature study, foreign language, physical training, etc.) than that prescribed to religious State schools." Even the ministry's inspection powers are curtailed. In contrast to the standard system of district inspection, there is one special national inspector who supervises all of Agudat Israel's primary schools. This inspector, however, is not empowered to give compulsory instructions to any Agudat Israel personnel. The Ministry of Education has imposed its standards on Agudat Israel in only two ways: first, it has insisted that the formal qualifications of their teachers be equivalent to those required in other official institutions; and second, the language of instruction must be Hebrew, not Yiddish, the customary language of the ultra-Orthodox. (Yiddish is permitted for the study of Talmud.) In exchange Agudat Israel was granted the status of a "recognized" school network and, perhaps more importantly, gained considerable financial subsidies. At present the state pays 85 percent of the salaries of the teachers and principals in the Agudat Israel schools, an increase of 25 percent from 1953 when the Education Law was enacted. Furthermore, in the majority of local authorities, by astute use of local coalition pressure tactics, Agudat Israel has obtained for its schools the same municipal services generally extended to "official" schools. "In short," to quote Kleinberger again, "Agudat Israel, owing to the political pressure it is able to exercise on Mapai, has succeeded in securing for its independent system of education almost all the benefits of State institutions, without accepting most of the obligations and controls involved in that status." [17]

With the State Education Law well established, the distribution of Jewish pupils in primary schools is relatively stable: approximately 64.5 percent attend state schools, 29 percent attend religious state schools, and 7 percent attend recognized independent schools.[18] In the past the religious parties have resisted educational changes (the proponents of these changes call them reforms) in the structure of the elementary system. The religious parties feared that the transfer of the seventh- and eighth-grade pupils from primary to postprimary education would weaken their position because their relative share of pupils in postprimary education is much smaller than their share of pupils in primary education.[19]

In Israel, secondary education is neither compulsory nor free although there is a system of scholarships and graduate tuition. The overall pattern of secondary education consists of secular and religious academic, vocational, and agricultural schools. (In recent years there has been a tendency to develop comprehensive secondary schools.) Within religious education there has been a considerable adjustment to the needs of a modernizing technological society. An increasing number of religious educational institutions have combined modern secondary secular education with the traditional studies. Since the beginning of the 1960s, the number of religious postprimary schools has increased dramatically, and the relative strength of the religious sector in postprimary education has increased, although it has not yet achieved the numerical strength it has reached in elementary education. (A factor which deserves notice in this connection is that yeshivot are for boys only.)

The talmudic academies (yeshivot) are of various types, but they all have one central educational goal: the study of Torah so as to "make a man good and straight." Character training, the implanting of moral-humanistic values, and concern for the students' welfare are their primary educational objectives. The Ministry of Education exerts no supervision over the yeshivot, but the state, through the Ministry of Religious Affairs, provides subsidies for them and their students.[20]

No description of religious education in Israel is complete without mention of Bar-Ilan University. Named after Rabbi Meir Bar-Ilan, a leader in the Mizrachi movement, the university, situated in a Tel Aviv suburb, began operating in 1955. It is sponsored by the Mizrachi movement and is an avowedly religious institution that offers a good secular education. All students, irrespective of their specialization, are required to take up Bible and talmudic studies "in the spirit of Orthodox teaching." Bar-Ilan is one of the main suppliers of teachers for Israel's religious secondary schools. Along with all the other institutions of higher education in Israel, Bar-Ilan receives a government subsidy.[21]

While all the religious schools are oriented toward Orthodox Judaism, the secular schools have never completely ignored Jewish subjects. Despite the fact that some Jewish content had been taught in the secular schools, in the late 1950s a concerted attempt was made to teach Jewish religious tradition as a "secular" subject in the nonreligious state schools. This arose out of deep concern over the prospect of the secular schools producing a generation of sabras almost ignorant of some of the basic elements of Judaism. Religion, which had served to bind Jews in the past, was becoming a barrier not only between the Orthodox and the non-Orthodox in Israel but also between Israelis and fellow Jews in the Diaspora. Sabras frequently tended to skip over 2000 years of Diaspora history and seek their roots in biblical times. This produced an unhealthy, unbalanced, and historically inaccurate chauvinism that reached its extreme in the so-called Canaanite movement. The Canaanites, a small but vocal minority, believe that the Israelis have to rid themselves of all specifically Diaspora-oriented characteristics and reestablish a direct continuity with the Canaanite-Palestinian biblical past.

In order to counter the indifference of so many young Israelis toward their religious heritage and their lack of identification with the Jews in the Diaspora, a Jewish consciousness (*toda'ah yehudit*) program was incorporated into the principles of the coalition government that came into being in 1955, after the election of the Third Knesset. This declaration reads

In primary, secondary and higher education the Government will endeavor to deepen the Jewish consciousness of Israel's youth, to root it in the past and the historical heritage of the Jewish people, and to strengthen its moral ties with world Jewry founded upon the recognition of the community of fate and of the historical continuity which unite the Jews throughout the world, in all generations and countries.[22]

It was not until 1959, however, that the Ministry of Education and Culture published a directive concerning a definite program of Jewish consciousness. The directive, designed particularly for nonreligious state primary schools, comprised five points: (1) Jewish Diaspora history was to be taught so that young Israelis would develop pride in their past. To that end, emphasis was to be laid upon the struggle for national survival, the perseverance and heroism

demonstrated by Jews in the face of persecution, the autonomy and solidarity of the Diaspora Jewish communities,
and the continuity of immigration to the Holy Land from
these communities in the hope of redemption. (2) Systematic study was to be undertaken of the various Diaspora Jewish communities—their structure, status, culture, customs,
and links to Israel. Jewish unity and mutual help were to be
emphasized as well as the emotional ties with Jews of the
Diaspora. (3) Pupils were to receive classroom instruction
in religious subjects as well as Jewish prayers, rites, customs,
folklore, and religious symbolism. The schools were to hold
celebrations on the eve of the Sabbath and Jewish holidays
so as to create a "Jewish atmosphere" and make the children more positively receptive to the values of their religious heritage. (4) Each week the respective weekly portion of the Pentateuch that is read in the synagogue on the
Sabbath would be discussed in class. This related the Bible,
the foundation of traditional observance, to the ritual cycle
of the Jewish year. The Bible, heretofore treated essentially
as a humanistic or nationalistic literary heritage, was now
given religious significance. (5) The traditional religious
elements in Hebrew literature would be reenforced by including larger portions of Oral Law and talmudic commentary, relating traditional Jewish values to current and
perennial problems of mankind. In all of these areas, the
culture, traditions, and literature of the Oriental Jewish
communities were to be included, in order to restore the
pride of non-European children in their specific cultural
heritage and mitigate their feelings of inferiority brought
about by the dominance of European Jewry.[23]

The directives of the Jewish consciousness program precipitated a Knesset debate. The program was supported in the main by Mapai, the Progressives, and the General Zionists. Acrimonious opposition came from the anticlerical left and the extreme religious parties. Mapam and some of the Achdut ha-Avodah Knesset members viewed the directives as religious compulsion and an unwholesome attempt to inject religious education into the secular state schools. The extreme religious parties opposed the program because they believed that religious tradition could not be taught by nonbelievers in a secular setting and that unless one accepted divine revelation of the scriptures and the obligations of Orthodox Judaism the Jewish consciousness program was an impossibility. Aside from these extremes, partisan polemic was largely absent. Almost all of the members who participated in the debate argued in favor of the program. Three themes were persistent: (1) the danger of an Israeli generation uprooted from the past and detached from Diaspora Jewry, (2) the need to prevent insularity and provincialism, and (3) the recognition that all students should have a deeper understanding of the religious aspects of Israeli and Diaspora society. One could not overlook the fact that many Jews, both in Israel and the Diaspora, were committed to a religious way of life. The program would bring children educated in secular schools closer to those who practice a religious life.[24]

The Jewish consciousness program has had only modest success. There has been some progress in eradicating the ignorance of things Jewish, but the objectives of the program are far from realized. Even if effective, a Jewish consciousness program can only narrow the gap between the secularists and the religious. As long as theopolitics persists,

142

the gap will not be bridged. The NRP-controlled state religious schools and the Agudat Israel ultra-Orthodox "recognized" schools are the fruits of theopolitics and their students the seeds of future theopolitical endeavors. The present students in the religious schools are future voters and potential adherents of the religious parties. Any changes in the educational system which might reduce the strength of the religious parties are certain to be resisted by them. Religion in the educational system will remain as one of the state's continuing problems.

10
Orthodoxy
and the
Military

CHAPTER 10

The Israeli military forces are a strong factor in the education of Israeli youth, ranking alongside the public schools, since national service is nearly universal for both men and women. The military can, therefore, either reinforce or undermine those values that have been inculcated by the educational system and the family. It is for this reason that the Orthodox have fought for establishment in the military and battled in the Knesset over national service requirements.

Orthodox Judaism has become firmly established in Israel's armed forces. One of the first laws passed by the Provisional Government gave the ministers of defense and religious affairs the joint authority to ensure the supply of kosher food to the army. From this modest beginning there has developed a well-organized and staffed Military Chaplaincy Department. Chaplains and religious affairs officers (Orthodox personnel not ordained as rabbis) are attached to every large unit, and each such unit has a mobile synagogue that is properly equipped and contains a Scroll of the Law (Sepher Torah). Even submarines are provided with small holy arks and miniature Torah scrolls. The religious personnel are responsible for the supervision of Orthodox dietary practice, the organization and conduct of religious services and celebrations, and the enforcement of Orthodox norms of Sabbath observance. All kitchens in military units are kosher and are supervised by the chaplaincy. The idea of separate religious and nonreligious units is logistically impractical and psychologically undesirable.

Chief Army Chaplain Major-General Shlomo Goren at the Western Wall.

146

Orthodox norms, such as those prohibiting smoking on the Sabbath and eating on the fast of Yom Kippur are prescribed by regulations and apply to all military areas. (The non-Orthodox violate these regulations with impunity in the privacy of their quarters.) All soldiers are required to participate in the devotional exercises prior to the High Holy Days (a practice some constitutional experts believe to be of doubtful legality).[1] On major festivals the chaplaincy distributes even to the most remote frontier positions the religious objects associated with that particular holiday. Thus, the chaplaincy corps attempts to provide every squad with a shofar for the High Holy Days and a seder meal and matzot on Passover. Senior commanders make it a point to participate publicly in holiday celebrations, generally in an uncomfortable field camp, as much for morale and nationalistic reasons as out of religious conviction. Nonetheless, whatever the reason, their presence helps to legitimize the Orthodox chaplaincy.

The chaplaincy issues its own journal, prints a special prayer book to be read before going into battle, and supplies every soldier with a Bible. During combat, the chaplains are on the front lines for personal ministrations and to take charge of the dead. Aside from considerations of observance, the chaplaincy, formerly under the direction of Chief Chaplain, Major-General Shlomo Goren, has attempted to reconcile traditional halakhic norms with the requirements of technology, security, and modern military administration. Questions, for example, as to the nature and permissibility of work on the Sabbath have continuously cropped up. The halakhah, however, is flexible, and the traditional doctrine of *pikuah nephesh* (to save a hu-

147

man life one may go to any lengths and annul all other prescriptions in Judaism) has been freely used. In this regard
the Military Rabbinate has been a force for the modernization of Orthodoxy. The chaplaincy has also acted to unify
the various Jewish communities. Chaplains conduct prayer
services according to a specially prepared unified order of
service, thereby facilitating worship by military personnel
coming from divergent Ashkenazic, Sephardic, and Oriental backgrounds.[2]

The formal incorporation of Orthodox norms into the
military has not produced much secular-Orthodox conflict.
This, however, was not the case with the issue of military
service for females. In 1949 when the Knesset discussed the
scope of the national service requirements, the secularists
wanted to include both men and single women. However,
the Orthodox strenuously opposed the drafting of women.
Members of the United Religious Front warned the Knesset that military service was morally damaging to young
women. A compromise was arrived at whereby Orthodox
females could obtain an exemption from military service.
But the secularists argued that this was a form of discrimination against non-Orthodox women and urged an amendment to the law so that religious women who refused to
serve in the army would be assigned to some form of sub-
stitute national service such as agricultural work in a religious settlement or some form of public welfare work,
nursing, or teaching. Nothing came of this attempt to equal-
ize the obligations of Orthodox and non-Orthodox women.
Some time later Ben-Gurion sought to have some form of
alternate service for Orthodox women approved by the

Knesset, but his urgings only further antagonized the Orthodox.[3]

In 1951, Ben-Gurion challenged the Orthodox by presenting to the Knesset a series of secularist bills, among them, an amendment to the Compulsory Military Service Law that abolished the exemption granted to religious females. Orthodox young women would, under the amendment, serve in military offices, farm settlements, hospitals, and other social and national welfare positions. The amendment offended Orthodox views of female modesty. Minister of Social Welfare Rabbi Yitzchak Meir Levin of Agudat Israel warned the Knesset that any amendment to the Military Service Law that infringed on the rights of the Orthodox would be disobeyed, even at the risk of imprisonment or execution. The Chief Rabbinate threatened that "the rabbinical court would ban the military amendment, a world wide day of fast would be proclaimed in protest, and Orthodox Jewry would 'fill the prisons in Israel with their daughters rather than comply with the law. . . .'" Rabbi Amram Blau, leader of the ultra-Orthodox Natore Karta, urged Orthodox females to commit suicide rather than accept conscription. Feelings ran high, and a few extremists went beyond rhetoric and attempted antigovernment action. The police foiled a group of fanatics who had plotted to blow up the Knesset and seized a small arsenal of weapons that were to be used by a minute band of zealots planning a "holy war." [4] The amendment, however, was shelved before coming to a final reading. Two years later, despite protests in Israel and abroad, the Defense Service Act was amended so that unmarried women aged eighteen to twenty-six who were exempted from military conscription on the grounds of religious objection were required to render equivalent national public service. The extreme Orthodox groups were incensed, but in fact they were not affected because relief from national service could be administratively granted for a number of reasons, including "a family's special way of life." The moderate Mizrachi factions were placated by the provision that during their period of national service religious girls were to be assured of an opportunity to maintain a religious way of life. And, as a modest quid pro quo for the secularists, the law provided that it was to be implemented by a minister designated by the government, which meant that the law was to be administered by the Ministry of Labor, a longtime Mapai stronghold.[5] In actual practice, because of NRP objections, the 1953 National Service Law has never been applied. Nonetheless, many moderate Orthodox girls voluntarily fulfill their military or national service. The great majority of ultra-Orthodox girls, however, have refused to perform any national service.

Following the Six-Day War, military personnel requirements increased dramatically; the period of military service was extended and the frequency of reserve call-ups increased. In order to ease the resultant labor shortage in health, education, and welfare services, the cabinet in late 1971 decided to organize a form of volunteer service for Orthodox girls exempted from military service on religious grounds. This decision touched off a furore. Some moderates in the National Religious Party agreed to the proposal, others, recognizing that abuses had crept into the exemption privilege, agreed with the volunteer principle but opposed the establishment of any mechanism that would lead from voluntarism to coercion. The ultra-Orthodox remained unyielding. To them young girls belonged in the home. Religious extremists assembled at the Wailing Wall, blew the shofar, and prayed: "Our Father, Our King, repeal the evil sentence." The cabinet decision has not as yet been carried out, and the controversy over national service continues.

The conflict over national service for Orthodox girls is the only significant area relating to the military where there is secular-religious discord. Within the military itself, in contrast to other areas of public life, the Orthodox rabbinate's position is secure, unchallenged, and essentially uncontroversial. This difference, however, may be explained by a unique combination of factors. Israelis esteem the military and are unwilling to involve it in polemic; they are aware that to ensure survival and not jeopardize national defense the functioning of the military cannot be impaired, even in the slightest. The military rabbinate recognizes these facts and has proved more flexible than has the Chief Rabbinate in other areas of public policy.

11
Orthodox
Pressure
Tactics

The Orthodox rabbinate has been given exclusive control over a number of areas of public life, including dietary supervision. The rabbinate often uses the power of dietary supervision as a lever to exert still greater influence in broad areas of secular public life. In this the rabbinate has several sources of potential support beyond the actual bargaining power of the religious parties. Pressure from Orthodox Jews in the Diaspora often can be quite effective. Observant Jews frequently come to the support of the rabbinate with petitions, protests, and demonstrations. Distinguished rabbis exhort their followers to resist fiercely any incursions into Orthodox norms. Two specific controversies are particularly illustrative: the fight over the S.S. *Shalom* and the Marbek abbatoir incident.

Despite its name, *Shalom*—Hebrew for peace—the luxury ocean liner that was the pride of Israeli shipping was launched only after a fierce struggle over whether or not it was to sail with two kitchens: kosher and nonkosher. Because the *Shalom* was owned by the Zim Israel Navigation Company, Ltd., a government-supported corporation, the resolution of the issue had consequences for the public order. The Zim management wanted to equip the *Shalom* with two kitchens so that its services would be competitive with those of other transatlantic carriers. The "international" cuisine, that is, the nonkosher kitchen, would satisfy the palates of those passengers who did not wish to be restricted to dietary regulations. For those who observed the dietary regulations there was to be a kosher kitchen. And thus the *Shalom* would be in a position to compete

Antielection propaganda on a wall in the Mea Shearim quarter of Jerusalem.

154

with ships of other lines, maximizing her economic return. Zim asked only that the rabbinate certify one kitchen as being kosher, a practice that the rabbinate performed for non-Israeli ships that had both kosher and nonkosher kitchens.

The rabbinate, however, refused to go along with this reasoning. If the *Shalom* was to be the Zim line's flagship, the maritime image of Israel, it should represent the traditions of the country. The existence of both kosher and nonkosher kitchens on non-Israeli liners was not analogous. Kashrut on the *Shalom* was similar to kashrut on other Zim line ships and the government airline El Al; failure to have only one kitchen was a breach of the status quo agreements. And, the Orthodox argued, it was doubtful that Zim would lose revenues if the *Shalom* was a one-kitchen ship: the loss of patronage by the nonobservant would more than be made up by the increased allegiance of the observant. Nor should economics interfere with religious observance.

As a ministerial committee debated the issue, the rabbinate warned that it would withhold the kashrut certification of the *Shalom* if it sailed with two kitchens, and hinted that it would go further and rescind the kashrut certificates of Zim's other ships. Although the revocation of the kashrut certificates would have had grave economic consequences for Zim, Zim at first refused to bow to the rabbinate and tried to fight back. Zim announced that it had signed a contract with the Associated Legislative Rabbinate of America, Inc. (a relatively small Orthodox faction based in New York, which had left the Union of Orthodox Rabbis), for supervision of the kosher facilities aboard the *Shalom*. When the American group that was to oversee the kosher

155

kitchen advertised for a "kashrut supervisor for a roving community," the Jerusalem rabbinate threatened to withdraw its recognition from any Israeli rabbi accepting the post.

As the kitchen controversy continued, the NRP vigorously reiterated its grave concern that a government-financed company was trying to circumvent another government organ, the Kashrut Division of the Chief Rabbinate. Meanwhile, in the United States, Rabbi Joseph B. Soloveitchik, respected dean of the American Orthodox rabbinate, took the unprecedented step of threatening to pronounce a *cherem,* a ban and boycott, on both Zim and El Al airlines if the *Shalom* sailed with two kitchens. In the face of these pressures the Zim board of directors canceled its arrangement with the New York rabbinical group and asked for a meeting with Chief Rabbi Nissim. This meeting was inconclusive, and the Chief Rabbinical Council (which in effect, because of vacancies, consisted only of Chief Rabbi Nissim and then Tel Aviv Chief Rabbi Unterman) issued an ultimatum: Zim had two weeks to announce its intention of abandoning the two kitchens on the *Shalom* or else the kashrut certification of all Zim's other ships would be withdrawn.

Counterpressure was now applied by the militant secularists. In an open letter to the minister of transport, the national executive of the League Against Religious Coercion stated its position:

We appeal to you to exercise all your authority in support of the decision of the ZIM Company to provide two kitchens on the s.s. SHALOM—not because the international kitchen is essential financially, but because the ship is an integral part of the State of Israel whose Declaration of Independence promised freedom of conscience and religion to all its inhabitants.

In our State all citizens live in peaceful coexistence in accordance with their various religions, traditions, and food habits. The same should apply to our "floating territory," the s.s. SHALOM. Do not let it be turned into a floating ghetto!

The vast majority of Israelis are disgusted with the way "kashrut" has become a matter of "selling" certificates—especially as it costs the population millions of pounds to support a parasitic array of "kashrut" supervisors.

We appeal to you not to stand aside in this struggle which now concerns not only the ZIM Company, but all the progressive elements of the population. Your stand will strengthen them and all progressive friends of Israel abroad who are concerned for the image of Israel as an enlightened State.[1]

The NRP threatened a cabinet crisis. If the *Shalom* was put into operation with two kitchens, the NRP would resign from the coalition. It was a touchy situation, but a crisis was averted when Zim's management reluctantly agreed to a formula whereby the *Shalom* would sail as a one-kitchen ship. When sailing as a kosher ship, there would be no nonkosher cuisine; on other sailings the kosher kitchen would be closed and the nonkosher kitchen open. The ship would be either "kosher" or "nonkosher" but not both, depending on the sailing. The rabbinate issued a certificate of kashrut for the vessel's one kitchen, and the *Shalom* sailed. For a while the battle over the *Shalom* seemed to have ended. The *Shalom* sailed the transatlantic route to Israel with a kosher kitchen and ran winter cruises in the Caribbean with a nonkosher kitchen. However, after a while the Chief Rabbinate objected to the practice of alternating kitchens, and it appeared that another storm might break. The issue smoldered for a while but was ultimately put to rest when Zim sold the *Shalom* to a West German company in 1967 because its operation was unprofitable.

The sailing of the S.S. *Shalom* as a one-kitchen ship was, in the main, a victory for the Chief Rabbinate, the religious parties, and their Orthodox allies. The Chief Rabbinate's threat to revoke the kashrut certificate for all of Zim's ships had proved a potent weapon. Once again theopolitics had been successful; in the face of its numerous secular problems the Eshkol government could not abide a cabinet crisis provoked by the religious parties. For the militant secularists, the abstract principle of freedom of choice was paramount; but for the great majority of Israelis, the question of one or two kitchens was purely academic— they would have little opportunity to avail themselves of the *Shalom*'s luxuries. Furthermore, the Rabbinate's concession to Zim, which permitted the *Shalom* to sail parttime as an "international" cuisine ship on the lucrative cruise run, tempered, for many, the feeling that the Orthodox were unreasonably intransigent. Although some compromise had prevailed, Orthodox values were further entrenched in an area of public activity.

The threat to withhold or revoke certificates of kashrut has also been used by the rabbinate against hotels. There have been occasional disputes in which the local rabbinates have threatened to revoke a hotel's kashrut certificate, an important economic asset, unless the hotel followed complete Sabbath observance. (For the Orthodox, Sabbath observance means abstention from all forms of work so as to honor the precept "remember the Sabbath Day and keep it holy.") For the hotel, total Sabbath observance would mean, among other things, that guests could not be registered or checked out (because employees would be prohibited from writing), smoking would not be permitted in the public rooms, telephones and manually operated elevators would not work, and many other hotel services would be limited or halted. When this issue erupted with particular intensity in Jerusalem in 1968 (shortly after Agudat Israel joined the Religious Council), the hotel owners fought back, refusing to paralyze their operations from sundown Friday to sundown Saturday. When the hotel owners announced that they would be willing to surrender the certificates of kashrut, and if necessary, maintain kosher kitchens without official supervision, the rabbinate backed down. The attempt to impose Orthodox Sabbath observances on hotels has been put into abeyance.[2]

The tactic of kashrut approval was also used by the established rabbinate in the Marbek slaughterhouse case. In the early months of 1964 a regional slaughterhouse neared completion and prepared to market its meat. The abattoir, Marbek, was established by a cooperative of agricultural settlements (including some Orthodox ones) in the south, covering an area governed by a number of regional councils. Before distribution began, however, obstacles were thrown up by the Chief Rabbinate. According to the Rabbinate, a kashrut certificate could not be given because ritual slaughtering must be supervised in the locality where the meat is to be consumed. Marbek disputed this idea, arguing that if meat is certified as kosher at the abattoir, wrapped, and refrigerated, it could not possibly become nonkosher on the journey from the slaughterhouse to the market. The concept of local supervision might have been valid in the past, and in the Diaspora, but it was not relevant to modern conditions in Israel. The Rabbinate's ruling, Marbek contended, was merely an excuse for protecting the Rabbinate's vested interests, since the new slaughterhouse was in competition with the slaughterhouse and kashrut supervision of the Tel Aviv municipality and religious council. The Rabbinate's reply to the charge that they were attempting to maximize the fees of the religious councils was that ritual slaughter (*shechitah*) was primarily a religious and not an economic matter. The Rabbinate was interested in making certain that the slaughterers were employees of society and, as such, answerable to the public, freed of possible influence or pressure by the seller. Since the seller wants to have as much meat as possible certified as kosher, if the seller employed the slaughterers, the latter's independence might be compromised. Furthermore, the Rabbinate contended, kashrut inspection also includes supervision in the meat markets, and the principle of continuous supervision must not be breached.

Marbek answered that they had insulated the ritual slaughterers from Marbek control by working out an arrangement whereby the slaughterers were paid by a union composed of slaughterers from some of the religious councils in the area, and that management thus could not (and would not) want to exert any influence on its employees.

The situation seemed resolved when the Chief Rabbinical Council decided to establish a special body to supervise the slaughtering and marketing operations of Marbek. Until the body was operative, the local religious councils could determine whether and under what conditions local butchers could sell Marbek meat as kosher. Trouble, however, developed when the Rabbinate dragged its feet in formalizing the commitment and insisted that Marbek limit its sale only to kosher butchers and dispose of its nonkosher meat for industrial uses. In order to market its meat, Marbek employed a Natore Karta rabbi to supervise its ritual slaughtering. The Rabbinate, incensed that a nonestablishment rabbi was being used to thwart them, warned shops and supermarket chain stores that the meat probably was not kosher and that they should stop selling Marbek meat as kosher or risk losing their certificates of kashrut. This threat was followed by action. A number of stores selling Marbek meat as kosher had their kashrut certification withdrawn. The withdrawal of certification affected not only meat but all products sold. The meat war was on.

Marbek's management now went to the secular courts. They requested an order nisi requiring the Chief Rabbinate to show cause why they refused to undertake kashrut supervision at the abattoir. At this stage, Prime Minister Eshkol and the ministers of agriculture, interior, and religious affairs entered the scene. As a result of their efforts, the Tel Aviv chief rabbinate, under Rabbi Unterman, retreated slightly. It was proposed that some form of kashrut supervision be instituted at Marbek, that the abattoir limit its production, and that a mutually acceptable means of disposing of Marbek's nonkosher meat be worked out. The Chief Rabbinical Council now made a decision: Marbek would not receive a countrywide *hechsher* (certificate of fitness), but local rabbinates could work out their own arrangements with the slaughterhouse; and also the Rab-

161

binate was to inform the High Court of Justice that it did not consider the secular court competent to review Rabbinical Council decisions on matters of a purely halakhic nature. (The Rabbinate contended that the granting of kashrut certificate was a subject solely within the purview of halakhah.)

In August 1964, the Supreme Court, sitting as a five-man high court of justice, ruled that it was competent to hold hearings on the order nisi. Marbek requested that the court make the order nisi absolute because, they contended, the Rabbinate's refusal to give them a nationwide kashrut certificate was based on grounds other than halakhah. The attorney general, whose presence attested to the importance of the case, stated that, in his opinion, the Rabbinate was within its legal right to base its decisions on halakhah, but the high court certainly had the power to determine whether or not the Rabbinate was basing its decisions on halakhic principles. The court did not go into the merits of the case and postponed a hearing on the order until the fall so as to give the Chief Rabbinate an opportunity to present its case.

(When the court subsequently published its rationale for holding the Rabbinical Council subject to its jurisdiction, it pointed out that the Rabbinate exercises its public functions by state law, and therefore, in the absence of a Knesset declaration to the contrary, its acts are like any other public body in that they are subject to high court surveillance. Significantly, the decision was written by the president of the Supreme Court and concurred in by the remaining four justices.)

The Rabbinate was now faced with a problem. They

were respondents to a court order nisi, and if they refused
to appear in court, the order could be made absolute. If
they refused to comply, that is, grant Marbek a nationwide
hechsher, the secular high court then could issue a contempt of court proceedings against the Rabbinate. There
was now the possibility of a clear-cut confrontation between
the Rabbinate and the secular High Court. The confrontation, however, never came. A compromise was arrived at.
Marbek withdrew its application for an order nisi against
the Rabbinate, and in exchange the Chief Rabbinate
agreed to negotiate a formula whereby Marbek would be
granted a hechsher. Under this agreement, the Rabbinate
placed the slaughterhouse under the kashrut supervision of
Tel Aviv and three other nearby municipalities. Marbek
was allocated a quota of half of the average weekly production of the slaughterhouses serving these four towns; the
remaining half of the meat would be supplied by the existing local abattoirs. Additional religious councils could enter into similar arrangements with Marbek. The agreement, in testimony to the efforts of the religious parties,
also stipulated that the minister of agriculture would com-
pensate the religious council and the Tel Aviv municipality
for the slaughterhouse fees lost by Marbek's competition.

This agreement was a victory for Marbek. Its goal—the
right to market meat authorized as "kosher" by the Rabbinate—had been achieved. For the Rabbinate, the local
arrangements clause was a face-saving fiction, while the
compensation clause, involving a direct state subvention to
offset the loss in slaughtering fees, ensured that there would
be no diminution of the rabbinate's economic base. The
public at large was convinced that the Rabbinate's insis-

tence on local inspection was less motivated by religious considerations than by a desire to safeguard their vested economic interests. The compensatory payment clause only reenforced this feeling. An editorial criticizing the compensatory provisions of the agreement noted:

> Nobody suggests that, having in the past been financed in part by the slaughterhouses, the Rabbinate should suddenly be faced with a curtailed budget. But the proper source for its budget is the Ministry of Religions, whose allocation is calculated in accordance with the share of national tax-money available for the maintenance of religious services, as compared with health, education and all other needs. For this money to be paid by the Ministry of Agriculture, as the only practical way of getting Marbek into operation, is nothing short of grotesque even if it solves the problem for the time being. This is a subject to which the State Controller might usefully give his attention. Perhaps in time it will be possible to produce a ruling to prevent the arbitrary paying of "compensation" to organizations and vested interests whom modernization deprives of traditional perquisites.
>
> . . . In a state of two million, we can no longer finance religious services by what amounts to a secret tax on the Sabbath chicken.[3]

The Rabbinate lost in overall public esteem. Unlike the contretemps over the *Shalom,* the prospect of regional slaughterhouses with hygienic conditions and the promise of lower meat prices was of vital concern to the average Israeli consumer. Furthermore, the Rabbinate's withholding or revoking certificates of kashrut, in order to compel obedience, was successfully challenged in the courts. Although the Rabbinate refused to contest the issue and avoided a direct showdown with the secular court, it is important to remember that the secular court clearly articulated its right of judicial scrutiny of certain of the Rabbinate's acts, a premise in derogation of the Rabbinate's position.

The marshaling of Diaspora support as was done in the *Shalom* incident is not a tactic used only by the rabbinate. It is also used by the religious parties as a means to effect the passage, defeat, or amendment of legislation touching on Orthodox norms. An interesting case in point is the on-going controversy over postmortems.

The Anatomy and Pathology Law of 1953, viewed with dismay by the Orthodox, permits postmortem operations without the prior consent of the deceased or his family only when necessary to establish the cause of death or to use part of the body for the curative treatment of another person. As a safeguard, three doctors are required to sign a certificate of necessity before the postmortem operation takes place. The extremely Orthodox were (and still are) opposed to this law because they consider the mutilation of the dead a desecration. Rabbi Immanuel Jakobovits, a distinguished scholar, has summed up the Orthodox position:

The conflicting interests are really between those of life and those of the dead. The living are free agents, and as such charged with the supreme duty to preserve life at all costs. Not so the dead. Their bodies are not our property, and their title to undisturbed rest may be as great as the claim of the living to life.[4]

By 1965, as a condition of the National Religious Party joining the cabinet in the Sixth Knesset, it was agreed that changes in the Anatomy and Pathology Law were to be made. The government sponsored amendments enabling hospital patients or their relatives to object to postmortems except in cases where the public interest takes precedence.

These proposed changes, however, were considered inadequate by the Orthodox, who began to mount an extensive campaign inside and outside Israel to achieve their objectives.[5]

Protest meetings were held in Israeli cities, and in London and New York. In the United States a group calling themselves the American Committee for Safeguarding Human Dignity in Israel sponsored a prominent statement in the *New York Times*. This statement appearing under a large headline proclaiming "DO NOT DESECRATE THE DEAD!" presented the Orthodox position and appealed for support. The pertinent parts read as follows:

In Israel, mass autopsies are being performed without permission, and despite the expressed objection, of the deceased and their family. A wave of protest has engulfed Israel in recent months. Would you want *your* close relative to be dissected after death?

One of the basic tenets of Jewish tradition prescribes that a person's body, after death, should not be tampered with in any way (except in unusually urgent circumstances) and that burial of the body and any of its limbs or organs should take place as soon as possible. These principles, based on the concept of Divine Image and the respect for human dignity prevalent in all civilized nations, have been affirmed and reaffirmed by rabbinic authorities for many centuries. As recently as several months ago 400 Israeli rabbis, including the Chief Rabbinate, issued a public proclamation condemning the practice of autopsies. In deference to these hallowed, universally-accepted attitudes, and in consideration of the sacred rights of man to determine the fate of his own body, governments throughout the world (including the United States) legally require written consent of the deceased and/or his next of kin before an autopsy may be performed. In Israel, unfortunately, the situation is drastically different.

In recent years there has been a vast increase in the number of autopsies performed in Israel. Prompted in part by foreign-financed research grants, many Israeli doctors and scientists go far beyond the normal need of performing autopsies for scientific purposes in cases of suspicious deaths and potentially dangerous epidemics. In some hospitals and institutions, the autopsy or dissection rate has reached up to 80% of all deaths, as reported in the Israeli press, including the Hadassah Hospital in Jerusalem. The autopsy "campaign" has apparently been undertaken with such zeal that many instances of unseemly haste and gross disrespect to bodies and organs have been reported by eyewitnesses. Furthermore, until recently a patient entering a hospital could request an affidavit from his doctor that in case of death his body be immediately returned to his family for burial. A Ministry of Health edict dated June 7, 1966 ordered that no such guarantees be given, and all patients who insist upon such prior conditions *be refused admittance to hospitals.*

. . . .

A battle against indiscriminate, compulsory autopsies in Israel has been raging for several years. Government commissions have been appointed, hearings held, recommendations reported (and ignored), protest meetings, demonstrations, delegations—all in vain. So-called attempts to introduce new amendments to the law to correct this situation were exposed as mere smokescreens that could not rectify this serious situation. It would seem that certain elements in Israel are so obsessed with their antipathy to anything that smacks of religion, that they do not hesitate to even go to the extreme of trampling upon the rights of the dead.

We seek to impose our will upon no one. At stake is not only a religious issue but what all civilized countries recognize as a basic human right; that the wishes of the deceased and/or his next of kin—and not the State—determine the disposition of his body. We demand that anyone, whether out of religious conviction or humanitarian feelings, be legally allowed to insist that no autopsy or dissection be

167

performed on his—or his relative's—body after death (granting the exceptions practiced in the United States, such as in cases of suspicious deaths or dangerous epidemics.)[6]

In the Knesset, Rabbi Menachem Porush of Agudat Israel charged that the bodies of 70 to 80 percent of patients who die in Israeli hospitals were dissected. These allegations were denied by a Ministry of Health official who contended that the frequency of postmortems was much lower. Prime Minister Eshkol, under pressure from the National Religious Party, announced that he would support an amendment to the Anatomy and Pathology Law which would provide for greater consideration of the wishes of the deceased and/or his family but which would also be mindful of the needs of public health and the advancement of science. A group of American rabbis living in Israel requested the protection of the United States Embassy against autopsies that might be made on them if they died in Israeli hospitals. By the late spring of 1967 the antiautopsy campaign had reached a fever pitch. Billboards urged the Orthodox to support the fight against autopsies. Pictures of dissected bodies and horror stories about the treatment given to bodies were circulated. Pathologists were threatened. Public prayers and fasts were held. And at a meeting organized by the Committee for Safeguarding Human Dignity a riot occurred and police were stoned. The medical profession and its supporters felt obliged to counterattack. Hebrew University and Tel Aviv University medical school faculties issued a statement defending the need for postmortems as necessary to scientific advancement and human betterment. Journalists were shown people who had their vision restored by transplating the corneas of deceased persons. And the medical profession submitted respected rabbinical opinion that held that postmortems were a vital need of the community. Just as the controversy reached a boiling point, the battle over autopsies was suddenly suspended as problems of security, the Six-Day War, and its aftermath took national precedence.[7] After the Six-Day War, however, when, along with the immediate threat to survival, the euphoria of national unity diminished, the Orthodox resumed their fight against autopsies. Currently, the issue remains unsettled, a continuing source of secular-religious antagonism.

Orthodox pressure tactics of protest and demonstration often are effective in that they tend to modify governmental positions. No democratic government wishes to alienate a portion of its population. Nor do Israeli leaders wish to disrupt the close ties with Israel of Jews in the Diaspora, by giving the impression that the government is hostile to Orthodox Judaism. On the other hand, when the actions of the rabbinate become detrimental to the Israeli public at large, as in the Marbek incident, the secular machinery, either through cabinet pressure and compromise or by judicial dictate, has restrained the rabbinate and reminded it of its dependence on secular authority.

12
"Who
Is
a Jew?"

Even the issue of Jewish nationality, though in many instances a wellspring of unity between the religious and the secularists, has acted to divide them. The fundamental question "Who is a Jew?" touching, as it does, on questions of belief, has exposed a deep division between the two groups. Though the issue was fought and resolved politically—in the cabinet, in committee, and on the floor of the Knesset—there was a consciousness that the final decision would have implications, not just for Israel, but for Jews in the Diaspora as well.

While the laws of Israel forbid discrimination, Jews in the Diaspora enjoy a special privilege, the Law of Return. The Law of Return, enacted in July 1950, was the statutory embodiment of the Zionist belief, articulated in the Proclamation of Independence, that Israel was created for any Jew in the Diaspora who wished to come, and that his return to Zion, the Land of Israel, was his absolute right as a Jew. To a large extent also, the Law of Return was an emotional response to restrictive national immigration policies that prevented many Jews from escaping the Holocaust or finding entry into new host countries after World War II. A Jew, unless it is determined that he is a danger to the public health or security, is entitled to settle in Israel as an immigrant.[1] A non-Jew who wishes to migrate to Israel must receive permission to do so, and the state may withhold such permission. If the non-Jew settles in the country, he may become a naturalized citizen.

The Registry of Population, under the minister of the interior, issues each resident an identity card on which are listed "religion" and "nationality." In an attempt to

A service at a Sephardic synagogue in Tel Aviv.

introduce some consistency into the registration of Israeli residents, Israel Bar-Yehudah of Achdut ha-Avodah, the minister of the interior, issued a directive in March 1958 to the offices of the Registry of Citizens: "Any person declaring in good faith that he is a Jew, shall be registered as a Jew and no additional proof shall be required." The Bar-Yehudah directive, in effect, allowed each person to be registered in accordance with the information given by him or his parents. This meant that if a non-Jewish woman declared in the Registry office that she was Jewish, she and her child would be so registered. The National Religious Party representatives in the cabinet (Mosheh Shapira, minister of social welfare and religious affairs, and Yoseph Burg, minister of posts) reacted sharply to the directive, charged a violation of the status quo set by the coalition agreement, and demanded a discussion. The rabbinate and certain Orthodox factions objected to the classification as Jews of the Karaites, a sect that rejects the Oral Law, and of the children of a number of families in which the wife was not Jewish that had recently immigrated from Poland. Rabbinic law holds that the child has the religion of the mother. The children of these unions were not yet converted to Judaism, or their conversion was not satisfactory to the religious authorities. However, it was argued—especially since both parents of the children had suffered because of their Jewish affiliation—that if the children of such mixed (that is, Jewish and non-Jewish) couples were declared Jewish on their identity cards, it would ease their absorption into Israeli society. (At one point Bar-Yehudah, to the great agitation of the Orthodox, had announced that "it is possible that not the laws of the Torah but other

173

human laws and considerations characterize the child.")[2]

Since the directive had practical as well as ideological import, it was decided that a committee consisting of the ministers of religion, interior, and justice be formed to solve the problem. The resultant interministerial discussions, however, did not fundamentally alter the situation, and the following instructions were issued by Bar-Yehudah's office in regard to

> any person declaring in good faith that he is a Jew and is not of another religion. . . . If both members of a married couple declare that their child is Jewish, this declaration shall be regarded as though it were the legal declaration of the child itself. . . . The registering official need not be concerned over the fact that according to the law of the Torah (in case one of the parents is non-Jewish) the child has the same status as its mother. . . . The parents' declaration that their child is Jewish suffices to register him as Jewish.

The implications of this directive were clearly unacceptable to the religious ministers and they resigned. According to the instructions, anyone, no matter what his faith, could identify himself as Jewish for purposes of national identification. The secularists argued that, since the Registry had a civil and not a religious purpose and the religious authorities need not have relied on it, religious criteria for determining Judaism were not relevant. Halakhah would still determine marriage and burial. The Orthodox retort was that according to halakhah one was considered Jewish either by birth or conversion and not by declaration. The fact that the rabbinical courts did not have to consider the identity card was irrelevant. What was at stake, for the religious, was the inseparability in Judaism of religion and nationality as well as the fear of creating disunity in the national religious character.

Shapira and Burg, in Knesset speeches, explained their resignations from the government. Shapira said,

In these days, the State of Israel has permitted itself to engage in polemic over the Jewish religion, over the national character and national distinctiveness of the Jewish people. . . . Who is a Jew? Today this question has been placed on our agenda in the State of Israel. For thousands of years we knew who was a Jew, and for what we were willing to suffer as Jews. Yet the State of Israel, which has just completed its tenth year, has seen fit to raise this question and render a decision which deliberately ignores thousands of years of Jewish history.

Dr. Burg was equally blunt:

Is it conceivable that an administrative act can remove the boundary between Jew and non-Jew? Is this an issue to be decided by a majority of 3 or 6 votes in the Government?

Bar-Yehudah, representing the secular point of view, reiterated that no consequences of legal importance would follow from his instructions and stated the following:

Our registrars do not determine what the law of the Torah is. That is done by the rabbis. But who is of Jewish nationality? That question shall be determined by us, the Knesset of Israel elected by the people. If that is the subject of the debate, it is a serious debate. For this purpose the State has come into being and on this I am prepared to take my stand.[3]

The issue was now squarely joined: Could Jewish nationality in Israel be separated from the Jewish religion?

Did the legislature in a Jewish state have the right to pass a law separating Jewish nationality from Judaism? But now the pressures of practicality intruded.

Prime Minister Ben-Gurion, it appeared, was not particularly desirous of remaining in a cabinet with secular parties that disagreed with him on economic matters. He feared that the two left-wing coalition partners, Achdut ha-Avodah and Mapam, would obstruct his economic programs and pending foreign-policy decisions regarding West Germany. He needed the leverage of the religious parties.

Looking for a way out of the "Who is a Jew?" impasse, Ben-Gurion employed a classic political technique: he set up a committee. This committee of three—the prime minister (Ben-Gurion), the minister of the interior (Bar-Yehudah), and the minister of justice (Pinchas Rosen of the Progressives)—was to examine the problem of the registration of children of mixed marriages and then "formulate a registry procedure in consonance with the tradition accepted by all circles of Jewry, be they Orthodox or liberals." The Orthodox were furious, for they felt that seeking outside "liberal" advice demonstrated flagrant disrespect for the Chief Rabbinate of Israel. A few days later the committee announced that the local registry officers should not register children of mixed marriages, that previous directives affecting such cases were null and void, and that all such registration was to be brought to the ministerial committee.

In the fall of 1958 Ben-Gurion sent out a letter to forty-five "sages of Israel" asking them to address themselves to the problem. The recipients of Ben-Gurion's letter covered a wide range—over half live in the Diaspora and included, in addition to Orthodox rabbis, rabbis of the Reform and Conservative branches of Judaism, writers, poets, jurists, and scientists. This letter is significant in its implication that others, even others outside Israel, might answer the question "Who is a Jew?" as well as the Chief Rabbinate in Israel. In his letter Ben-Gurion asked for an opinion as to the course that the Israeli government should pursue in the registration of children of mixed marriages. His letter revealed that he considered the issues to be multifaceted. He wrote, among other things,

Four considerations should be taken into account for the understanding of the problem as a whole

(1) The principle of freedom of conscience and religion has been guaranteed in Israel both in the Proclamation of Independence and in the Basic Principles of the governments that have held office until now, which have included both "religious" and "secular" parties. All religious and anti-religious coercion is forbidden in Israel, and a Jew is entitled to be either religious or non-religious.

(2) Israel serves in our time as a center for the ingathering of the exiles. The immigrants come from East and West, from both progressive and backward countries, and the merging of the various communities and their integration into one nation is one of Israel's most vital and difficult tasks. Every effort must therefore be made to strengthen the factors that foster cooperation and unity, and to root out as far as possible everything that makes for separation and alienation.

(3) The Jewish community in Israel does not resemble a Jewish community in the Diaspora. We in this country are not a minority subject to the pressure of a foreign culture, and there is no need here to fear the assimilation of Jews among non-Jews which takes place in many prosperous and free countries. On the contrary, here there are, to a slight extent, possibilities and tendencies making for the assimilation of non-Jews among the Jewish people, espe-

cially in the case of families coming from mixed marriages who settle in Israel. While mixed marriages among those who come here, especially from Eastern Europe, result in practice in the complete merging with the Jewish people.

(4) On the other hand, the people of Israel do not regard themselves as a separate people from Diaspora Jewry; on the contrary, there is no Jewish community in the world that is inspired by such a profound consciousness of unity and identity with the Jews of the world as a whole as the Jewish community in Israel.[4]

In general the replies displayed a high degree of consensus as to "Who is a Jew?" Most of the respondents concurred with the rabbinical definition: one was a Jew if born to a Jewish mother or admitted to Judaism as a proselyte according to the requirements of Jewish law. Those, however, who chose to delve into related issues showed a wider variety of opinions. (Examples of related issues would be these queries: Do Jews form a religious community with national characteristics? Are Jews a nation, a religion, or both? What should be the relationship between the faith of Israel and the people of Israel? and so on.) But well before all the answers were in, Ben-Gurion moved to placate the religious elements. He appointed as minister of religious affairs Tel Aviv Sephardic Chief Rabbi Yaakov Mosheh Toledano, a distinguished scholar unaffiliated with any party.

The question of "Who is a Jew?" for identity card registration was solved after the elections to the Fourth Knesset. Coalition stability once again required the presence of the National Religious Party in the government. The NRP returned to the coalition, and Mosheh Shapira, who had resigned six months previously over Bar-Yehudah's directives, was given the Ministry of the Interior. Shapira immediately issued new instructions to the registrars. A Jew was defined as "a person born of a Jewish mother who does not belong to another religion, or one who was converted in accordance with religious law." The first "who clause" in Shapira's directive, however, contradicts a number of generally accepted rabbinic interpretations which hold that apostates remain Jews. The "who clause" was designed to exclude apostates such as Brother Daniel, the monk who was born a Jew, and wanted to claim Israeli citizenship under the Law of Return. It was an interesting situation, an Orthodox minister who had resigned because the secular definition of "Who is a Jew?" for registration purposes would not square with halakhic doctrine was now issuing an order that partly upheld and (in the view of some halakhic authorities) partly violated halakhic reasoning, in order to be logical in his interpretation of Israeli religious nationalism. The definition of a Jew had been resolved temporarily for secular registration purposes. The definition, however, was based on an administrative order, not Knesset legislation, thereby inviting future "Who is a Jew?" problems.

The first "who clause" in Interior Minister Shapira's definition of a Jew—"a person born of a Jewish mother who does not belong to another religion"—reached the High Court for adjudication in November 1962 in the Brother Daniel case. Brother Daniel was born Oswald Rufeisen in Poland in 1922 to Jewish parents. He was reared and educated as a Jew. In his youth he was active in the Zionist youth movement, and after his secondary schooling he underwent pioneering training in Vilna for two years in preparation for his immigration to Palestine. In June 1941 he was caught by the Gestapo and imprisoned. He escaped and succeeded in obtaining false papers certifying that he was a German Christian. As such he worked as an interpreter in a German police station, where he used his position to warn the local Jews of the Germans' intention to liquidate the Mir ghetto. Acting on this information, some 150 Jews were able to escape from the ghetto and join the partisans. He was betrayed by a Jewish informer and under questioning revealed himself as a Jew. He was again imprisoned and again he escaped, finding refuge in a convent. In 1942, while in the convent, he embraced Christianity, and in 1945, at the end of the war, he became a priest and entered the Carmelite Order. He entered this order deliberately, knowing that it had a chapter in Palestine. In 1958 his superiors acceded to his request that he be allowed to live in the order's monastery in Israel. He secured an Israeli entry visa and applied to the Polish authorities for permission to leave the country. In his application for exit permission, he stated that it was based on his "belonging to the Jewish people," even though he was a monk. The Polish authorities granted him exit papers only after he waived his Polish citizenship. He received a travel document that is issued only to Jews who are emigrating to Israel and leaving Poland permanently. When Brother Daniel arrived in Israel, he applied for an immigration certificate and for registration on his identity card as a Jew. This was refused. A personal appeal to Bar-Yehudah, the minister of interior, was to no avail. Although personally sympathetic to Brother Daniel, Bar-Yehudah felt compelled to uphold the refusal as being consonant with registration directives. When Bar-Yehudah was succeeded by Shapira as minister of the interior, Brother Daniel again applied for an immigrant's visa under the Law of Return. Again his application was rejected and Brother Daniel sought redress in the courts. He brought a petition for an order nisi calling upon the minister of the interior to defend his refusal to grant him an immigrant's visa under the Law of Return.

The High Court was now faced with determining the meaning of the term "Jew" within the framework of a national context. By a four-to-one decision the High Court upheld Minister Shapira and affirmed that one who converts to Christianity, although born a Jew, is not entitled to claim the right to automatic Israeli citizenship under the Law of Return. In arriving at the majority decision, Justices Moshe Silberg, Moshe Landau, and Zvi Berinson discoursed on the meaning of the term "Jew" as did Justice Haim Cohn in his dissent.[5]

Justice Silberg began his lengthy judgment by acknowledging his "deep sympathy and great sense of obligation" to Brother Daniel for his deeds in rescuing Jews from the Nazis. But despite his feeling for Brother Daniel, he could not desecrate the concept of "Jew" in name and in meaning. He reached the conclusion that what Brother Daniel was asking was to "erase the historical and sanctified significance of the term 'Jew' and to deny all the spiritual values for which our people were killed during various periods of our long dispersion. . . . It would make our history lose its unbroken continuity and our people begin counting its days from the emancipation which followed the French Revolution." According to the prevailing opinion in Jewish law, Silberg noted, "a Jew who becomes converted to another religion or becomes an apostate continues to be regarded as a Jew for all purposes save perhaps in relation to certain 'marginal' laws." He then analyzed this principle according to halakhic authorities and came to the conclusion that the term "Jew" as used in the Law of Return is not identical in meaning with the term "Jew" as interpreted according to Jewish religious law and as it is used in the Rabbinical Courts Jurisdiction (Marriage and Divorce) Law. If "Jew" meant the same in the Law of Return as in the Marriage and Divorce law, which is interpreted according to Jewish religious law, Silberg felt, he would have been bound to honor Brother Daniel's request. But this was not so. The term "Jew" used in the Marriage and Divorce Law is to be understood in its religious sense, "whereas in the Law of Return the term 'Jew' has a secular meaning, that is, as it is usually understood by the man in the street." The Law of Return is a secular law, and, in the absence of definitions either in the statute itself or in the decided cases, its terms must be interpreted according to the ordinary man. The ordinary meaning of the term "Jew," usually understood by the ordinary Jew in the street, is that a Jew who has become a Christian is *not* called a "Jew."

Justice Silberg then began an analysis of Jews and Israeli nationalism. He pointed out that

there is one thing that is shared by *all* Jews who live in Israel (save for a mere handful) and that is that we do not sever ourselves from our historic past and we do not deny our heritage. We still drink from the waters of our past. The channels have changed but we have not sealed the wells; without our past we would be "as the poor that are

182

cast out." Only the naive could believe or think that we are creating in this country a new culture; for this it is much too late. A people which is almost as old as the human race cannot start ab ovo, and our new culture in this land—however new it may be—cannot be but a *new expression* of the culture of the past.

Whatever national attributes may be possessed by a Jew living in Israel—whether he is religious, non-religious or anti-religious—he is bound willingly or unwillingly by an umbilical chord [*sic*] to historical Judaism from which he draws his language and its idiom, whose festivals are his own to celebrate, and whose great thinkers and spiritual heroes—not the least of whom are the martyrs of 1096 who perished at the stake in Spain—nourish his national pride. Would a Jew who has become a Christian be able to feel at home in all this? What can all this national sentiment mean to him? Would he not see through different eyes, would he not regard in a different light, our draining to the dregs the bitter cup from which we drank so deeply in those dark Middle Ages? I have not the least doubt that Brother Daniel will love Israel. This he has proved. But this Brother's love will be from without—the love of a brother far away. He will not be a true part of this Jewish world.

He then rejected out of hand the contention of Brother Daniel's counsel that if the court refused to recognize Brother Daniel as a Jew, it would make Israel a theocratic state. Israel, Silberg wrote,

is not a theocratic state, because as the present case demonstrates, the life of its citizens is regulated by the law and not by religion . . . it is according to the *religious,* and not the secular, provisions of Israel Law that the petitioner would be regarded as a Jew, were such provisions to be applied to him.

Justice Cohn, in his dissent, agreed with three of Silberg's conclusions and disagreed with one. Cohn concurred with Silberg that, according to Jewish law, Brother Daniel remained a Jew, that the Law of Return ought not to be construed according to religious law, and that the Law of Return ought not to be interpreted in such a way as to conflict with the prophetic purpose of the establishment of the State of Israel. However, Cohn, despite his agreement with Silberg on these three points, could not agree that Brother Daniel should be deprived of his right to return under the Law of Return. For Justice Cohn, Brother Daniel had this right as a Jew. Cohn supported this conclusion by elaborating on his conception of historic continuity and postulating a subjective test:

And because the petitioner is a Christian, he may not be registered as having Jewish nationality, and consequently he is not "included in the Law of Return." . . . The only obstacle in his path is the fact that he professes another religion. I am willing to agree with that part of the decision of the Government that anyone declaring in good faith that he is a Jew is to be regarded as a Jew for the purposes of the Law of Return. I cannot agree, however, to the proviso to that decision which restricts the effectiveness of such a declaration to cases where the person concerned has no other religion. . . . In the absence of an objective test, contained in the Law itself, there is no alternative, in my opinion, but to assume that the Legislature intended to content itself with the subjective test, that is to say, that the right to return to Israel belongs to any person who declares that he is a Jew returning to his homeland, and that he wishes to settle there. The additional requirement of a declaration of good faith prescribed in the Government's decision is completely valid, for it was not the purpose of the legislature to grant the right of return to anyone who wishes to abuse it for purposes other than those contemplated in the Law. The further provision, however, that that right belongs only to those who profess no religion other than the Jewish faith exceeds, in my opinion, the powers of the Government, whose duty it is merely to carry out the Law. It is therefore invalid, and of no binding effect. Had it been desired to apply the Law only in the case of Jews not practicing any other but the Jewish religion or only to those who believe in the God of Israel, or had any other similar religious qualification been intended, the legislature could and should have said so in clear language. Since it did not do so, the Law must be construed and applied as it is and as it reads, without adding to or subtracting from the term "Jew" any religious qualification.

Justice Landau began his opinion by stating that he concurred with Silberg without hesitation and, without derogating from Silberg's judgment, wanted to add a few remarks. For Landau the question before the bench was "What was meant by the Legislature when it used the term 'Jew' in the Law of Return?" In order to answer this question, Landau resorted to an interpretation of Zionist thought. It was legitimate to seek guidance from the fathers of Zionism. He cited a letter from Theodor Herzl to a man by the name of De Jong who had been a Jew and had become a Christian, and as a Christian applied for membership in the Zionist Organization. Herzl had written quite simply: "Mr. De Jong being a Christian cannot become a member of the Zionist Organization. We would be grateful to him for any assistance he may give us as a non-member." Landau also cited quotes from Achad Ha-Am, mentioned phrases in the Proclamation of Independence to show that the Law of Return was enacted for the *sons* of the nation returning home. The meaning of the Law of Return cannot be severed from the sources of the past from which its content is derived, and in these sources nationalism and religion are inseparably interwoven.

A Jew who, by changing his religion, severs himself from the national past of his people ceases therefore to be a Jew in the national sense to which the Law of Return was meant to give expression. And it makes no difference whether the change was effected for opportunistic reasons or out of sincere personal conviction, as in the case of the present petitioner. He has denied his national past, and can no longer be fully integrated into the organized body of the Jewish community as such. By changing his religion he has erected a barrier between himself and his brother Jews, especially as this change has assumed so extreme a form as entering the gates of the monastery. . . .

. . . Zionism has always emphasized the national aspect of Judaism, in contrast to its antagonists who regard Judaism merely as a religious creed. Nonetheless, it is a fact that today too religious identification, even though this might be through the flimsiest participation in religious ceremonies, continues to be the principal force that links together the Jews of the Diaspora. For the Jew in the Diaspora conversion is the first step towards assimilation, and it is for this reason that the Diaspora Jew undergoes conversion. The Law of Return was enacted for the benefit of Jews who immigrate to Israel from the Diaspora and this fact emphasizes all the more strongly the basic weakness of the interpretation suggested by the petitioner for the term "Jew" in that Law.

Justice Many confined himself to a statement associating himself with the opinions of Justices Silberg and Landau.

Justice Berinson began his opinion with a history of Brother Daniel and the events leading to the case at bar. Inter alia, he said,

. . . were I at liberty to decide this question according to my own convictions, I would not have the slightest hesitation in regarding this particular petitioner as a member of the Jewish people. Ben Yehuda in his dictionary defines a "nation" as a group of people who have the same origin, who speak the same language, who have a common history and who live for the most part in the same country. There is no mention of religion being a feature common to all members of the nation whereby they are recognized and we must not assume that the author overlooked the Jewish nation when he came to give that definition. . . .

Such was the opinion of Ahad Haam, which was similar to the Jewish religious ruling which said that "A Jew who sins, remains a Jew all the same" and even though he may change his religion he does not cease to be part of the Jewish people.

But the people themselves, however, because of a well developed sense of preservation, have believed differently and have behaved differently throughout the centuries. In their opinion a Jew who has embraced another religion has withdrawn himself not only from the Jewish faith but also from the Jewish nation, and has left no further room for himself amongst the Jewish people. It is not for nothing that a Jew who has changed his religion is called in Hebrew a "meshumad" (meaning destroyed) because he was considered as a man who from the national point of view had destroyed himself and become lost to the nation, both he himself and his descendants. And the rest of his family would mourn for him by making a rent in their clothes as they would when mourning for someone who had really died. . . .

I believe that the Law of Return was enacted in this spirit and in using the word "Jew" therein the Knesset intended the term to be understood in its popular meaning.

The variety of opinions and the fact that there was a dissent attest to the centrality and controversy surrounding the issue. The strands of peoplehood, Judaism, nationalism, and the State of Israel were interwoven into the fabric of Israeli society. But distinctions, which not all agreed with, had to be made. By and large, most Israelis accepted the decision as the correct and logical one. For the man in the street, a Jew who converted and who was now practicing another religion was not entitled to return to Israel as an automatic right. Rabbinical dicta to the effect that a Jew who has sinned nonetheless remains a Jew just did not square with the average Israeli's commonsense definition of a Jew by nationality. Chief Rabbi Nissim expressed his disagreement with the court's view that in terms of most rabbinical laws Brother Daniel would have to be considered a Jew. In the Diaspora the organizational wings of Orthodox, Conservative, and Reform Judaism approved of the decision. But the American Council for Judaism, an anti-Zionist group, found fault with the court's holding. In the summer of 1963, after fulfilling naturalization requirements under the terms of the citizenship law, Brother Daniel was given Israeli citizenship. *Oswald Rufeisen* v. *The Minister of the Interior* settled only one legal aspect of the dilemma of Judaism and Israeli nationalism. Other aspects of the problem soon agitated the public and permeated the political process in the Eitani Affair.

The Eitani Affair touched on but never really came to fundamental grips with the subjective meaning of the term "Jew" as used in the Law of Return. The Eitani Affair erupted into the headlines in December 1964 and was settled finally sixteen months later. It involved Mrs. Rina Eitani, who was the daughter of a German Gentile mother and a Polish Jewish father. Her father was killed by the Nazis, and she, with her mother and sister, were confined to the Warsaw Ghetto as Jews. She survived the war and after a year in a British detention camp in Cyprus arrived in British Palestine in 1947 as a Youth Aliyah ward. She was registered as being of Jewish nationality. She served in the Israeli army and then lived in a border settlement. A rabbi married her to an Israeli Jew; she considered herself Jewish, and was bringing up her children as Jews. In 1952 she received Israeli citizenship under the law that granted citizenship to all Jews entering Israel under the Law of Return. In 1961 she applied for and received an Israeli passport that was renewed in the spring of 1964. The following fall Mrs. Eitani, then a Mapai city councillor in Upper Nazareth, was engaged in a political quarrel with her fellow councillors who belonged to the National Religious Party. Somehow in the heated atmosphere the charge was made that Mrs. Eitani was born of a non-Jewish mother and had never been converted to Judaism. Accordingly, her citizenship granted to her under the Law of Return was subject to question because it was predicated on her declaration that she was a Jewess. The Ministry of the Interior, then being run by the NRP, demanded that Mrs. Eitani return her passport—standard procedure in citizenship cases in which questions have arisen. Mrs. Eitani announced her intention to retain her passport and threatened that if the ministry did not withdraw its demand for her passport she would take the issue to the Supreme Court. In the Knesset, the opposition parties lost a motion for a debate on the status of Mrs. Eitani. The League Against Religious Coercion had another cause célèbre. With such a furore unleashed, officials in the Ministry of the Interior backed down and permitted Mrs. Eitani to retain her passport until such time as a decision unfavorable to her was made. In March 1966 the Ministry of the Interior decided that her passport was valid. The

189

decision was based on a judgment handed down by Supreme Court Justice Yitzchak Kister when he had been a Tel Aviv district court judge. In that decision, Judge Kister had invoked the doctrine of estoppel under which authorities are prevented from revoking a right granted in error to a person if that person has already made use of that right in good faith.[6]

When the Eitani affair was finally concluded, although it involved much personal heartache and contributed much acrimony to secular-religious relations, its legal impact amounted only to an aberrational footnote in the complexities of defining Israeli Jewish nationalism. It remained for the Shalit case again to bring the problem squarely to the legal and political foreground.

In the fall of 1968 in a case initiated by an Israeli naval officer, Lieutenant Commander Binyamin Shalit, the High Court of Justice was presented with another variant of the "Who is a Jew?" problem. Shalit, a Jew born in Haifa, married a Gentile woman of French-Scottish origin in Edinburgh. The couple considered themselves to be "nonbelievers." In 1964 their son Oren was born. When Commander Shalit answered the questionnaire for the Population Registry, he entered the baby as Jewish by nationality or ethnic affiliation (*le'um*) and left the space for religion blank. The registrar struck out the entry under nationality, and in the space for religion wrote, "Father Jewish, mother Gentile." When a daughter, Galia, was born in 1967, Commander Shalit did not fill in the spaces for religion or nationality. But another registrar wrote in the space for nationality, "Father Jewish, mother Gentile," and in the space for religion he wrote, "Not registered."

Shalit was dissatisfied and wrote to the minister of the interior requesting that his children be registered as Jews by nationality and of no religion. When his request was denied, he filed an order in the High Court calling upon the Ministry of the Interior to show cause why his children should not be registered as being Jewish by ethnic affiliation.

The High Court was now faced with the issue: Was Jewish nationality in its ethnic connotation identical with Jewish religious affiliation? A far-reaching principle was involved—the link between religion and nationality. For the Orthodox, religion and nationality, or "peoplehood," were indivisible. Shalit's children, being born of a non-Jewish mother, under halakhah could not be considered Jewish. For the militantly secularist Israeli, Shalit's request was reasonable and represented a principle of secularist thinking. It was possible for the child of a non-Jewish mother to embrace Jewish nationality and belong in the sense of historical, intellectual, and emotional but not religious identification. One could cast away the religious tie but in Israel still be a Jew. The court was faced with a dilemma: Should it, as a legal body, firmly address itself to the issue of "Who is a Jew?" as it relates to Israeli nationality and Judaism and, in the process, involve itself with ideological conflict? To do so, might create an irreparable gap in Israel between the secularists and the religionists and also create problems for worldwide Jewish unity. An unprecedented nine-member full bench heard Commander Shalit argue his case. Then, in a dexterous move designed to dodge the issue and avoid tangling with the principle involved, the High Court asked the attorney general to convey to the cabinet the court's recommendation that the law requiring the description of a citizen's nationality in identity cards and the Population Registry be abrogated, and that in the future only details of an individual's religion and citizenship be noted. Justice Shimon Agranat, president of the court, announced that the tribunal would defer its decision on Commander Shalit's application, pending the government's response to the court's suggestion. The government, however, felt that an entry of nationality was needed for security reasons and rejected the court's recommendation. The High Court now had to adjudicate Shalit's right to have his children registered as being of Jewish nationality.

The High Court decided in January 1970, by a split vote of five to four, that the Ministry of the Interior had to register the Shalit children as Jewish by nationality even though their mother was non-Jewish. Each of the justices found it necessary to write an opinion. Significantly, however, the case was primarily decided on the technical procedural issue of registration; the broader implications of judicially defining "Who is a Jew?" were avoided. Nevertheless, there were some interesting obiter dicta by some of the justices who tried to come to grips with the fundamental question of defining Jewish nationality.[7]

Justice Cohn held that the only question before the court was whether the minister of the interior had been entitled to instruct registration officers to refuse to register as Jewish children of mixed marriages, where the mother is not Jewish. The registration official, he stated, is neither judge nor policy maker, and his duty is to record the facts given to him by the citizen. The legislature was well aware of the circumstances of religion and personal status in Israel. The registration of these particulars did not provide even prima facie or probative evidence of their correctness as far as matters of religion and divorce are concerned. Where the legislature had not imported religious law, the courts were not entitled to apply it.

Justice Sussman declared that it was not necessary for the Court to decide "Who is a Jew?" because the only issue before the bench was whether the Ministry of the Interior was, or was not, obliged to register the Shalit children as members of the Jewish nation without any religion. For Sussman the registration clerk was duty bound to register the particulars unless he had reasonable grounds for believing them incorrect. As religion and ethnic affiliation are based on subjective feelings and generally cannot be objectively examined, they do not have to stand up to the test of objectivity. Previous Supreme Court rulings, he reasoned (particularly the Rufeisen case), and the study of various laws showed that the term "Jew" had no fixed and immutable meaning. One had to ask "Who is a Jew for purposes of such and such a law?" In any event, this registration was not binding for other purposes, such as marriage and divorce.

Justice Witkon agreed with Justices Cohn and Sussman that the case should be decided narrowly. The purpose of the Registration Law was statistical, and it was not necessary for the registration officer to enter into ideological controversy. It was the duty of the registration officer to register the particular the way it was given to him by the citizen in good faith.

Justice Many opined that the question of whether or not

the Shalit children were members of the Jewish nation was not at issue. The holding of the case could be confined to the fact that neither the Registration of Inhabitants Ordinance nor the Population Registry Law empowered the minister of the interior or the registration officer to establish criteria concerning nationality, and that in the circumstances at bar, for the reasons given by Justices Cohn and Sussman, the Shalit children had to be registered as ethnically Jewish.

Justice Berinson acknowledged his concurrence with Justice Sussman's judgment, but since the Rufeisen case had been mentioned, he wanted to clarify some points. The majority in that case had decided that secular law and not religious law should be applied to the question of whether or not Brother Daniel was a Jew. In that case, he noted, he had been of the opinion that the word "Jew" in the Law of Return referred not to the halakhic sense of Jew but to the everyday sense of the word. In the Shalit case the halakhic concept was not consistent with the reality of the present day. Mixed marriages occur in Israel. In a marriage between a Jewish woman and a non-Jewish man, the woman usually cuts her ties with her people and follows her husband. According to Jewish law the children of this marriage are Jews. On the other hand, the daughter of a Jewish father, and non-Jewish mother, even if born, reared, and educated in Israel as a Jew, would always be considered non-Jewish by religious law. Whatever the halakhah may be, the registrar of inhabitants is not a registrar for halakhic purposes, he is a registrar for the whole population. It would be a sad day if potential immigrants were discouraged by the fear that their children would not be accepted into the ranks of Jewry because of the halakhah. Should the floodgates of Russia ever be opened, thousands seeking reunion with their people would be cut off from Jewry because of their non-Jewish wives. The halakhic conception of the ethnic affiliation of an Israeli citizen cannot serve as a basis for a ruling by a secular court.

Justice Silberg said that the question before the High Court was the most important question ever to come before it. In his view the task of deciding whether ethnic affiliation and religion could be separated should be decided not by the High Court but by a representative body of world Jewry. But no such body exists, and in the circumstances the High Court had no alternative but to determine the attitude of Jewry to the problem. He did not intend to bury the issue beneath the procedural formal provisions of the laws. The question was whether a person could be a Jew ethnically without at the same time being a Jew by religion, that is, whether any other test besides that of halakhah could be applied to the national identity of a Jew. Silberg dismissed the Brother Daniel case, noting that it dealt with the extreme example of a Jew who had converted to Christianity but wanted to be considered a Jew for purposes of the Law of Return. That law, he reasoned, talks in the language of the ordinary man, which would not include a convert to Catholic monasticism and should be given preference over the halakhic rule of "once a Jew always a Jew." In the present case there was no question of interpreting the term "Jew" according to any secular law, since the Population Registry does not contain the word "Jew" but does talk of "ethnic group." The consequence of adopting Shalit's subjective definition of "Jewishness," Silberg felt, would be a catastrophe. Anyone who argues that a person can be Jewish ethnically without being Jewish by religion must inevitably be forced to the conclusion that Christians and Moslems, if they feel a close affinity with Israeli culture and values, can also demand to be registered as ethnically Jewish. The objective test of the halakhah (the Jewishness of the mother) was the easiest way of establishing the ethnic affiliation of a Jew.

Justice Landau noted that the Shalit request to the court raised the question of whether in Israel a person may be deemed a Jew by ethnic affiliation even though he is not Jewish according to halakhah. This was so laden with ideological conflict that the High Court had taken the unprecedented step of advising the government to remove the ethnic affiliation listing from the Population Registry. A solution by way of a judicial decision was an illusion. However, a temporary political solution was reached by the Knesset when it gave its implied consent to the directives issued from time to time by the minister of the interior. On two occasions when the Knesset had an opportunity to do so—in 1965 when the Population Registry Law replaced the Registration of Inhabitants Ordinance and in 1967 when amendments to the later law were introduced —the Knesset refrained from discussing this directive. The silence on the part of the Knesset must be, he reasoned, implicit approval of the directive. The registering official, in Landau's view, was correct in following the minister's directives and not registering the children according to Shalit's evaluation of ethnic affiliation.

Justice Kister, among other things in his opinion, pointed out that in 1958 the minister of the interior had issued directives for registering the children of mixed marriages. According to these directives, a child had to be registered as a Jew if both parents had so registered him. The government of the time was willing to introduce a new type of Jew, that is, a Jew who is not a Jew according to halakhah. However, the government was persuaded that this was not a wise step, and those directives were withdrawn and replaced by new directives in 1960 to which Shalit had taken exception. These new directives are not repugnant to the laws of Israel, and the minister of the interior's decision not to register the Shalit children as being ethnically Jewish should be upheld.

The president of the court, Justice Agranat, affirmed his belief that the Jewish nation and the Jewish religion have been inseparable. However, the question of whether it is possible, in modern Israel, to regard a child born of a non-Jewish mother and a Jewish father as ethnically Jewish because he does have some Jewish blood and it can be assumed in the course of time that he would become affiliated with the Jewish people among whom he is brought up, even without a formal act of conversion, was an ideological one toward which there is no common approach. He was, therefore, of the opinion that the court should not intervene in the decision of the registration officer.

The High Court's attempt to avoid deciding the issue, the fact that the majority of the justices stressed that they were deciding the case on the limited technical question, the need exhibited by each justice to go on record setting forth his reasoning, and the close vote, all indicate the depth of the ideological controversy. As soon as the decision was announced, a furore exploded. The religious sec-

tor was dismayed and condemned the verdict, while the
secularists welcomed it. Ashkenazic Chief Rabbi Unterman
and Sephardic Chief Rabbi Nissim, in unequivocal statements, deplored the ruling. Mr. Maurice A. Jaffe, president of the Union of Israel Synagogues, on the Sabbath
following the court's decision, at the Hechal Shlomo synagogue delayed the reading of the weekly Torah portion in
order to complain about the court's action before God and
the congregation. In the United States, leaders of Orthodox Judaism denounced the ruling.[8] The Orthodox viewed
the court decision as tantamount to creating a schism in
the Jewish community in Israel and the Diaspora. On the
other hand, the secularists, resentful of rabbinical power
and chafing under the restrictions imposed by religious
law on nonbelievers, viewed the decision as a victory for
personal liberty and a blow against the established rabbinate.

The decision itself and the outcry against it within their
constituency prompted the leaders of the National Religious Party to serve notice on Premier Golda Meir that
they would defect from the coalition unless legislation nullifying the effect of the High Court's ruling was enacted
speedily. The situation was reminiscent of the 1958 cabinet crisis when Bar-Yehudah issued his registration directives in contravention of halakhah. This time, however,
an attempt was made immediately to accommodate to
Orthodox demands. Premier Meir hoped to forestall a bitter national debate. In the face of some opposition in the
cabinet (Mapam, the representatives of the Independent
Liberals, and some members of the Liberal wing of Gahal),
Justice Minister Yaakov Shimshon Shapira of the Labor

Alignment attempted to work out a compromise solution that would be acceptable to the Orthodox and at the same time not totally alienate the secularists. The Shapira formula provided that the Shalit children would be registered as ordered by the court. (An attempt to overturn the specific decision as it applied to the Shalits would have been an unwarranted affront to the dignity and prestige of the High Court as an institution.) The registration of the children would be, nonetheless, in contravention of a warning issued by the Chief Rabbinical Council that any official issuing a document certifying that someone was Jewish, when in fact, according to religious law, he was not, would be bearing false witness and transgressing the Torah. The rabbinate had put NRP minister of the interior Mosheh Shapira in an untenable position: signing the Shalit documents would be defying the rabbinate, while failing to do so might subject him to action for contempt of court. In the future, however, under an amendment to the Population Registry Law, a Jew would be defined as one born of a Jewish mother, or a convert, provided the person concerned held no other religion. The criteria henceforth for defining a Jew for registration purposes basically would be the halakhah. A subjective test to determine nationality was no longer legally permissible; Jewish nationality and religion, as far as they related to registration, were inseparable. On this the rabbinate and its Orthodox allies had won.

This definition of "Jew" also would be applied to the Law of Return; but now a practical problem affecting future immigration had to be faced. If obstacles were placed in the way of the non-Jewish partner or the children of a mixed-marriage union, immigration might be discouraged, particularly from the Soviet Union and other eastern bloc countries. Accordingly, the Shapira compromise also provided for another provision to the Law of Return which would give all immediate members of an immigrant family, if either one of the parents was Jewish, all the privileges of the immigrant, including Israeli citizenship, but not recognition of Jewish nationality. And finally, a special ministerial committee was appointed to inquire into the ways of speeding the process of conversion to Judaism. This would be of special importance to the children of mixed marriages who ultimately would want to marry in Israel.

Explaining in part the reasons why she supported the Shapira formula, Mrs. Meir, whose record had been that of a hard-liner against Orthodox demands, was quoted as saying that she was "ready to make any concessions to prevent any possible sanction of inter-marriage originating in Israel." She also was reported to have observed, "We are a small state, and a very small part of the Jewish people. The very moment we shrug off the responsibility— that rests on us more than any other Jewish community— of maintaining the Jewish people, there will be no point to the State whatsoever." [9]

Public reaction to the proposals, as reflected in newspaper comments, was mixed. The influential independent newspaper *Ha-Aretz* (*The Land*) gave voice to what many felt: the proposals were an attempt to rush through legislation before public opposition could organize itself. The paper recalled a 1968 public opinion poll which found that 59 percent of those questioned favored the separation of nationality and religion and only 32 percent favored linking them. As expected, Mapam's *Al ha-Mishmar* (*The Daily Guardian*) termed the proposals "coercion" and predicted that the struggle to rescind the sanction given to religious law would continue without letup. In general, the Orthodox press welcomed the proposals, although they expressed some reservations about them. *Ha-Tzopheh* (*The Observer*), the newspaper of the National Religious Party, wanted to strengthen the amendments. The paper of the Agudat Israel party was doubtful about granting immigrant rights to those who did not wish to convert. And the paper of the Poale Agudat Israel party declared that the proper way to join the people of Israel was through appropriate conversion. The question of the nationality clause in the Population Register was also aired. Views ranged the entire gamut of options: eliminating the nationality category, retaining it in its present form, or modifying it somehow.[10]

Despite the rabbinical warning, the Shalit children were duly registered. The cabinet, sensitive to the public outcry, continued its jockeying over the Shapira proposals and softened them somewhat so that (1) halakhic definitions would apply, but the burden of proof would be on the registering official (in marriage cases, the rabbis traditionally have put the burden of proof on the applicant); (2) the privileges extended to non-Jewish spouses of Jewish immigrants under the Law of Return would extend beyond the original proposal that covered the immediate family, so that the spouses of children and grandchildren would also be covered; and (3) the wording in the definition regarding conversions was to be simply "convert."

Religious leaders wanted to insert the word *kadin* (that is, "according to law"). A *kadin* convert would be one who met the standards of conversion of the established Orthodox rabbinate.

In the Knesset the debate during the first reading of the bills incorporating the changes was stormy. Mr. Shalom Cohen of the tiny Ha-Olam ha-Zeh (This World) party, in concluding his remarks against the government-sponsored legislation, shocked the chamber when he passionately tore a page from his identity booklet. (Defacing an identity booklet is a crime punishable with up to a year in prison, but Cohen as a member of the Knesset enjoyed parliamentary immunity.) When Speaker Reuven Barkatt, the following day, submitted to the Knesset the House Committee's decision to suspend Mr. Cohen for five consecutive sessions, Uri Avnery, the other representative of Ha-Olam ha-Zeh, began shouting that the committee's decision was illegal. Avnery persisted in his shouting, and the speaker, to restore order, was forced to adjourn the meeting for five minutes. When the session resumed, Barkatt put to a vote a motion to expel Avnery for a breach of order. The motion carried, Avnery refused to leave despite appeals to do so and finally was carried out of the chamber by ushers. The Knesset then approved the suspension of Shalom Cohen, who walked out quietly.[11]

In defending the government's bill, Justice Minister Shapira pointed out that the proposal talks of "conversion" and not of "conversion according to halakhah." He made it clear that an immigrant presenting a conversion certificate of any kind from any Jewish community in the world would be registered as a Jew and would receive full immigrant's rights. He also pointed out that the amendment departed from some versions of halakhah in that it denied immigrant's rights to an apostate. (The Brother Daniel judgment, which refused to accept the generally held halakhic principle of "once a Jew, always a Jew," was now being incorporated into the law.) In an impassioned speech in support of the government legislation the prime minister, Mrs. Meir, spoke as follows:

We in the Labor Party do not deny that we made compromises, and we are not sorry. Nor are the religious parties sorry, I believe. It is slander, to say that our compromises were made in order to discriminate against others. The opponents of this amendment have no right to talk about coercion, when they accepted the situation for 10 years, down to the Supreme Court judgment in the Shalit case.

The amendment is no more than a compromise. It makes it possible to return to the situation prevailing before the Court judgment, while correcting an important lacuna affecting immigrants' rights.

We have decided on the Committee of Ministers to study conversion procedures that will be simpler and faster for the good of all of us, for the good of the immigrants as well as we who absorb them, so that no problems be created with the family.

I understand that the conversion procedure may not always be pleasant for a non-Jewish woman. But if she leaves her home, family and relatives as well as her language and faith, to come and live among Jews, where she knows her children will be brought up as Jews, with the obligations of Jews, then she has made a sacrifice to start with. But if she wants her children to have a good life here, then she must make a second sacrifice, and I do not know of any mother who is not prepared to offer one further sacrifice for the sake of her children.

I do not support this law for the sake of Government unity, or the welfare of the religious parties. Nor do I believe that if it is passed, intermarriage will cease in the Diaspora. But at least the Diaspora will know that Israel has not established a license to intermarriage.

Other debaters emphasized other facets of the pending legislation, while outside the Knesset building the secularists and the religionists massed separately to underscore their positions.[12]

Those protesting the legislation carried placards reading: "Golda and Shapira Must Not Decide Who Is a Jew," and "We're 20th-Century Jews; Not the Generation of the Exodus." Those supporting the government proposals mounted a rally that was quieter than the preceding one by the protesters. The religionists began their demonstration with the blowing of a shofar by a man wearing a prayer shawl and concluded with a prayer and the singing of "Hatikvah." Some of the signs carried by the Orthodox proclaimed: "Five Judges Can't Change the Halakhah." "Our Right to This Land Is Judaism," "We're an Ancient People; We Weren't Born in 1948," and "Jews Yes, Canaanites No."

Prior to the final passage of the bill the rabbinate, hoping to drive home to the NRP its views on the issue of conversion, issued statements to the effect that conversion to Judaism is not a formality but a process with meaning. The rabbinical court judges stated that only a conversion according to halakhah by a properly established rabbinical court admits a non-Jew to Judaism, and a person converted in any other way is not properly converted and would not be considered a Jew. The statement then rejected the charge that the religious courts put difficulties in the way of would-be converts. The Chief Rabbinical Council also issued a statement reaffirming its regret that the govern-

ment bill did not specify that only conversions according
to halakhah would be accepted.[13]

The sessions accompanying the final passage of the legislation defining a Jew were as tumultuous as the debate on
the first reading. This time, it was an Orthodox member
who precipitated a vote of expulsion. The Knesset was particularly disturbed by the actions of Rabbi Menachem
Porush of Agudat Israel. Rabbi Porush, speaking against
the pending changes, warned of the consequences that
would ensue if strict halakhic conversions were not ad-
hered to unyieldingly. It would create, he said, two classes
of Jews in Israel: Jews under the Law of Return and Jews
under the Marriage and Divorce Law. Porush castigated
the National Religious Party for assisting Reform Judaism
to take root in Israel. In a fury of rhetoric he called Reform rabbis anti-Jewish, anti-Zionist, and anti-God. And
just to round out the picture, he asserted that Conservative
and Reconstructionist Jews were no better than Reform
Jews. His rhetoric would have attracted no more than the
usual notice given to any ultra-Orthodox spokesman in
similar circumstances except, in a moment of passion,
Porush held up a Reform prayer book, spat on it, and then
threw it to the floor. Justice Minister Shapira characterized
Porush's action as "scandalous behavior" and called for
disciplining him. In a personal statement at the end of the
session, Rabbi Porush apologized and requested that his
apology terminate the incident. The Knesset, however, felt
differently and subsequently endorsed the House Committee's suggested penalty of expulsion for one session.
When the vote enacting the legislation came, the ultra-
Orthodox Agudat Israel and Poale Agudat Israel parties

voted against it, because they believed it compromised Orthodoxy. Also voting against it, but obviously for different reasons, were Mapam, the Independent Liberals, most of the Liberal wing of Gahal, State List, Free Center, Ha-Olam ha-Zeh, and both the Jewish and Arab Communist parties. But the measures were enacted on the strength of the votes of the Labor Alignment, the National Religious Party, the Herut wing of Gahal, and some Liberals affiliated with Gahal.[14]

When the law was finally passed, the religionists had achieved their basic objectives, while some concessions had been incorporated for the secularists. A Jew was defined as "a person born of a Jewish mother or having converted to Judaism, not being a person affiliated to some other religion." Prime Minister Golda Meir and Justice Minister Shapira, along with the ultra-Orthodox, seemed to agree that the intent of the legislation would include non-Orthodox conversions abroad. The NRP could not accept this premise; for them, conversion obviously had to mean conversion according to halakhah, even if it were not clearly spelled out in the legislation. The NRP leadership took a practical turn of mind, and Dr. Zerah Warhaftig of the NRP, the minister of religious affairs, suggested the possibility of creating a school for conversions and special rabbinical courts to specialize in conversion cases, thereby making the process of conversion speedier.

The final legislation was more liberal than originally proposed and attempted to mollify the secularists. Immigrants' rights were to accrue to children and grandchildren of Jews and also their spouses. The Jewish member of the family bestowing these rights need not be still alive, nor need he himself immigrate to Israel for these rights to become effective. Immigrants' rights will accrue to former Jews who left the Jewish faith involuntarily. Where differences arise in proving the "Jewishness" of a registrant, the chief registration officer, not the local registering clerk, will decide. Documents purporting to show that a registrant is not Jewish may be nullified by a declaratory court judgment.[15]

The entire legislative process—preparation by the minister of justice, discussion and approval by the cabinet, presentation, debate, committee revision, final Knesset passage, and promulgation—took only a few weeks. (The High Court decision in the Shalit case was handed down on January 23, 1970, and by March 16 the legislation had been enacted.) While the celerity of the legislation's passage was designed to inhibit prolonged public controversy and damp down the religion-state controversy, its swiftness could in no way conceal the depth of the ideological divisions within the country. The "Who is a Jew?" formula, as finally enacted, did not really resolve Israel's identity crisis as it relates to state and religion. No one really thought it would. At best, like the compromise over the constitution and other religion-state problems, it can hope to offer only a basis for a modus vivendi, not a solution. The established rabbinate with its exclusive jurisdiction in marriage and divorce has made it abundantly clear that conversions abroad will not be acknowledged by rabbinical courts unless they have been executed in accordance with the Orthodox rabbinate's standards of halakhah. Individual cases are certain to arise and produce continued controversy and agitation if not coalition crises.[16]

13
The Languishing Soul: Religion in the Body Politic

The State of Israel, the Third Jewish Commonwealth, has been confronted with the need to work out a viable religion-state accommodation. The resultant religion-state arrangements, based as they are on Jewish history and theology, will of necessity be unique and not totally congruent with religion-state patterns in other parts of the world. In the established Western nations, the religion-state relationship and derivative question of the position of religion in a free society, traditionally, have been set in the framework of Christian theology. Within this context, and ofttimes after a violent and tortuous history, the religion-state association has generally settled into one of three broad patterns: (1) a state religion (established church); (2) several religions recognized by the state; and (3) separation of the state from religion.[1]

In contrast to the variety of historical trends of Western church-state relations, the traditional relationship between religion and political authority in non-Western countries where Hinduism, Buddhism, and Islam prevailed was primarily one of extensive interdependence. Hindu, Buddhist, and Muslim rulers built and endowed places of worship and customarily were the protectors of the faith. But with the profound social changes that followed World War II, old ways were displaced. Despite the fact that the young polities of Asia have encountered a multitude of problems having little prototype in the West, the religion-state positions that are now appearing may be seen to

A bar mitzvah celebration of eighteen 13-year-olds from a primary school in Nahariya, held in the ruins of the first-century synagogue at Masada.

parallel some of the patterns already established in the West.

In contemporary India, religion, perhaps the strongest single factor in the growth of Indian civilization, has been made legally subordinate to the secular state. Constitutionally, religious pluralism prevails because there is neither a state religion nor official recognition of the religion of the majority. But emerging secularism might be a more accurate description of the extraordinarily complex Indian state-religion mosaic. The strong influence of ancient Hindu values (religious toleration, absence of ecclesiastical organization, traditional differentiation of political and religious functions among different castes, and a historical theory that is not antagonistic to secular political authority), the legacy of communalism, and the leadership of the religious Gandhi and the agnostic Nehru have all contributed to this complexity.[2]

In contrast, India's neighbors, Buddhist-oriented Burma and Islamic Pakistan, although they shared with her a heritage of British colonial rule, embarked, after their independence, on different paths of state-religion legislation. In Burma, before the establishment of Buddhism, there was no official state religion, but neither was there separation of religion and state. Buddhism enjoyed a special position as the faith professed by the great majority of Burmese. In August 1961, Buddhism was established as the state religion; but an army coup in March 1962 terminated the life of the Burmese Buddhist state. A more secular orientation of the government process now prevails, and religious issues and problems remain in flux.[3]

211

Similarly in flux, but operating against a significantly different religious background, is Pakistan, where conflicting theories of the nature of an Islamic state have preoccupied the political process since independence. Unlike Hinduism and Buddhism, Islam, despite occasional Koranic dicta to the contrary, is theologically and historically (the sword or the Koran) an intolerant religion and has traditionally fused temporal and spiritual authority (Muhammad and the Caliphate). The last constitution of Pakistan, now abrogated, required that no law be repugnant to Islam and provided for an advisory council of Islamic ideology to inform the executive and the legislature if new laws were consonant with traditional Islamic principles. Muslim law is comprehensive and regulates "within its powerful and precise sweep everything from prayer rites to property rights." Despite its totality, Islamic law (*shari'ah*) in modern practice is enforced only in religious courts with jurisdiction over religious and personal law, while secular courts adjudicate disputes arising out of statute law. However, the process of secular circumscription of personal law has begun. The status of Islam, then, and its relationship to developing Pakistani federalism remain fluid. In Bangladesh, formerly East Pakistan, secularism has been adopted as one of the new nation's ideological tenets.[4]

In the Middle East the new polity of Israel is in the process of working out a modus operandi with the ancient religion of Judaism. Israel is a secular state characterized by a plurality of attitudes toward Judaism and its national mission. At the extremes are the minority views espoused by the Canaanites and the Natore Karta. The Canaanites hold that Israel is a new nation, created in the Land of the Canaanite, rooted only in the ancient traditions of the land and its soil. For the Canaanite, the sole connection with the Jews in the Diaspora is the tenuous one of a common origin. "One who comes from the Jewish dispersion, is a Jew and not a Hebrew. . . . A Jew and a Hebrew can never be identical." Only Hebrews are legitimate heirs to the historic destiny of the land. Diaspora Jewry had been deprived of a history and were merely incidentals of other people's histories. Zionism, a Dispersion movement, is foreign to the true Hebrew. "The whole of Jewry, with all its values and with all the products of its historical inheritance, is alien to the generation of the sons of the land." [5] The Canaanites are the quintessential secularists; contrarily, the Natore Karta are the quintessential religionists.

Like the Canaanite, the member of the Natore Karta sect will ascribe no Jewish significance to the State of Israel. Ultra-Orthodox and extremist, he believes Jewish education is properly limited to the study of the Bible, Talmud, and commentaries. Hebrew, the holy tongue, cannot be used in everyday life, only for prayer and study. The establishment of the State of Israel is the evil result of Zionist ideology and politics and is a denial of the divinely ordained order. In the days preceding the establishment of Israel the Natore Karta organized demonstrations, prayers, and fasts and sent a memorandum to the United Nations protesting the creation of a Jewish state. They believe that a Jewish state can be established only by the Messiah. The modern state of Israel is not a messianic state; it is a secular society that does not keep the commandments or recognize the totality of halakhah. Refusal to accept halakhah in every facet of life is a denial of the existence of God. Although the Natore Karta are irreconcilably opposed to the state, the government has tacitly permitted them to go their own way, free of the obligations of defense service and school attendance.

Between the extremes of the anti-Jewish secularists and the antistate religionists are a number of other positions, including that held by the significant group of Orthodox and ultra-Orthodox Jews (organized in the National Religious Party and the two Agudah parties), who consider the State of Israel to be an instrument of Divine Providence. For these believers Israel primarily has religious significance. The state is a legitimate outgrowth of the Jewish destiny: the people of Israel and the religion of Israel are one. Despite present deficiencies, a total halakhic system will ultimately prevail. In the meantime, theopolitics is the earthly device that will help to bring about redemption in the holy land of Zion.

There is also another category of Israeli Jews, organized in a handful of Conservative and Progressive congregations and the small "Seekers of the Way" group (which shares some common ideas with the Reconstructionist philosophy), who do not accept Orthodoxy and the entire halakhic system but nonetheless view Israel as having a religious significance. For these non-Orthodox, the State of Israel is an organic part of Jewish history in which religious norms must continue to evolve. Their emphasis on evolving Jewish norms and their rejection of the totality of halakhah and traditional Orthodox ritual has caused these non-Orthodox to clash with the Orthodox and ultra-Orthodox.

And finally, there are those Israelis who approach Judaism as a national culture. They relate to the biblical past and the Diaspora experience, but for them the values of Judaism are expressed primarily in a national secular culture that recognizes the role of traditional Judaism but believes that traditional attitudes must accommodate themselves to the new national status of Judaism.

At times, secularist and religionist find common ideological ground; but these shared attitudes are not sufficiently large to resolve the religion-state debate. Here the differences are too great. The result is the functioning of a democratic political system characterized by theopolitics. Theopolitics, buttressed by its strong but sometime ally, nationalism, has succeeded in grafting onto the secular body politic, by a series of piecemeal steps (Days of Rest Ordinance, Kosher Food for Soldiers Ordinance, Religious Services Budget Law and Amendment, Hours of Work and Rest Law, Marriage and Divorce Law, Pork Prohibition Law, the National Service Law, the Dayyanim Law, Religious Courts Law, and Who Is a Jew Amendment), some Orthodox norms.

For the great majority of Israelis the Knesset enactment of these laws did not involve a primary question of belief. The average Jewish Israeli was, and is, willing to tolerate a number of Orthodox theopolitical demands. This is so because so many secularly oriented Israelis remain sympathetic to Orthodox Judaism: Judaism embodies a moral and humanistic value system that they respect and are

215

proud of; through the millennia of persecution in the Diaspora the Jewish people drew strength from their religion; and the roots of contemporary Israel reach back through a religious heritage to biblical times. These three premises are deeply ingrained in the average Jewish Israeli and explain, in part, why theopolitics has achieved some of its successes. But Knesset enactments cannot bring about the private observance of dietary rules and religious rituals, ensure the sanctity of the Sabbath, or compel one to live his life according to the ethical code of Judaism. There is, moreover, a limit to the leverage of theopolitics. The general population simply will not accept any situation that borders on theocentrism.

There have, on the other hand, been a number of significant secular incursions into religious areas. The established Orthodox rabbinate, as a state-supported institution, is subject in certain areas to the jurisdiction of the secular courts. And the rabbinate's courts, even though they have been given exclusive jurisdiction (via a secular process) in matters of marriage and divorce, are subject to the incursions of certain inhibitory secular legislation (Women's Equal Rights Law, Marriage Age Law, and so forth). Their original jurisdiction is only that given to them by the Knesset, and their penal decisions are dependent on secular authorities for enforcement.

Paradoxically now in Israel, under what should be the most benign of conditions, theopolitics, by eliminating the aspect of voluntary acceptance of the yoke of religion, has created a crisis for Judaism. The monopolistic establishment of the Orthodox rabbinate has had a deleterious effect on Judaism. Its very establishment is a secular political act. The rabbinate, maintained and supported out of the public treasury, has become a dependent outgrowth of the state. In order to protect its position and preferments, the rabbinate must concern itself with temporal matters. Budgets and buildings have assumed priority over teaching and spirituality. The Ministry of Religious Affairs, that part of the bureaucracy which works most closely with the rabbinate, is a political ministry no different in its basis of authority from any other secular ministry. The Ministry of Religious Affairs, in this sense, is akin to the Ministry of Police or Social Welfare. This interdependence with a political branch of the government acts in derogation of the rabbinate's spiritual standing. It is no wonder that the critics of the rabbinate refer to the seat of the Chief Rabbinate in Jerusalem (Hechal Shlomo) as the "Datican"—a pun on the Hebrew *dati,* meaning religious. The rabbinate, which should be concerned with the sacred, is in fact concerned with its secular institutional underpinnings. This unhealthy situation has been compounded by the character and attitudes of the rabbinate itself.

The established religionists have concerned themselves primarily with issues of orthopraxy and religious behavioralism which have been characterized pejoratively as "conspicuous" religion. "Conspicuous" religion touches on form and not inner substance. One does not protect the values of Judaism by having the state pass coercive laws that have loopholes and can be circumvented with slight effort. Piety, like morality, cannot be legislated. The rabbinate's attempts to ensure conformity by threats to withhold certificates of dietary fitness (as exemplified by the *Shalom* kosher kitchen dispute and the Marbek abbatoir incident) are examples of rabbinical power being used in a temporal manner: in the *Shalom* instance, to enforce ritual observance, and in the Marbek case, to maintain institutionalized economic prerogatives. These exercises in rabbinical authority are perversions of religious values. They are no less misguided than the motives of the unsophisticated religionist who, in order to prevent the desecration of the Sabbath, throws a rock at the passing motorist.

To a large extent the rabbinate's almost exclusive interest in religious behavioralism and cultic forms, rather than Judaic humanistic values, is a direct result of traditional Orthodoxy's inability to come to grips with the realities of existence in a modern Jewish state. It has been shown that at present halakhah cannot sustain a legal system satisfactory to a corporate-technological system. Some things as fundamental as the state's functioning and providing needed public services on the Sabbath have never been resolved according to halakhic norms. Rabbinical committees, during the Mandate and after the creation of the state, have wrestled occasionally with the halakhic problems of the state services on the Sabbath. And while various rationales have been advanced, there are conflicting interpretations, and the overall question has never been disposed of systematically and satisfactorily.[6] But halakhah need not be static. The obstacles to its modernization are not in the halakhah but in the established rabbinate's intransigent attitudes.

Politicization, the stress on behaviorism, and the inability of the rabbinate to react promptly and positively to the realities of a modern Jewish commonwealth have created a double crisis: a crisis of authority between the established rabbinate and the state, and a crisis of religious values among the Orthodox themselves, the average Israeli Jew, and Conservative and Reform Jews throughout the Diaspora. The institutionalized rabbinate has become detached from the larger Jewish community. Its concern with "conspicuous" religion has caused it to become intellectually fossilized and spiritually sterile.

Since the establishment of the Jewish state and the subsequent institutionalization of the Orthodox rabbinate, the rabbinate has been silent on significant moral and humanistic issues. And when the rabbinate has spoken and acted, more often than not, its pronouncements have created ill will and detracted from the respect and support that it should be worthy of. Accordingly, there are a growing number of Jews in Israel and the Diaspora, many of them observant, who are becoming increasingly disillusioned with the Orthodox rabbinate. They are worried about the rabbinate's politicization, with its concomitant possibility of secular encroachment; and they are equally worried about the rabbinate's stress on rigid habit and ritualistic convention at the expense of spiritual understanding and creativity. Moreover, the rabbinate's unwillingness to recognize that the Conservative and Reform branches of Judaism have a stake in Israel as a Judaic spiritual center has created still another set of strains within the overall Jewish community. Reform and Conservative Jews share with Orthodox Jews the emotion-charged symbol of Israel as a Jewish national home. Sustained Jewish aid from the Diaspora and Diaspora Jewry's involvement in and reaction to the Six-Day War attest mightily to this.

The established rabbinate must allow Reform and Conservative Judaism an opportunity to relate to Israel and cultivate ties there. But Reform and Conservative Jews cannot hope to influence and depoliticize the Israeli rabbinate. Only the Orthodox can do that. Happily, there seem to be some hopeful glimmers in the direction of change. The rabbinate is no longer being criticized solely by the secularists. More and more of the Orthodox are questioning some of the cherished premises of theopolitics and the tactics of the rabbinate. They are beginning to see that faith and personal commitment cannot be legislated. Out of this Orthodox disillusionment, initially sparked by isolated alarm and protest, additional voices urging reform are being heard. One group, led by the distinguished Orthodox scholar, Professor Efrayim E. Urbach, has assumed the beginnings of organizational form, calling itself the Movement for Torah Judaism.[7]

The Movement for Torah Judaism is dedicated to the depoliticization of the institutions of the rabbinate. It eschews theopolitics and stresses teaching as the proper way to inculcate Jewish values. It has called for a restructuring of Jewish religious life in Israel on a voluntaristic basis. Organized religious life would be the responsibility of kehillot organized on the basis of free association. Under this proposal, once again private faith would be free of the restrictions of public policy, and Orthodoxy, by not exerting a claim upon the secular authority, would no longer need nonreligious sanction for essentially religious activities. But to achieve a voluntaristic religious life, the reformers will have to alter the established institutions of the religious parties and the rabbinate—a task that will meet with resistance.

The prospects are not good that in the near future the rabbinate will relinquish its institutionalized position. Equally dim is the possibility that the Orthodox and the ultra-Orthodox will abandon the practice of theopolitics. Furthermore, the continuation of the educational trend system will ensure a constant flow into the electorate of religious-school graduates, likely to support the religious parties. Future religion-state issues will continue to be resolved (as were, for example, the conflict over the written constitution and the Who is a Jew Amendment) on an ad hoc basis of political compromise. In the legal system, tension will continue between rabbinic and secular authorities, and it is likely that the secular side will prevail. Moreover, some issues that appear to have been settled do not, in reality, lend themselves to facile solutions, and thus such questions as that of the relationship between Judaism and Israeli nationalism, or of civil marriage and divorce, and of conversion to Judaism are certain to inflame either secularists or religionists, leaving both dissatisfied. But the political system will remain viable, and a Kulturkampf will be postponed, no small achievement.

Throughout the centuries, religious Jews hoped for "Next year in Jerusalem." It is an irony of history that with the establishment of the Third Jewish Commonwealth and the incorporation of Jewish institutions into the Israeli body politic the spirit of Judaism is languishing.

Appendix
Results of Knesset Elections 1949–1969*

Knesset	First	Second	Third
Date	January 25, 1949	July 30, 1951	July 26, 1955
Electorate	506,567	924,885	1,057,795
Actual Votes Cast	440,095	695,007	876,085
Valid Votes Cast	434,684	687,492	853,219

Party, Percentage, Seats

Secular Parties			
Communists 3.5% 4	Communists 4.0% 5	Communists 4.5% 6	
Mapam 14.7% 19	Mapam 12.5% 15	Mapam 7.3% 9	
		Achdut ha-Avodah 8.2% 10	
Mapai 35.7% 46	Mapai 37.3% 45	Mapai 32.2% 40	
Progressives 4.1% 5	Progressives 3.2% 4	Progressives 4.4% 5	
General Zionists 5.2% 7	General Zionists 18.9% 23	General Zionists 10.2% 13	
Herut 11.5% 14	Herut 6.6% 8	Herut 12.6% 15	

Religious Parties	United Religious Front 12.2% 16 Mizrachi Ha-Poel ha-Mizrachi Agudat Israel Poale Agudat Israel	Mizrachi — National Religious Party 1.2% 2 9.1% 11 Ha-Poel ha-Mizrachi 2 Agudat Israel — Torah Religious Front 6.7% 2 4.7% 6 2.0% 3 Poale Agudat Israel 1.6% 2	
Other Lists	Arab Parties (Mapai Affiliated) 3.0% 2 Sephardim 4 Yemenite 1 WIZO (Women's International Zionist Organization) 1 Fighters 1 6.9% Not Placing 3.7% 0	Arab Parties (Mapai Affiliated) 4.7% 5 Not Placing 0.7% 0	Arab Parties (Mapai Affiliated) 4.9% 5 Not Placing 1.9% 0

* Based on Misha Louvish, ed. *Facts About Israel: 1968* (Jerusalem: Information Division, Ministry for Foreign Affairs, 1968), p. 77; *Statistical Abstract of Israel, 1967*, No. 18 (Israel: Central Bureau of Statistics, The Government Press, 1967), pp. 574–576; and Central Election Committee Tally, *Jerusalem Post*, November 10, 1969, p. 3.

223

Results of Knesset Elections 1949–1969

Fourth	Fifth	Sixth	Seventh
November 3, 1959	August 15, 1961	November 2, 1965	October 28, 1969
1,218,483	1,274,280	1,449,709	1,748,710
994,306	1,037,030	1,244,706	1,427,981
964,337	1,006,964	1,206,728	1,367,743
Communists 2.8% 3	Communists 4.1% 5	New Communists (Arab) 2.3% 3	New Communists (Arab) 2.8% 3
		Israel Communists (Jewish) 1.1% 1	Israel Communists (Jewish) 1.1% 1
			Alignment—Israel Labor Party 46.2% 56
Mapam 7.2% 9	Mapam 7.6% 9	Mapam 6.6% 8	Mapam
Achdut ha-Avodah 6.0% 7	Achdut ha-Avodah 6.5% 8	Alignment 36.7% 45	Achdut ha-Avodah
Mapai 38.2% 47	Mapai 34.7% 42	Achdut ha-Avodah	Mapai
		Mapai	Rafi
		Rafi 7.9% 10	State List (Ben-Gurion) 3.1% 4

224

Progressives
4.6% 6

General Zionists
6.1% 8

Herut
13.6% 17

National Religious Party
9.9% 12

Torah Religious Front
4.7% 6

Arab Parties
(Mapai Affiliated)
3.5% 5

Not Placing
3.4% 0

Liberals
13.6% 17

Herut
13.7% 17

National Religious Party
9.8% 12

Agudat Israel
3.7% 4

Poale Agudat Israel
1.9% 2

Arab Parties
(Mapai Affiliated)
3.5% 4

Not Placing
0.7% 0

Independent Liberals
3.8% 5

Gahal
21.3% 26

General Zionists

Herut

National Religious Party
8.9% 11

Agudat Israel
3.3% 4

Poale Agudat Israel
1.8% 2

Arab Parties
(Mapai Affiliated)
3.8% 4

Ha-Olam ha-Zeh
1.2% 1

Not Placing
1.7% 0

Independent Liberals
3.2% 4

Gahal
21.6% 26

General Zionists

Herut

Free Center
1.2% 2

National Religious Party
9.7% 12

Agudat Israel
3.2% 4

Poale Agudat Israel
1.8% 2

Arab Parties
(Mapai Affiliated)
3.5% 4

Ha-Olam ha-Zeh
1.2% 2

Not Placing
1.4% 0

Notes

2 The Restoration of Zion

1. For an excellent selection of basic readings and a provocative analysis of the diverse intellectual currents that contributed to the Zionist movement, see Arthur Hertzberg, *The Zionist Idea: A Historical Analysis and Reader* (New York: Doubleday and Company, Inc., and Herzl Press, 1959), passim. The quote from Kalischer is on pp. 109–110.

2. Ibid., p. 19. Ben Halpern, *The Idea of the Jewish State* (Cambridge: Harvard University Press, 1961), p. 61.

3. The phrase "to bigotry no sanction, to persecution no assistance," made famous by President George Washington in his 1790 classic document to the Hebrew Congregation of Newport, Rhode Island, was taken initially from the Congregation's letter to him, expressing their gratitude for America's blessings of liberty:

Deprived as we heretofore have been of the invaluable rights of free citizens, we now, with a deep sense of gratitude to the Almighty Disposer of all events, behold a government erected by the majesty of the people—a government which to bigotry gives no sanction, to persecution no assistance—but generously affording to all liberty of conscience and immunities of citizenship;—deeming everyone, of whatever nation tongue or language, equal parts of the great governmental machine.

Quoted in Edmond Cahn, "How Democracy Unites Us," *Congress Bi-Weekly*, Vol. 31, No. 14 (November 9, 1964), p. 37.

4. D. R. Elston, *Israel: The Making of a Nation* (London: Oxford University Press, 1963), p. 11. Professor Sachar chronicles an interesting vignette in the history of the Jewish Emancipation in Great Britain. Lord Lionel Rothschild, a Whig, beginning in 1847 was elected, and thereafter occasionally reelected, as the city of London's member of Parliament. But the House of Commons refused to seat Rothschild because he refused to take the oath "on the true faith of a Christian." After each election Rothschild "engaged in an embarrassing little pantomime: he approached his seat in Commons, paused, sighed audibly, and walked out. . . . An Act was passed in 1858 that allowed each house of Parliament to establish its own rules of oath-taking; and Lionel Rothschild was seated in Commons that year." But it was not until 1871 that Parliament authorized Oxford and Cambridge to award degrees to Jews and Nonconformists. Howard Morley Sachar, *The Course of Modern Jewish History* (New York: Dell Publishing Company, 1963), pp. 114–115.

5. Sachar, *The Course of Modern Jewish History*, pp. 86, 182, 244.

6. Shtetl life came to a tragic and abrupt end with World War II. For a superb anthropological study of the culture, see Mark Zborowski and Elizabeth Herzog, *Life Is With People: The Culture of the Shtetl* (New York: Schocken Books, 1962); Lucy S. Dawidowicz, *The Golden Tradition: Jewish Life and Thought in Eastern Europe* (New York: Holt, Rinehart & Winston, 1967).

7. The Jewish nationalism movement of this period produced many leaders and almost as many philosophical variants. Peretz Smolenskin emphasized cultural nationalism. Eliezer Perelmann, better known by his Hebrew name, Eliezer Ben-Yehudah, struggled to revive Hebrew in a modern secular form (his differences with the Orthodox residents of Jerusalem presaged the current religious-secular clash). Moses Leib Lilienblum advocated Jewish colonization of Palestine. Asher Ginzberg, who wrote under the pen name Achad Ha-Am, espoused cultural and spiritual revival. Chaim Nachman Bialik developed elements of the old and the new in his writings. Micah Joseph Berdichevsky tried to construct a compromise between traditional rabbinic values and the secular learning of Haskalah. Joseph H. Brenner wrote proletarian-oriented social criticism. Jacob Klatzken ultimately became a political Zionist, while Nachman Syrkin, Ber Borochov, Aharon David Gordon, and Berl Katzenelson urged variants of ethical and socialist Zionism. Religious Zionism had its advocates in Samuel Mohilever, Yehiel M. Pines, Rabbi Avraham Issac Kook, and Rabbi Meir Bar-Ilan. Jewish nationalism also gave rise to such diverse and controversial activists as Valdimir Jabotinsky, Chaim Weizmann, and David (Green) Ben-Gurion.

8. Hertzberg, *The Zionist Idea*, p. 181.

9. The name BILU is derived from the Hebrew initials of the Biblical verse, "House of Jacob, come ye, and let us walk." (Isaiah, 2:5, Bet Yaakov, lekhu ve-nelkhah.) BILU was organized by young Russian Jews in the early 1880s to establish agricultural settlements in Palestine.

10. Berl Katzenelson, himself a leading member of the Second Aliyah, has expressed the ethos of aliyah:

There are many meanings to the word *"Aliyah."* "Aliyah" means climbing the rungs of a ladder, and it also means going to Palestine. Going to any other land we call "Immigration," but returning to Zion, and to Zion alone, is *"Aliyah."* "Aliyah" is a rise from the depths of the *Galuth* to the homeland to the land of liberty. We use *Aliyah* in both the material and the spiritual sense. There is an

Aliyah of will and of hope. There is an *Aliyah* of the class and of the nation, and there is also an Aliyah of the individual. We have always looked upon ourselves as *Halutzim,* the pioneers of the people. Behind us, thousands await redemption. They shall come, and, together with us, shall build this land.

Berl Katzenelson, quoted in A. Revusky, *The Histradrut: A Labor Commonwealth in the Making* (New York: New York League for Labor Palestine, 1938), pp. 27–28.

11. For a brief but interesting chronicle of some of the personalities who immigrated to Israel before the First Aliyah, see David Ben-Gurion, "First Ones," in *Israel Government Yearbook 5723 1962/63,* ed. Reuben Alcalay (Israel: The Government Printer, 1963), pp. 7–72. An accurate and handy compilation of immigration statistics may be found in *Statistical Abstract of Israel, 1965, No. 16* (Central Bureau of Statistics, State of Israel, Jerusalem: Jerusalem Academic Press Ltd., 1965), p. 95.

12. Richard Gottheil, "Zionism," *The Jewish Encyclopedia,* ed. Isidor Singer (New York: Funk and Wagnalls Company, Vol. 12, 1905), p. 673.

13. Robert G. Weisbord, *African Zion: The Attempt to Establish A Jewish Colony in the East Africa Protectorate, 1903–1905* (Philadelphia: The Jewish Publication Society of America, 1968), p. 9.

14. Nadav Safran, *The United States and Israel* (Cambridge: Harvard University Press, 1963), p. 67.

15. Gordon and Katzenelson died before the creation of the State of Israel and, unlike Ben-Zvi and Ben-Gurion, are but little known outside Israel. Aharon David Gordon (1856–1922), the most influential Israeli exponent of the "religion of labor," believed that redemption was possible only through physical labor. Berl Katzenelson (1887–1944), a leading spokesman and organizer in the socialist-labor-Zionist movement, founded the Histadrut, the Tel Aviv newspaper *Davar,* and fostered the development of Palestinian labor culture. Lester G. Seligman, *Leadership in a New Nation: Political Development in Israel* (New York: Atherton Press, A Division of Prentice-Hall, Inc., 1964), p. 31.

16. Leonard Stein, *The Balfour Declaration* (New York: Simon and Schuster, 1961), passim; Chaim Weizmann, *Trial and Error: The Autobiography of Chaim Weizmann* (New York: Harper & Brothers, 1949), pp. 176–211; League of Nations Association Research Committee, *The Palestine Mandate* (Geneva: League of Nations Association, 1930), pp. 6–8.

17. League of Nations, *The Palestine Mandate,* pp. 8–9.

18. Bernard Joseph, *British Rule in Palestine* (Washington: Public Affairs Press, 1948), p. 124.

19. Irving Miller, *Israel: The Eternal Ideal* (New York: Farrar, Straus and Cudahy, 1955), p. 33.

20. Albert M. Hyamson, *Palestine Under the Mandate: 1920–1948* (London: Methuen and Company, Ltd., 1950), p. 123. For an interesting personal account of the Mandate, see Norman and Helen Bentwich, *Mandate Memories: 1918–1948* (New York: Schocken Books, 1965).

21. While all the members of the Shaw Commission signed the report, Mr. Snell, the Labour M.P., added a special note in which he took exception to the Commission's recommendations on the crucial matters of immigration and the constitutional grievances of the Arabs. League of Nations, *The Palestine Mandate,* p. 16; Harry Sacher, *Israel: The Establishment of a State* (London: George Weidenfeld and Nicholson, 1952), pp. 11–12; Elston, *Israel,* p. 26.

22. Oscar I. Janowsky, *Foundations of Israel: Emergence of a Welfare State* (Princeton: D. Van Nostrand Company, Inc., 1959), pp. 145–147.

23. Harry Sacher, *Israel,* p. 13; Halpern, *The Idea of the Jewish State,* p. 138.

24. Harry Sacher, *Israel,* pp. 12–17.

25. Churchill is quoted in Arthur Koestler, *Promise and Fulfillment: Palestine 1917–1949* (New York: The Macmillan Company, 1949), p. 46. In February 1940 the Land Transfer Regulations were published and effectively curtailed any possibility of the Jews purchasing land in viable amounts. Harry Sacher, *Israel,* p. 16.

26. Elston, *Israel,* p. 31.

27. Koestler, *Promise and Fulfillment,* p. 41.

28. Ibid., p. 58. Koestler quoting from Statements and Memoranda, presented by the Jewish Agency to the Anglo-American Committee of Inquiry, Jerusalem, 1947. One of these floating coffins, the *Struma,* in its heyday a nondescript Danube cattle boat, captured world attention when it sank 8 kilometers off the coast of Turkey on February 24, 1942. Of the 777 persons on board, only 1 survived.

29. J. C. Hurewitz, *The Struggle for Palestine* (New York: W. W.

Norton and Company, Inc., 1950), p. 208. Halpern, *The Idea of the Jewish State,* p. 358; Sachar, *The Course of Modern Jewish History,* pp. 464–465.

3   The Institutions of Theopolitics

1. M. Z. Frank, "God of Abraham in the State of Israel," *Middle East Journal,* Vol. 5, No. 4 (Autumn 1951), 407.

2. For a brilliant analysis of the Kehilla, see Jacob Katz, *Tradition and Crisis: Jewish Society at the End of the Middle Ages* (New York: The Free Press of Glencoe, Inc., 1961), passim.

3. Moshe M. Czudnowski and Jacob M. Landau, *The Israeli Communist Party and the Elections for the Fifth Knesset, 1961* (Stanford: The Hoover Institution on War, Revolution, and Peace, Stanford University, 1965), pp. 4–8. For discussions of the Israeli Communist party split, see Maurice Friedberg, "The Split in Israel's Communist Party," *Midstream,* Vol. 12, No. 2 (February 1966), 19–28, and Kevin Devlin, "Communism in Israel: Anatomy of a Split," *Survey,* No. 62 (January 1967), 141–151. Also outside the mainstream of Israeli political life are the Arab lists. For a comprehensive discussion of the Arabs in the Communist party and the Israeli political process, see Jacob M. Landau, *The Arabs in Israel: A Political Study* (London: Oxford University Press, 1969), passim. See Appendix, "Results of Knesset Elections 1949–1969."

4. Shlomo Katz, "Mapam—A Case of Political Neurosis," *Jewish Frontier,* Vol. 17, No. 10 (October 1950), 16–19; L. Berger, ed., *The Israel Yearbook: 1971* (Israel: Israel Yearbook Publications Ltd., 1971), p. 338.

5. For a fuller text of Mapai's first platform, see "Mapai," *The Standard Jewish Encyclopedia,* ed. Cecil Roth (New York: Doubleday and Company, Inc., 1966), p. 1266.

6. L. Berger, ed., *The Israel Yearbook: 1965* (Israel: Israel Yearbook Publications Ltd., 1965), p. 351.

7. For a more detailed description of the development of Herut, see Scott D. Johnston, "Politics of the Right in Israel: The Herut Movement," *Social Science,* Vol. 40, No. 2 April 1965), 104–114.

8. See Don Peretz, "Reflections on Israel's Fourth Parliamentary Elections." *Middle East Journal,* Vol. 14, No. 1 (November 1959), 15–27; Eliahu Salpeter, "Israel Knesset Elections," *Middle Eastern Affairs,* Vol. 12, No. 9 (November 1961), 262–268; Scott D. Johnston,

"The Multi-Party System of Israel; Some Aspects of Party Politics in the Parliament (Knesset)," *Studies on Asia,* Vol. 3 (1962), 59–75; Norman L. Zucker, "Israel's Multipartyism," *Jewish Spectator,* Vol. 27, No. 3 (March 1962), 18–22; Norman L. Zucker, "Israel's Politics: Retrospect and Prospect," *Jewish Frontier,* Vol. 29, No. 4 (May 1962), 12–16; Shlomo Avineri, "Israel in the Post-Ben-Gurion Era," *Midstream,* Vol. 11, No. 6 (June 1965), 20. Achdut ha-Avodah was originally one of the constituent factions of Mapai. It broke from Mapai to join in the formation of Mapam in January 1948.

9. See Jon Kimche, "Succession and the Legacy in Israel," *Journal of International Affairs,* Vol. 18, No. 1 (January 1964), 43–53; E. A. Bayne, "Israel's Government by the People: The Background of the Israeli Elections of 1965" (New York: American Universities Field Staff Report, 1966), pp. 1–14; Scott D. Johnston, "A Comparative Study of Intra-Party Factionalism in Israel and Japan," *Western Political Quarterly,* Vol. 20, No. 2, Part I (June 1967), 288–307; Eliezer Livneh, "The Elections in Israel," *Midstream,* Vol. 12, No. 1 (January 1966), 48–55; Jon Kimche, "A Mandate for Change," ibid., 51–61.

10. Joseph Dunner, *The Republic of Israel: Its History and Its Promise* (New York: McGraw-Hill Book Company, Inc., 1950), p. 131.

11. L. Berger, ed., *The Israel Yearbook: 1963* (Israel: Israel Yearbook Publications Ltd., 1963), p. 306.

12. Reuben Alcalay, ed., *Israel Government Yearbook: 5723 (1962/ 63)* (Israel: The Government Printer, 1963), p. 380.

13. See Appendix for the results of the 1949–1969 Knesset elections and the flow of party faction and fusion. There are a number of good recent books on Israeli politics. The following are particularly useful: Alan Arian, *Ideological Change in Israel* (Cleveland: The Press of Case Western Reserve University, 1968); Ervin Birnbaum, *The Politics of Compromise: State and Religion in Israel* (Cranbury, New Jersey: Fairleigh Dickinson University Press, 1970); Leonard J. Fein, *Politics in Israel* (Boston: Little, Brown and Company, 1967).

14. Terence Prittie, *Israel: Miracle in the Desert* (New York: Frederick A. Praeger, Inc., 1967), p. 113. It is now more than two decades since the establishment of the state, and the Natore Karta leaders have not softened their hostility to political Zionism. While the Natore Karta membership in Israel includes only a few hundred families, the movement also has adherents outside Israel. The United States branch of the Natore Karta is fond of placing statements in

ZIONISM:
BETRAYAL OF THE JEWISH PEOPLE

(Third in a series)

Zionism has succeeded in confusing Jews and non-Jews alike, and there is an urgent need for clarification.

In the last two generations, the image of the Jewish people in the eyes of the world has changed completely, and a picture has been presented that is entirely alien to the true concept of the people that has proudly borne the name of Israel through the centuries and millennia.

Since its very inception Zionism has deliberately aimed at breaking the eternal bond between G-d and the people of Israel, substituting for the lofty Jewish deals a belated narrow nationalism and chauvinism. On this basis of secular nationalism, there have inevitably followed political and military conflicts with other countries and nationalities.

Actually, the life and the very existence of the Jewish people is based solely on one fundamental idea: the observance of the commandments as specified in the Torah.

At the birth of Zionism, great rabbis strongly condemned it as a TOTAL FALSIFICATION, AS TREASON AND TOTAL DISOBEDIENCE to the laws of the Torah which forbid the establishment of any Jewish state before the coming of Moshiach (the Messiah). Talmudic law admonishes the Jewish people not to rebel against the nations of the world, and emphatically enjoins all Jews to be loyal to the countries of their abode.

ZIONISM, IN ORDER TO FURTHER THE BREAK WITH JEWISH TRADITION AND OVERCOME THE OPPOSITION OF JEWS TO ZIONISM, USED ALL MEANS AT ITS DISPOSAL TO UNDERMINE THE PEACEFUL STAY OF JEWS IN COUNTRIES THROUGHOUT THE WORLD. The books and other writings of the founders of Zionism clearly show this anti-Jewish and anti-religious attitude, and the same policies and methods were used by the later leaders of Zionism. Ultimately, this led to the great tragedy of the Jewish people in our time. The unbelievable climax was the Zionist collaboration with the Nazi murderers, a perfidy which is irrefutably documented by the Kastner trial.

AND EVEN TODAY THIS CONTINUES. BOYCOTTS AGAINST VARIOUS COUNTRIES ARE PROCLAIMED FROM TIME TO TIME BY INDIVIDUALS OR ORGANIZATIONS "IN THE NAME OF THE JEWISH PEOPLE"; DEMONSTRATIONS ARE HELD TO "IMPROVE THE SITUATION" OF THE JEWS IN THE SOVIET UNION (WHEREAS THE REAL AIM IS TO FIND IMMIGRANTS FOR THE ZIONIST STATE). THE WORLD MUST KNOW THAT THE ZIONISTS DO NOT REPRESENT US AND THEY CAN NOT SPEAK IN THE NAME OF THE JEWISH PEOPLE.

Those who have suffered or may suffer through Zionist military or political activities should not blame the Jewish people for deeds committed by the Zionists—who have all turned their backs on Jewish tradition.

Zionist politicians and their fellow travelers do not speak for the Jewish people. Indeed, the Zionist conspiracy against Jewish tradition and law makes ZIONISM—AND ALL ITS ACTIVITIES AND ENTITIES—THE ARCHENEMY OF THE JEWISH PEOPLE TODAY.

*"Guardians of the Holy City"; authentic Orthodox Jews, under the leadership of the rabbinical sages, who remain loyal to the teachings of the Patriarchs.

NETUREI KARTA OF U.S.A.*
P.O.B. 2143
BROOKLYN, NEW YORK 11202
Rabbi Chaim Blau

233

the *New York Times.* The statement reproduced on page 233 appeared in the *New York Times* on March 12, 1971, 43:1.

15. The text of the pertinent parts of the status quo agreement reads:

The Executive of the Agency has authorized the signatories to formulate its attitude towards the questions which you have raised in conversation, and we are now informing you of the attitude of the Executive of the Agency:

(a) *Sabbath.* It is clear that the legal day of rest in the Jewish State should be the Sabbath, with Christians and members of other faiths naturally being granted the right to rest on their own festive day of the week.

(b) *Dietary Laws.* All necessary measures should be taken to guarantee that in every state kitchen intended for Jews the food will be kasher.

(c) *Marriage.* All members of the Executive appreciate the gravity of the problem and its great difficulties, and on the part of all the bodies represented by the Executive of the Agency everything possible will be done to satisfy in this respect the profound need of adherents of the faith, so as to prevent the division of the House of Israel into two parts.

(d) *Education.* The full autonomy of every 'trend' in education will be guaranteed. (Incidentally, this practice also prevails in the Zionist Federation and in the official Jewish community at the present time.) There will be no interference on the part of the government with the religious conviction and the religious conscience of any section in Israel. The State will naturally determine minimal compulsory studies, the Hebrew language, history, sciences, &c. and supervise the fulfilment of this minimum, but it will give full freedom to every 'trend' to conduct education according to its own conviction and will refrain from any interference with religious conscience.

Emile Marmorstein, *Heaven at Bay: The Jewish Kulturkampf in the Holy Land* (London: Oxford University Press, 1969), pp. 86–89. Marmorstein quotes the entire letter. S. Clement Leslie, *The Rift in Israel: Religious Authority and Secular Democracy* (New York: Shocken Books, 1971), pp. 29–30.

"Kosher," the Ashkenazic form, or "kasher," the Sephardic form, means "fit" or proper." In reference to food it means that the food is ritually clean. The laws of kashrut are based on biblical prohibitions as elaborated by the Talmud and later authorities. Jewish dietary laws divide all food into three classifications: (1) Those foods that are inherently kosher and may be eaten in their natural state (for example, grains, fruit, vegetables, and so on). (2) Those foods that require some form of processing to be kosher—meat, poultry, or fish. Animals and fowl must be killed in a prescribed manner by a ritual slaughterer (*shohet*) and then examined by a ritual health inspector (*bodek*).

Traditionally the slaughterer and the inspector were the same. Certain portions of the animal may not be eaten, and these must be excised or purged from the freshly slaughtered beast. (3) Those foods that are inherently not kosher (for example, pork, shrimp, and so on). For fish to be kosher they must have fins and easily removable scales. Meat may come only from peaceful, cloven-hooved creatures that graze and chew their cud. Furthermore, according to dietary regulations, meat and milk products must not be cooked or eaten together.

16. In June 1967, prior to the Six-Day War, Prime Minister Levi Eshkol's coalition government was widened to include all the important parties and became the National Unity government. Gahal departed from the National Unity coalition in August 1970 when Prime Minister Meir acceded to pressure from the United States and agreed to accept a cease-fire and enter into peace talks with the United Arab Republic. Beigin insisted that since the talks included a willingness to withdraw from some of the occupied territories, Gahal could no longer remain in the coalition. His position was narrowly upheld by the vote of the Joint Central Committee of the Herut and Liberal parties. The vote was mainly along party lines, the Liberals being opposed to pulling out of the coalition, with the Herutists supporting such a move. *Israel Digest,* Vol. 13, No. 17, August 21, 1970, 2.

17. The quote is from remarks of Esther Raziel-Naor of Herut. The childhood recollections are those of Menachem Beigin. *Newsweek,* Vol. 59, No. 13 (March 26, 1962), 64; *New York Times,* March 11, 1962, 9:1; *Jerusalem Post Weekly, Overseas Edition,* March 2, 1962, 8:4; ibid., July 27, 1962, 2:8.

18. Rafi's decision to merge was by no means a clear-cut endorsement. See Lea Ben Dor, "A Vote for Labor Unity," *Hadassah Magazine,* Vol. 49, No. 5 (January 1968), 6. Two interesting approaches to the creation of the Israel Labor Party are Lea Ben Dor, "A Two Party System?" *Congress Bi-Weekly,* Vol. 35, No. 3 (February 5, 1968), 16–17, and Ervin Birnbaum, "Old Problems in a New Guise," *Midstream,* Vol. 14, No. 5 (May 1968), 23–31. For some insights into Mapam's ideology and reasons for joining the ILP, see "Inside Israel," *New Outlook: Middle East Monthly,* Vol. 11, No. 9 (November–December 1968), 67, and Dan Sachs, "Mapam Joins the Alignment," ibid., Vol. 12, No. 1 (January 1969), 38–40.

19. Two good analyses of the 1969 election are Herbert Smith, "Israel Elections, 1969." Mimeographed (New York: The Foreign Affairs Department, The American Jewish Committee, n.d.), and Amnon Ru-

binstein, "Hectic Aftermath to Dull Elections," *Hadassah Magazine,* Vol. 51, No. 4 (December 1969), 15, 31.

20. Aaron Antonovsky, "Israeli Political-Social Attitudes." Research paper, The Israel Institute of Applied Social Research, n.d., pp. 2–6. In August 1971 Gallup Israel issued the results of a public opinion survey which showed that of those Israelis polled 55 percent opposed separating religion from state, 36 percent were in favor, and 9 percent gave no opinion.

21. *Sabra,* the term for a person born in Israel, is an Arabic word that literally means "prickly pear," or "cactus." The Israelis use the word to connote that the nonimmigrant Israeli is supposed to be a special type of person, outwardly strong and tough but inwardly tender and kind.

4.   The Conflict over the Constitution

1. Emanuel Rackman, *Israel's Emerging Constitution: 1948–51* (New York: Columbia University Press, 1955), p. 38.

2. Yehuda Leo Kohn, "The Emerging Constitution of Israel," in *Israel: Its Role in Civilization,* ed. Moshe Davis (New York: Harper & Brothers, 1956), pp. 132–133.

3. "Constitution of Israel: Proposed Text," *Jewish Frontier,* Vol. 16, No. 1 (January 1949), 4–9.

4. Rackman, *Israel's Emerging Constitution,* p. 43.

5. Hayim Greenberg, "Notes on the Israeli Constitution," *Jewish Frontier,* Vol. 16, No. 5 (May 1949), 49.

6. Joseph Badi, *The Government of the State of Israel: A Critical Account of Its Parliament, Executive, and Judiciary* (New York: Twayne Publishers, Inc., 1963), pp. 120–122; Max M. Laserson, "On the Making of the Constitution of Israel," *Jewish Social Studies,* Vol. 14, No. 1 (January 1952), 13–14; Eliezer Goldman, *Religious Issues in Israel's Poltical Life* (Jerusalem: Mador-Dati, 1964), pp. 55–66.

7. Rackman, *Israel's Emerging Constitution,* p. 113. For Ben-Gurion's argument why a written constitution should be postponed, see David Ben-Gurion, *Rebirth and Destiny of Israel* (New York: Philosophical Library, 1954), pp. 363–380.

8. Rackman, *Israel's Emerging Constitution,* pp. 30–31.

9. Oscar Kraines, *Government and Politics in Israel* (Boston: Hough-

ton Mifflin Company, 1961), p. 30; Rackman, *Israel's Emerging Constitution*, p. 173.

10. Henry E. Baker, "Legal System," in *The Israel Yearbook: 1969*, ed. L. Berger (Israel: Israel Yearbook Publications Ltd., 1969), pp. 97–98; Peter Elman, "Basic Law: The Government, 1968," *Israel Law Review*, Vol. 4, No. 2 (April 1969), 242–259; Amnon Rubinstein, "Israel's Piecemeal Constitution," in *Studies in Israel Legislative Problems, Scripta Hierosolymitana*, Vol. 16, ed. G. Tedeschi and U. Yadin (Jerusalem: The Hebrew University, 1966), pp. 207–208; Eliahu Likhovski, "Can the Knesset Adopt a Constitution Which Will Be the 'Supreme Law of the Land'?" *Israel Law Review*, Vol. 4, No. 1 (January 1969), 61–69. The Ministry of Justice has prepared drafts for Basic Laws on "Legislation" and "The Courts," and a special subcommittee of the Knesset's Constitutional, Legislative and Judicial Committee is working on a Basic Law dealing with a Bill of Rights.

11. Hannelore Zander, "The Israeli Draft Constitution," *Common Cause*, Vol. 3 (August 1949), 46.

5 The Establishment of the Orthodox Rabbinate

1. Norman Bentwich, "Chief Rabbis—and An Office that Dates from Ottoman Times," *Jerusalem Post Weekly, Overseas Edition*, March 13, 1964, p. 7; Amnon Rubinstein, "Law and Religion in Israel," *Israel Law Review*, Vol. 2, No. 3 (July 1967), 384–388.

2. Reuven Alcalay, ed., *Israel Government Yearbook 5728* (1967/68) (Central Office of Information, Prime Minister's Office, Israel: The Government Printing Press, 1968), pp. 271–273. The quote is on page 272.

3. The councils and committees are under the general supervision of the Ministry of Religious Affairs and their staffs come under the civil service regulations. The number of council members is determined by the minister of religious affairs, but in no case may this number exceed the number of members of the local authority. Appointments to the religious councils are renewed quadrennially on a shared basis. The minister of religious affairs and the local authorities each appoint 45 percent of the total of the council membership, leaving the selection of the remaining members to the local rabbinate, and the appointments must be approved by all parties. If the minister of religious affairs, the local authority, and the local rabbinate cannot reach an agreement, the question is referred to a committee composed of the ministers of religious affairs, justice, and the interior, or

their representatives. Should the committee be unable to reach agreement, the matter is brought before the government for a final decision. This peculiar arrangement for the division of religious council seats is a result of an agreement between Mapai and the NRP. An attempt to challenge in the courts this formula for the allocation of council seats was unsuccessful. Where a local authority has no religious council, such as in a new development town, the minister for religious affairs is empowered to establish one.

In 1964 the Jerusalem Religious Council, one of the more important councils, for the first time had its activities scrutinized by the state controller. In his report the controller took note of, among other things, the sloppy accounting procedures used, a quarrel between the council members belonging to the dominant National Religious Party and the council members of Agudat Israel (who do not recognize the Chief Rabbinate and only recently had begun to participate in the council), the inactivity of the council's committees, failure to maintain complete records of kashrut inspections, and failure to give written explanations of refusals to renew kashrut certificates. The present system of religious councils was last extended in 1967. At that time during the Knesset debate, it was generally conceded that the religious council system had numerous defects, but, in the absence of working out a more satisfactory system, the councils were to be extended. As of 1969 there were 179 religious councils and 320 religious committees. For further details concerning religious councils, see Yehoshua Freudenheim, *Government in Israel* (Dobbs Ferry, New York: Oceana Publications, Inc., 1967), pp. 95–96; Rubenstein, "Law and Religion in Israel," 398–399; Alcalay, *Israel Government Yearbook 5728*, p. 37; Misha Louvish, ed. *Facts About Israel: 1969* (Jerusalem: Information Division, Ministry for Foreign Affairs, Keter Books, 1969), p. 66.

4. In 1935 the Electoral Assembly was composed of 42 rabbis recognized by the Jewish Community rules and 28 laymen nominated by the General Council (Vaad Leumi). Under the 1954 election rules, the outgoing Chief Rabbinical Council and the minister of religious affairs each appoint 4 members to a committee that selects 42 rabbis for the electoral college. These rabbis, together with 28 laymen chosen by the local religious councils comprise a 70-man electoral college. Joseph Badi, *Religion in Israel Today: The Relationship Between State and Religion* (New York: Bookman Associates, 1959), pp. 32–35; Freudenheim, *Government in Israel* pp. 92–95.

5. In order to resolve the anomaly of having a chief rabbi who would violate the Dayyanim Law if he served as president of the Grand

Rabbinical Court when over seventy-five, the law was amended in 1966. Under the new rules the principle of a chief rabbi not serving as a dayyan when over seventy-five was retained, but a superannuated chief rabbi was permitted to exercise certain powers and duties he would have exercised in his capacity as a dayyan. See Henry E. Baker, "Legal System," in *The Israel Yearbook: 1967*, ed. L. Berger (Israel: Israel Yearbook Publications Ltd., 1967), pp. 85–86.

6. The 1964 rabbinical elections were held under regulations that specifically provided that they were to be in force for that election only. The Mandatory Regulations served as a model, as in the previous rabbinate election, but further changes were also introduced. The electoral committee consisted of nine members (previously eight) of which four were appointed by the government on the recommendation of the minister of religious affairs, and four were elected by the Chief Rabbinical Council. The chairman, the ninth member, was elected by the eight members of the committee. The membership of the Electoral Assembly was broadened to 125, the principles of parity between Ashkenazic- and non-Ashkenazic communities retained, along with the division of the Electoral Assembly members into two groups: 75 rabbis and 50 representatives of the religious councils. The latter group had to affirm by written statement that their attitude toward Jewish tradition was "positive." Freudenheim, *Government in Israel*, pp. 92–95, gives the details and nuances of the election mechanism.

7. *Jerusalem Post Weekly, Overseas Edition*, March 20, 1964, p. 2.

8. The reestablishment of a Sanhedrin, Rabbi Goren urged in a visit to the United States, could "fill the vacuum in world Jewish life because of the present lack of an effective rabbinic authority which could issue binding orders and rulings on difficult religious matters." A Sanhedrin would, Goren stated, "raise immeasurably the prestige, stature, and dignity of Orthodox Jewry" and would make "Talmudic and Biblical codes an accepted part of the behavioral patterns of Jews in their multifarious activities." The idea of a Sanhedrin to modernize archaic religious regulations was not new. Chief Rabbi Ouziel previously had called for the setting up of a Sanhedrin. And Rabbi Yehudah L. Maimon, the Mizrachi leader who was Israel's first minister of religious affairs, during his tenure of office, strongly supported the idea of convening a Sanhedrin. Maimon's call for a Sanhedrin was vigorously opposed by the ultra-Orthodox who disputed his belief that the establishment of a Jewish state marked the beginning of Messianic redemption. *New York Times*, December 2, 1962, 149:3 for Goren quote; ibid., February 4, 1950, 4:6 for Rabbi Maimon's views on the desirability of calling a Sanhedrin.

9. English language coverage of the rabbinate elections, background and results, appeared in both the *New York Times* and the *Jerusalem Post*. Specifically, see the *New York Times,* March 15, 1964, 46:6; ibid., March 18, 1964, 8:3; the *Jerusalem Post Weekly, Overseas Edition,* January 17, 1964, p. 2; ibid., January 24, 1964, p. 1; ibid., March 10, 1964, pp. 1 and 2.

10. *Jerusalem Post Weekly, Overseas Edition,* April 17, 1964, p. 2.

6 Reform and Conservative Judaism in Israel

1. *New York Times,* March 26, 1968, 11:1.

2. Ibid., July 25, 1956, 2:3. Dr. Glueck's remarks challenging the Orthodox establishment were not the first in this vein by authoritative spokesmen of the Reform movement. Similiar intentions were publically announced by Dr. Solomon B. Freehof, president of the World Union for Progressive Judaism, and Dr. Maurice N. Eisendrath, president of the Union of American Hebrew Congregations, a member of the world body, in 1960 at public ceremonies marking the move of the World Union from its former location in London to its new headquarters in New York. At that time Dr. Freehof remarked that Reform Judaism "is indispensable to the spiritual development of the Israelis," and that the Israelis "have modernized all relationships except the basic Jewish religious relationship." He challenged Israeli Orthodoxy by calling it "out of step" and offered the hope that Reform Judaism "with its world experience" would help the Israelis "to find an interpretation and practice of Judaism which will integrate their lives in basic harmony." Ibid., April 15, 1960, 14:6.

3. *Jerusalem Post,* July 8, 1963, p. 5. In December 1969, Dr. Glueck announced that from the beginning of the 1970–1971 academic year all rabbinical students at the Hebrew Union College in the United States would be required to spend at least the first of their five years of study at the college's Jerusalem school. He also took the occasion to announce that he had no intention of introducing American Reform Judaism into Israel. Any reform movement would have to grow organically out of local conditions. *Israel Digest,* Vol. 13, No. 2, January 23, 1970, 7.

4. *New York Times,* October 19, 1962, 8:4.

5. Ibid., January 29, 1966, 5:5.

6. Italics in the original. Mendel Kohansky, "Reform Judaism Meets in Israel," *Midstream*, Vol. 14, No. 9 (November 1968), 59–60.

7. The Western Wall, because of its symbolic significance, had served as a backdrop for previous religious controversy. Shortly after the Six-Day War, Rom Moav, chairman of the Jerusalem Branch of the League Against Religious Coercion, along with his wife, were involved in a disturbance at the Wall. They were taken into custody when a fracas arose because the Moavs offended Orthodox religious sentiments. Dr. Moav was bareheaded, and Mrs. Moav refused to abide by the Orthodox practice of devotional segregation of the sexes. The Moav incident highlighted the issue of whether the Western Wall is to be considered a historical site or a Holy Place. If the Wall is considered a Jewish Holy Place, only the Chief Rabbinate can decide what is permissible. The decision to erect barriers separating men and women at the Wall was made by the Chief Rabbinate. In practice, however, the Religious Affairs Ministry, by arrangement with the Chief Rabbinate, supervises the Wall and a de facto recognition of the Wall as a Holy Place seems to have been established.

8. Kohansky, "Reform Judaism Meets in Israel," p. 55.

9. *Jerusalem Post Weekly, Overseas Edition,* July 8, 1968, p. 5.

7 The Legal System

1. For an amplification of this point, see Izhak Englard, "The Problem of Jewish Law in a Jewish State," *Israel Law Review,* Vol. 3, No. 2 (April 1968), 254–255 and passim.

2. Menahem Elon, "The Sources and Nature of Jewish Law and Its Application in the State of Israel," Part I, *Israel Law Review,* Vol. 2, No. 4 (October 1967), 515–565; Part II, ibid., Vol. 3, No. 1 (January 1968), 88–126; Part III, ibid., Vol. 3, No. 3 (July 1968), 416–456; Part IV, ibid., Vol. 4, No. 1 (January 1969), 80–140. This is a brilliant, scholarly, and insightful treatment of the subject. The quote is from Vol. 4, No. 1, 138–139.

3. Shalev Ginossar, "Israel Law: Comments and Trends," *Israel Law Review,* Vol. 1, No. 3 (July 1966), 385–387.

4. Haim H. Cohn, "Secularization of Divine Law," in *Studies in Israel Legislative Problems, Scripta Hierosolymitana,* Vol. 16, ed. G. Tedeschi and U. Yadin (Jerusalem: The Hebrew University, 1966), pp. 55–103; Englard, "Problem of Jewish Law," passim, and Englard, "The Relationship Between Religion and State in Israel," in *Studies*

in Israel Legislative Problems, Scripta Hierosolymitana, Vol. 16, ed. G. Tedeschi and U. Yadin (Jerusalem: The Hebrew University, 1966), pp. 254–275.

5. As might be expected, there are a number of decided differences between the civil and the religious courts. Rabbinical courts apply Jewish law, which makes no distinction between material and procedural rules. This is so because all the rules have a single source: the Torah as interpreted by the Talmud and its commentators. A rabbinical court is composed of at least three judges (dayyanim), no matter how trivial the case might appear. The litigants themselves, and not their representatives, open the pleas and reply to questions put to them by their opponents and the court. The court takes an active part in the investigations, the examination of witnesses, and is competent to summon witnesses and call evidence on its own. The line between the pleadings of plaintiff and defendant is lightly drawn. Even after pleadings are concluded, the court may allow a litigant to resume. And even after issuing a decision, the court may stay execution of its judgment and on its own initiative reopen the case for further consideration. Any party, at any time, is allowed to petition the court to reopen the case on the grounds that he has fresh evidence to produce. This departure from the rigid procedural formalities usually associated with secular courts is based on the premise that nothing should be allowed to interfere with the determination of perfect justice. In order to qualify for the position of *dayyan,* one must pass an examination and be certified by the Council of the Chief Rabbinate. But before a candidate takes this examination he must possess an acceptable rabbinical certificate, be married, be thirty years old, and have "a manner of living and style of behavior in accord with the position of a Dayyan." After having qualified, the applicant is screened by a Selection and Appointment Board, and, if the board recommends, the candidate receives his appointment as a dayyan from the president of the state. Moshe Chigier, "The Rabbinical Courts in the State of Israel," *Israel Law Review,* Vol. 2, No. 2 (April 1967), 177–178, 180.

6. Secular enforcement of rabbinical judgments are detailed in the Rabbinical Courts Jurisdiction Law:

Where a rabbinical court by final judgement, has ordered that a husband be compelled to grant his wife a letter of divorce or that a wife be compelled to accept a letter of divorce from her husband, a district court, may, upon expiration of six months from the day of the making of the order, on the application of the Attorney General, compel compliance with the order by imprisonment.

The same provisions apply to a man being compelled to give chalitza, only that the district court may act on the application of the Attorney General after only three months. Joseph Badi, ed., *Fundamental Laws of the State of Israel* (New York: Twayne Publishers, Inc., 1961), p. 314.

7. Uri Yadin, "Reflections on a New Law of Succession," *Israel Law Review*, Vol. 1, No. 1 (January 1966), 132–141.

8. Joseph Badi, *The Government of the State of Israel: A Critical Account of Its Parliament, Executive, and Judiciary* (New York: Twayne Publishers, Inc., 1963), p. 255; Izhak England, "Relationship Between Religion and State," in *Studies in Israel Legislative Problems*, ed. Tedeschi and Yadin, p. 261. A comparison between the Declaration of Allegiance in the Judges Law and the Dayyanim Law is interesting. The Judges Law states:

A person appointed to be Judge shall, before assuming his functions, make the following declaration before the president of the State— "I pledge myself to bear allegiance to the State of Israel and to its law, to dispense justice fairly, not to pervert the law and to show no favour."

The Dayyanim law states:

A person appointed to be a *dayyan* shall, before taking his seat, make before the President of the State, in the presence of the Chief Rabbis of Israel, the following declaration: "I pledge myself to bear allegiance to the State of Israel, to dispense justice fairly, not to pervert the law and to show no favor."

Badi, ed., *Fundamental Laws*, pp. 304–305, and p. 376.

9. England, "Relationship Between Religion and State," in *Studies*, 269–270.

8   Marriage and Divorce

1. The applicable law in matters of personal status depends on whether or not the persons concerned are Jews, Moslems, Druzes, or members of one of the other recognized religious communities. No provision is made for civil marriage or civil divorce in Israel, although in some cases, non-Jewish foreigners may be married by their consuls in Israel. Whether Jewish foreigners may be married by their consuls in a nonreligious ceremony that would be in contravention of the Marriage and Divorce Law is probably doubtful and raises some interesting legal questions, which, however, are hardly a matter

of major social significance. See Henry E. Baker, *The Legal System of Israel* (Jerusalem: Israel Universities Press, 1968), pp. 159–160. Moslem religious courts (shari'ah hear matters of personal status between all Moslems, Israelis as well as foreigners, on the basis of Koranic law. The salaries of their religious judges (*Kadis*) and the expenses of their own court system are paid for by the government. In contrast, the recognized Christian communities, operating courts based on their respective canon law, are funded by the communities themselves. Some of the vagaries of personal status of the non-Jewish recognized communities may be found in Yehoshua Freudenheim, *Government in Israel* (Dobbs Ferry, New York: Oceana Publications, Inc., 1967), pp. 102–105, and Bernard M. Casper, "Religious Life," *Israel Today*, No. 24 (Jerusalem: Israel Digest, 1968), 8–12. The Jurisdiction in Matters of Dissolution of Marriage (Special Cases) Law of 1969 filled a gap in the existing system. Under the Special Cases Law matters of dissolution of marriage (divorce, annulment, and recognition of marriage as void ab initio) which do not lie within the exclusive jurisdiction of one of the religious courts are within the jurisdiction of the District Court or a Religious Court as determined by the President of the Supreme Court. In 1969 a Jerusalem District Court granted Israel's first civil divorce to a "mixed" marriage couple, the husband being Jewish, the wife Christian. Henry E. Baker, "Legal System," in *The Israel Yearbook: 1970,* ed. L. Berger (Israel: Israel Yearbook Publications Ltd., 1970), pp. 114–115; Isaac S. Shiloh, "Marriage and Divorce in Israel," *Israel Law Review,* Vol. 5, No. 4 (October 1970), 479–498; *Jerusalem Post Weekly, Overseas Edition,* November 23, 1970, p. 3.

2. The ab initio prohibition of the marriage of a cohen to a divorcee or a woman who has been granted chalitzah has resulted in some interesting case law regarding the validity of such marriages. In the 1964 Haklai case the Supreme Rabbinical Court registered as married a cohen and a divorcee who had wed in a private ceremony, holding that, under halakhah, the marriage was now valid. In the 1970 Rudnitski case, a cohen and a divorcee tried for five years to have the rabbinical courts recognize their marriage; the High Court ultimately did so. In 1972 a cohen and a woman who had received chalitzah were married in a private wedding ceremony, and the High Court of Justice later declared them legally man and wife. In a two-to-one decision the High Court ruled that insofar as the rabbinical courts were dilatory in determining the issue, the public interest demanded that the status of the couple be settled. *Jerusalem Post,* March 28, 1972, p. 10. For comments and details on the debate over civil marriage and divorce, see Joseph Badi, *The Government of the State*

NOTES FOR CHAPTER 8

of *Israel: A Critical Account of Its Parliament, Executive, and Judiciary* (New York: Twayne Publishers, Inc., 1963), pp. 253–254; Eliezer Goldman, *Religious Issues in Israel's Political Life* (Jerusalem: Mador Dati, 1964), pp. 74–80. Badi's view is prosecular, Goldman's view, proreligious. Also informative are Aaron Zwergbaum, "The Civil Marriage Controversy in Israel," *Congress Bi-Weekly*, Vol. 30, No. 15 (November 4, 1963), 18–20, and Trude Weiss-Rosmarin, "Comments and Opinions," *Jewish Spectator*, Vol. 28, No. 8 (October 1963), 3–8.

3. A mamzer, despite its colloquial definition of any illegitimate child, is, according to halakhah, a child born of incest or to a married woman in adultery. According to the Deuteronomic prohibition (23:3), such offspring "shall not enter into the assembly of the Lord; even to the tenth generation." Biblically, the only legal marriage permitted to a mamzer is to a freed bondswoman, a convert, or another mamzer. Interestingly, a child of an unmarried mother is not a mamzer, and a child having the status of a mamzer inherits from his father equally with legitimate children.

The Langer case was an instance of rigid rabbinical rulings that failed to alleviate the plight of mamzerim. Hanoch and Miriam Langer, a brother and sister, were denied permission to marry their affianced by a rabbinical court on the ground that their mother had not been divorced from her first husband when she had married their father. The mother had, in Europe, been married to a Polish convert to Judaism. During World War II the couple separated. Mrs. Langer emigrated to Israel and married an Israeli. The first husband subsequently appeared in Israel, and the rabbinate noted the situation in its records. When Hanoch and Miriam applied to the rabbinate to be married, they learned they had been categorized mamzerim, and could only marry others similarly stigmatized. They might have gone abroad for civil marriages, but the children eventually born to them would still have been considered mamzerim. Hanoch, in the armed forces at the time of the ruling, appealed to Defense Minister Moshe Dayan, who raised the matter in the cabinet. Rabbi Goren was then instructed to study the case. Rabbi Goren examined the circumstances and wrote a brief establishing Hanoch and Miriam's right to marriage on the basis of a flaw in the first husband's conversion procedure. Since a flaw in the conversion would make the first marriage invalid, no divorce would be required for the second marriage. Shortly after Rabbi Goren was elected Chief Rabbi, in a portent of future rabbinical flexibility, the stigma of being mamzerim was removed from the Langers, who thereupon married their affianced.

4. This paragraph is a generalized treatment of levirate marriage and chalitzah. For an additional discussion of some of the complexities and nuances of levirate marriage and the requirement of chalitzah, see, among others, the *Standard Jewish Encyclopedia* and the *Encyclopedia of the Jewish Religion*.

5. *Jerusalem Post Weekly, Overseas Edition,* June 14, 1963, p. 7; ibid., February 21, 1964, p. 1.

6. Philip Gillon, "Welcoming the Convert—With Love," *Jerusalem Post Weekly, Overseas Edition,* March 9, 1970, p. 13.

7. Ida G. Cowen, "Bene Israel and M'Dinat Israel," *Reconstructionist,* Vol. 30, No. 5 (April 17, 1964), 15.

8. Malka Hillel Shulewitz, "The B'Nei Israel versus the Rabbinate," *Jewish Frontier,* Vol. 30, No. 9 (October 1963), 9.

9. Cowen, "Bene Israel," 19–20.

10. *Jerusalem Post Weekly, Overseas Edition,* August 21, 1964, p. 2. The *Post*'s coverage of the Bene Israel incident was extensive. See also S. N. Eisenstadt, *Israeli Society* (New York: Basic Books, Inc., 1967), pp. 312–314, 318–319.

9   The Educational System

1. The educational systems of the non-Jewish population—Druze, Arab, and recognized Christian communities—while relevant to the total Israeli educational structure, are essentially outside the scope of the Israeli religion-state controversy and therefore need not be discussed in the context of this book.

2. Joseph S. Bentwich, *Education in Israel* (Philadelphia: Jewish Publication Society of America, 1965), pp. 7–8.

3. Moshe Avidor, *Education in Israel* (Jerusalem: Youth and Hechalutz Department of the Zionist Organization, 1957), pp. 27–28.

4. Randolph L. Braham, *Israel: A Modern Education System* (Washington: U.S. Government Printing Office, 1966), pp. 16–34.

5. Joseph S. Bentwich finds that the trend system was not "wholly pernicious." On the positive side he points out that under the trends education was "a live issue, compelling teachers to constant examination of their practice and beliefs." Bentwich, *Education in Israel,* p. 26. The weakness of the educational system was documented in 1946

by a British Commission of Enquiry headed by Sir Arnold McNair. For extracts from McNair see Braham, *Israel,* p. 34.

6. The five-to-thirteen age range was implemented in three stages during three years. In the 1949–1950 school year all children between six and eleven were included; in 1950–1951 it included all children between five and twelve; and in the 1951–1952 school year the five-to-thirteen range became fully operative. The range of free compulsory attendance was subsequently progressively extended upward. As of 1969, free education was compulsory for all children up to the age of fifteen.

7. In 1965–1966 there were some 5000 children attending nonrecognized Jewish traditional primary schools. In addition to these schools, exemptions also applied to certain Christian Mission schools. Aharon F. Kleinberger, *Society, Schools and Progress in Israel* (London: Pergamon Press, 1969), p. 117.

8. State of Israel, Central Bureau of Statistics, *Statistical Abstract of Israel 1965,* No. 16 (Israel: Jerusalem Academic Press, Ltd.), pp. 96–101.

9. Asher Zidon, *Knesset: The Parliament of Israel* (New York: Herzl Press, 1967), p. 307.

10. Joseph Badi, *The Government of the State of Israel: A Critical Account of Its Parliament, Executive, and Judiciary* (New York: Twayne Publishers, Inc., 1963), p. 192.

11. Oscar Kraines, "Israel: The Emergence of a Polity," *The Western Political Quarterly,* Vol. 6, No. 1 (September 1953), 529. During the previous year secular hostility to increased religious demands had surfaced. One manifestation of this was the founding in Jerusalem in 1950 of the League Against Religious Coercion. As its name implied, the League stood for the complete separation of religion and state and pledged itself to work for minimization of religious restrictions on Israeli life. The League mounted a vigorous campaign and soon had branches in Tel Aviv and Haifa.

12. Kleinberger, *Society, Schools and Progress in Israel,* p. 119.

13. Braham, *Israel,* p. 43.

14. Joseph Badi, ed., *Fundamental Laws of the State of Israel* (New York: Twayne Publishers, Inc., 1961), p. 291.

15. Naftaly S. Glasman, *Developments Toward a Secondary Education Act: The Case of Israel* (Ann Arbor, Michigan: University Microfilms, Inc., 1969), pp. 82–86.

16. The Council for Religious State Education, under the law, exercises veto power over the minister of education in religious areas. The Council controls the appointment of the director of the Religious Education Division of the Ministry and supplementary programs. The Council may, on "religious grounds" alone, disqualify a principal, inspector, or teacher at a religious state educational institution from appointment or further service. The phrase "religious grounds" has been interpreted by the Council most broadly so as to include within its scope the conduct of an employee and the employee's spouse. The Council also has dismissed teachers who sent their children to nonreligious secondary schools.

The composition of the Council indicates its theopolitical character. The members of the Council are appointed by the minister with the approval of the government for a period of four years. Two members are representatives of the minister, six members are appointed from a list of twelve proposed by the minister of religious affairs. Three are chosen from a list of at least six proposed by religious teachers' organizations, and three more from among the religious members of the Education Committee. Thus, of the fourteen members, nine are representatives of the National Religious Party. The six appointed by the minister of religious affairs are of his party, and because elections in the teachers' organizations are conducted along party lines, this ensures that the three representatives of the religious teachers will be from the NRP. The NRP enjoys additional leverage when the government must, with an eye to coalition building, approve the minister's appointments to the Education Committee and the Council for State Education. Insofar as the Council for Religious Education controls the appointment of the director of the Division of Religious Education, the supreme pedagogic authority of the religious state schools, the values of the National Religious Party infuse and characterize religious state education. Kleinberger, *Society, Schools and Progress in Israel*, p. 126.

17. Ibid., p. 132 and p. 133.

18. Ibid., p. 168; Misha Louvish, ed., *Facts About Israel: 1969* (Jerusalem: Information Division, Ministry for Foreign Affairs, Keter Books, 1969), p. 152.

19. Glasman, *Developments,* pp. 259–261; Kleinberger, *Society, Schools and Progress in Israel*, p. 189.

20. For an excellent discussion of the various types of *yeshivot,* see Zerah Warhaftig, *The Yeshivah in Israel* (Jerusalem: Ministry of Religious Affairs, The Government Printer, n.d.); J. Bentwich, *Education in Israel*, pp. 109–111; Louvish, ed., *Facts: 1969,* p. 160.

21. Braham, *Israel*, p. 81, p. 151; J. Bentwich, *Education in Israel*, p. 144.

22. Kleinberger, *Society, Schools and Progress in Israel*, pp. 326–327.

23. Ibid., pp. 327–328.

24. Eliezer Goldman, *Religious Issues in Israel's Political Life* (Jerusalem: Mador Dati, 1964), pp. 84–93.

10 Orthodoxy and the Military

1. Amnon Rubinstein, "Law and Religion in Israel," *Israel Law Review*, Vol. 2, No. 3 (July 1967), 412.

2. Reuven Alcalay, ed., *Israel Government Yearbook 5728* (1967/68) (Central Office of Information, Prime Minister's Office, Israel: The Government Printing Press, 1968), pp. 111–112; Leo Heiman "Religion in Israel's Army," *Jewish Frontier*, Vol. 22, No. 4 (April 1957), 25–27; Bernard M. Casper, "Religious Life," *Israel Today*, No. 24 (Jerusalem: Israel Digest, 1968), pp. 15–17. For a discussion of some of the problems involved in establishing a unified service, see "Symposium: Can a Unified Code of Religious Customs Be Introduced in Israel?" *Iggeret LaGolah*, No. 64 (September–October 1957), 10–22.

3. Emanuel Rackman, *Israel's Emerging Constitution: 1948–51* (New York: Columbia University Press, 1955), pp. 151–152; Joseph Badi, *Religion in Israel Today: The Relationship Between State and Religion* (New York: Bookman Associates, 1959), p. 27. Ben-Gurion also had to deal with the question of military service for Orthodox males who were studying in a yeshiva (talmudic academy). He solved this by entering into an informal agreement with Chief Rabbi Yitzchak Ha-Levi Herzog. Under this agreement those attending yeshivot were deferred as long as they remained full-time students. This understanding, based on instructions originally issued by Ben-Gurion, became standard government policy, although it never formally became law. In actual practice, the great majority—it has been estimated at about 90 percent—of yeshiva students at some point in their lives do some form of national service. *Jerusalem Post Weekly, Overseas Edition*, February 5, 1968, p. 9. The legality of the policy of deferring yeshiva students was challenged unsuccessfully in 1970. The High Court of Justice refused to consider the issue, ruling it was a purely political matter; ibid., March 2, 1970, p. 20.

4. Rackman, *Israel's Emerging Constitution*, pp. 151–152; Hal Lehrman, *Israel: The Beginning and Tomorrow* (New York: William

Sloane Associates, 1951), pp. 101–104; *New York Times,* May 16, 1951, 13:1; Alfred Werner, "Israel's Zealots in Gabardine: The "'Guardians of the City,'" *Commentary,* Vol. 11, No. 1 (January 1951), 61–67.

5. See "National Service Law, 1953," in *Fundamental Laws of the State of Israel,* ed. Joseph Badi (New York: Twayne Publishers, Inc., 1961), pp. 311–313.

11   Orthodox Pressure Tactics

1. *Jerusalem Post Weekly, Overseas Edition,* January 17, 1964, p. 5.

2. Ibid., February 10, 1969, p. 4.

3. Ibid., August 28, 1964, p. 8.

4. Immanuel Jakobovits, "The Dissection of the Dead in Jewish Law," in *A Treasury of "Tradition,"* ed. Norman Lamm and Walter S. Wurzburger (New York: Hebrew Publishing Co., 1967), p. 303.

5. *Jerusalem Post Weekly, Overseas Edition,* February 11, 1966, p. 2; *New York Times,* September 23, 1966, 2:6.

6. *New York Times,* April 7, 1967, p. 12. Italics in original.

7. *Jerusalem Post Weekly, Overseas Edition,* March 27, 1967, p. 10; *New York Times,* May 4, 1967, 6:1; ibid., May 28, 1967, 4:1.

12   "Who Is a Jew?"

1. The liberality of the Law of Return has been abused by some who want Israeli passports as documents of convenience. The Israeli Ministry of Interior has estimated that there were 80,000 to 110,000 holders of Israeli passports living outside of Israel, and of these 75 to 80 percent had dual nationality. The Law of Return was amended in 1966 so that (with some exceptions) a new immigrant is required to reside in Israel for a year before he may receive an Israeli passport. *New York Times,* August 4, 1966, 10:8.

2. Baruch Litvin, comp., and Sidney B. Hoenig, ed., *Jewish Identity: Modern Responsa and Opinions on the Registration of Children of Mixed Marriages* (New York: Philipp Feldheim, Inc., 1965), p. 314; *New York Times,* July 9, 1961, 76:2; Ervin Birnbaum, *The Politics of Compromise: State and Religion in Israel* (Cranbury, New Jersey: Fairleigh Dickinson University Press, 1970), pp. 178–189.

3. Eliezer Goldman, *Religious Issues in Israel's Political Life* (Jerusalem: Mador Dati, 1964), pp. 67–69.

4. Litvin and Hoenig, *Jewish Identity,* p. 310, pp. 14–15. Litvin's book contains the full texts of Ben-Gurion's letter and the replies to it.

5. See Judgment: *High Court Application of Oswald Rufeisen* v. *The Minister of the Interior,* State of Israel, The Supreme Court (Jerusalem: The Ministry of Justice: 1963); Justice Silberg's opinion goes from page 1 to page 26. The quotes in the text from Silberg are to be found on pages 3, 18, 19, 20, 21, 22, 23, 25, 26, and 27. Justice Cohn's opinion goes from page 26 to page 38. The quotes in the text from his opinion are to be found on pages 28, 29, 31, 32, 33, 34, 36, and 38. Landau's opinion runs from page 38 to page 50. The quotes in the text from Justice Landau's opinion are to be found on pages 41, 46, 47, 48, 49, and 50. Justice Many's opinion is on page 50. The opinion of Justice Berinson runs from page 50 to page 71. The quotes in the text from his opinion may be found on pages 61, 67, 68, 69, and 70.

6. *New York Times,* January 28, 1965, 7:5; *Jerusalem Post Weekly,* December 25, 1964, p. 1; January 1, 1965, p. 8; January 8, 1965, p. 2; March 25, 1966, p. 1.

7. *New York Times,* October 18, 1968, 3:1; November 22, 1968, 10:4; *Jerusalem Post Weekly, Overseas Edition,* November 25, 1968, 4:1. The nine opinions of the justices in the Shalit case (*Binyamin Shalit, Petitioner,* v. *1. Minister of Interior, 2. Haifa Registration Officer, Respondents*) are summarized by the *Jerusalem Post*'s law editor, Doris Lankin, in the issue of January 25, 1970, pp. 4–5. The text follows Lankin's summaries.

8. *Jerusalem Post Weekly, Overseas Edition,* January 26, 1970, p. 4; *New York Times,* January 28, 1970, 8:1.

9. *Jerusalem Post Weekly, Overseas Edition,* February 20, 1970, p. 4.

10. Zvi Ben-Moshe, "Reactions to the Shalit Case," *Congress Bi-Weekly,* Vol. 37, No. 4 (March 6, 1970), 4–5; *Israel Digest,* Vol. 13, No. 4 (February 20, 1970), 4–5.

11. *New York Times,* February 4, 1970, 4:4; ibid., February 5, 1970, 15:1; *Jerusalem Post Weekly, Overseas Edition,* February 9, 1970, pp. 6, 7. For an interesting account of Avnery and his views, see Uri Avnery, *Israel Without Zionists: A Plea for Peace in The Middle East* (New York: The Macmillan Company, 1968).

12. *Jerusalem Post Weekly, Overseas Edition,* February 16, 1970, pp. 10, 13.

13. Ibid., p. 10; ibid., March 9, 1970, pp. 4, 2; Moshe Brilliant, "A Ticklish Question," *Israel Magazine,* Vol. 2, No. 9 (June 1970), 36–42.

14. *Jerusalem Post Weekly, Overseas Edition,* March 23, 1970, p. 11.

15. *Israel Digest,* Vol. 13, No. 7 (April 13, 1970), 1, 8; Shalev Ginossar, "Who Is a Jew: A Better Law?" *Israel Law Review,* Vol. 5, No. 2 (April 1970), 264–267. For an interesting and provocative analysis of the Shalit case, see Robert Alter, "The Shalit Case," *Commentary,* Vol. 50, No. 1 (July 1970), 55–61.

16. The controversy over the legislative definition of a Jew had scarcely abated when the National Religious Party precipitated a crisis over a Reform conversion. A Mrs. Helen Zeidman, originally an American Christian, was converted to Judaism by rabbis of the Circle for Progressive Judaism, a Reform group in Tel Aviv. Mrs. Zeidman had filed a writ in the High Court to require her registration as a Jew by nationality after the Shalit decision but before legislation nullifying its effect was passed. Under the Shalit decision, her bona fide declaration that she was Jewish by nationality would have been sufficient to require her registration. The attorney general announced he would not challenge Mrs. Zeidman's writ, as she was on solid legal grounds, and advised NRP Minister of the Interior Mosheh Shapira to register Mrs. Zeidman as she requested. If Interior Minister Shapira had been forced to register Mrs. Zeidman, in effect recognizing Israeli Reform conversions, the NRP threatened to resign from the government. In an effort to avoid a cabinet crisis, Justice Minister Y. Shapira wrote to Interior Minister M. Shapira that the registration of Mrs. Zeidman, because of its unique timing, would not set a precedent and that in the future, all conversions in Israel must be confirmed by the Chief Rabbinate. While the interior minister's letter, based on a 1927 Mandatory Ordinance still in force, ruled out Israeli Reform conversions, it did not rule out Reform conversions performed outside Israel. The religious parties and the rabbinate, however, intransigently refused to permit the Zeidman registration, even as an exception. The NRP declared they would sooner resign from the government than be responsible for the registration of a person who had not been converted by the procedure sanctioned by halakhah. The crisis was resolved when Mrs. Zeidman was persuaded to apply for Orthodox conversion. An Orthodox conversion was arranged for, and performed, in record time by Rabbi Shlomo Goren, chief rabbi of the Israel Forces and Tel Aviv chief

rabbi-elect. A cabinet crisis had been averted, and the Orthodox made some small gains in that it was now spelled out that all conversions in Israel were subject to the authority of the Chief Rabbinate. Nonetheless, it is interesting to speculate on what might have happened if Mrs. Zeidman had refused to undergo an Orthodox conversion and had insisted on pressing her rights in the courts. In all probability, some form of coalition crisis would have occurred. For the text of Justice Minister Shapira's letter, see *Jerusalem Post Weekly, Overseas Edition,* June 1, 1970, p. 4. Details of the denouement of the Orthodox conversion may be found in ibid., June 22, 1970, p. 6.

In 1972 the High Court ruled against Dr. Georges R. Tamarin, a Jewish-born self-proclaimed atheist, who appealed to have the word "Jew" in his identity card changed to "Israeli." Tamarin contended that the 1970 amendments to the Law of Return had created "a new national category." The High Court rejected this and said, "There is no Israeli nation separate from the Jewish people. The Jewish people is composed not only of those residing in Israel but also of Diaspora Jewry." Shortly after the Tamarin ruling the High Court rejected an application by Binyamin Shalit to have his third child registered as a "Hebrew national." *Jerusalem Post Weekly, Overseas Edition,* January 25, 1972, p. 3; ibid., February 1, 1972, p. 5.

13 The Languishing Soul: Religion in the Body Politic

1. For a discussion of the traditional state-religion classifications, see Arcot Krishnaswami, "The Status of Religions in Relation to the State," *Journal of Church and State,* Vol. II, No. 1 (May 1960), 44–60.

2. Donald E. Smith, *India as a Secular State* (Princeton: Princeton University Press, 1963), pp. 106–108.

3. Fred R. von der Mehden, *Religion and Nationalism in Southeast Asia: Burma, Indonesia, The Philippines* (Madison: The University of Wisconsin Press, 1963), pp. 97, 100–101, 106–108; Donald E. Smith, *Religion and Politics in Burma* (Princeton: Princeton University Press, 1965), passim.

4. Wilfred Cantwell Smith, *Islam in Modern History* (Princeton: Princeton University Press, 1957), p. 29; Robert D. Campbell, *Pakistan: Emerging Democracy* (Princeton: D. Van Nostrand Company, Inc., 1963), pp. 39–42; Herbert J. Liebesny, "Legal Processes: Stability and Change, Islamic Law," unpublished paper delivered at the

Annual Meeting of the American Political Science Association (Chicago, Illinois, September 9–12, 1964), pp. 19–20; Leonard Binder, *Religion and Politics in Pakistan* (Berkeley and Los Angeles: University of California Press), passim. I am indebted to my friend Professor Donald E. Smith for the observation on Bangladesh.

5. Emile Marmorstein, *Heaven at Bay: The Jewish Kulturkampf in the Holy Land* (London: Oxford University Press, 1969), pp. 102–103.

6. Zvi Zinger, "Public Services on the Sabbath," in *A Treasury of "Tradition,"* ed. Norman Lamm and Walter S. Wurzburger (New York: Hebrew Publishing Company, 1967), pp. 268–283.

7. S. Clement Leslie, *The Rift in Israel: Religious Authority and Secular Democracy* (New York: Schocken Books, 1971), p. 65.

Glossary

Achdut ha-Avodah (Labor Unity).
A left-wing socialist Zionist party that splintered from Mapam after the 1951 elections, assuming an ideological stance to the right of Mapam and the left of Mapai. Achdut remained a separate party for the 1955, 1959, and 1961 Knesset elections, and in 1965 it joined with Mapai in an electoral alliance known as the Alignment.

Agudat Israel (Union of Israel).
An ultra-Orthodox party that in 1955 and 1959 ran with Poale Agudat Israel as the Torah Religious Front.

Alignment.
An arrangement in which the parties agree to retain their organizational autonomy while coordinating their electoral and parliamentary activities. Mapai and Achdut ha-Avodah entered into an alignment before the 1965 elections, but it terminated when Mapai, Achdut ha-Avodah, and Rafi merged to form the Israel Labor Party. Mapam then aligned with the Israel Labor Party for the 1969 elections.

Aliyah (pl. aliyot).
From the Hebrew word meaning "ascent" or "going up," it refers, in one context, to Jewish immigration to the Holy Land.

Ashkenazi (pl. Askenazim).
Jews who came from middle and northern Europe.

Bene Israel (Sons of Israel).
A Jewish group from India.

Canaanite.
One who believes that Israel must rid itself of all specifically Diaspora-oriented characteristics and reestablish a direct continuity with the Canaanite-Palestinian biblical past.

Dayyan.
A religious judge.

Emancipation.
The removal of civic, political, and economic restrictions imposed on Jews.

Free Center.
A party founded in 1967 by a Herut splinter faction.

Gahal.
An acronym for the Herut–General Zionist bloc, formed in 1965, with each party retaining its organizational autonomy.

General Zionists.
A secularist, capitalist-oriented party. The General Zionists united with the Progressives to become the Liberals in 1961 but split with the Progressives in 1965 and joined Herut in the formation of Gahal.

Halakhah.
Jewish law.

Ha-Olam ha-Zeh (This World).
An independent political movement that started in 1965. Also known as the "New Force," it advocates separation of religion and state.

Ha-Poel ha-Mizrachi (Spiritual Center Workers).
An Orthodox political party composed mainly of workers and farmers who believe in blending socialism, Zionism, and Orthodoxy. Ha-Poel ha-Mizrachi ran with Mizrachi in 1955 as the National Religious Party. The two Mizrachi parties merged in 1956, retaining the name National Religious Party.

Haskalah.
The Jewish Enlightenment movement of the eighteenth and nineteenth centuries that emphasized the need for secular education.

Herut (Freedom).
A secular rightist political party that emphasizes free initiative and less governmental control and advocates a highly nationalistic and expansionist foreign policy. Herut joined with the General Zionists in 1965 to form Gahal.

Independent Liberal Party.
Founded in 1965 by those Progressives who refused to join the General Zionists and Herut in the formation of Gahal.

Israel Labor Party.
A party formed in 1968 from the merger of Mapai, Achdut ha-Avodah, and Rafi. It aligned itself with Mapam for the 1969 elections, thereby consolidating the electoral strength of the secular left parties.

Kashrut.
Dietary fitness.

Kehillah (pl. Kehillot).
The Jewish community organization.

Knesset.
Israel's 120-member unicameral parliament.

Liberals.
The union of the Progressives and the General Zionists effected for the 1961 elections and dissolved in 1965.

Maabarot.
Semipermanent transitional settlements for immigrants.

Maki.
The Israel Communist Party. Outside the mainstream of Israeli politics, it is anti-Zionist and generally an apologist for Soviet policies.

Mapai (Israel Worker's party).
The largest and most important socialist-Zionist party, it favors a secular state but is not hostile to many historic and religious aspects of Judaism. The leader of all government coalitions, Mapai entered into an "alignment" with Achdut ha-Avodah for the 1965 elections and in 1968 joined with Achdut ha-Avodah and Rafi to form the Israel Labor Party.

Mapam (United Worker's party).
An antireligious very left-wing socialist Zionist party. Mapam entered into an alignment with the Israel Labor Party for the 1969 elections.

Mizrachi (Spiritual Center).
An Orthodox political party composed mainly of urban, middle-class Orthodox Jews who are devoted to building Israel according to the teachings of the Orthodox rabbinate. Mizrachi ran with Ha-Poel ha-Mizrachi in 1955 as the National Religious Party, and in 1956 the two Mizrachi parties merged, retaining the name National Religious Party.

National Religious Party (NRP).
The name given to the 1955 electoral alliance of Mizrachi and Ha-Poel ha-Mizrachi and subsequently retained when the two parties formally merged in 1956.

Natore Karta (Guardians of the City).
A group of ultra-Orthodox who believe that Jews must accept unquestioningly their fate on earth and must not try to change their condition or interfere with Divine Will. They reject the legitimacy of the government of Israel.

Poale Agudat Israel (Workers of the Union of Israel).
An ultra-Orthodox workers' party that in 1955 and 1959 ran with Agudat Israel as the Torah Religious Front.

Progressives.
A small secularist center party. In 1961 the Progressives united with the General Zionists to become the Liberals. They assumed the name Independent Liberals when in 1965 they refused to join the General Zionists and Herut in the formation of Gahal.

257

Rafi (Israel Labor List).
Formed in 1965 by Ben-Gurion, Moshe Dayan, and others when they split from Mapai. The main points of departure from Mapai involved an advocacy of the abandonment of the list system of proportional representation for a constituency system as well as contending personalities and political styles. Dissolved in 1968 when Rafi merged with Mapai and Achdut ha-Avodah to form the Israel Labor Party.

Sabra.
An Arabic word meaning "prickly pear" or "cactus," and applied to a person born in Israel.

Sephardi (pl. Sephardim).
The term applied to Jews, and their descendants, who came from Portugal, Spain, and parts of the Mediterranean basin.

State List.
A party formed by Ben-Gurion and a small coterie of adherents after Rafi dissolved in 1968.

Theopolitics.
The attempt by the Orthodox, organized in political parties, to establish a Torah state by means of political activity.

Toda'ah yehudit.
A Jewish consciousness program designed for nonreligious state primary schools.

Torah Religious Front.
The electoral alliance of Agudat Israel and Poale Agudat Israel in the 1955 and 1959 elections.

United Religious Front.
The 1949 electoral alliance of the four religious parties: Mizrachi, Ha-Poel ha-Mizrachi, Agudat Israel, and Poale Agudat Israel.

Vaad Leumi.
The national council of the organized Jewish community in Palestine.

Yeshiva (pl. yeshivot).
Theological academy.

Yishuv.
The Jewish settlement in Palestine.

Works Cited

Alcalay, Reuben, ed.
Israel Government Yearbook 5723 (1962/63). Israel: The Government Printer, 1963.

————.
Israel Government Yearbook 5728 (1967/68). Central Office of Information, Prime Minister's Office. Israel: The Government Printing Press, 1968.

Alter, Robert.
"The Shalit Case." *Commentary*, Vol. 50, No. 1 (July 1970), pp. 55–61.

Antonovsky, Aaron.
"Israeli Political-Social Attitudes." Research paper, Jerusalem: The Israel Institute of Applied Social Research, n.d.

Arian, Alan.
Ideological Change in Israel. Cleveland: The Press of Case Western Reserve University, 1968.

Avidor, Moshe.
Education in Israel. Jerusalem: Youth and Hechalutz Department of the Zionist Organization, 1957.

Avineri, Shlomo.
"Israel in the Post–Ben-Gurion Era." *Midstream*, Vol. 11, No. 6 (June 1965), pp. 16–32.

Avnery, Uri.
Israel Without Zionists: A Plea for Peace in the Middle East. New York: The Macmillan Company, 1968.

Badi, Joseph.
Religion in Israel Today: The Relationship Between State and Religion. New York: Bookman Associates, 1959.

————.
The Government of the State of Israel: A Critical Account of Its Parliament, Executive, and Judiciary. New York: Twayne Publishers, Inc., 1963.

Badi, Joseph, ed.
Fundamental Laws of the State of Israel. New York: Twayne Publishers, Inc., 1961.

Baker, Henry E.
"Legal System." In *The Israel Yearbook 1967*, edited by L. Berger. Israel: Israel Yearbook Publications Ltd., 1967.

———.

The Legal System of Israel. Jerusalem: Israel Universities Press, 1968.

———.

"Legal System." In *The Israel Yearbook 1969*, edited by L. Berger. Israel: Israel Yearbook Publications Ltd., 1969.

———.

"Legal System." In *The Israel Yearbook 1970*, edited by L. Berger. Israel: Israel Yearbook Publications Ltd., 1970.

Bayne, E. A.
"Israel's Government by the People: The Background of the Israeli Elections of 1965." New York: American Universities Field Staff Report, 1966.

Ben-Dor, Lea.
"A Vote for Labor Unity." *Hadassah Magazine*, Vol. 49, No. 5 (January 1968), p. 6.

———.

"A Two Party System?" *Congress Bi-Weekly*, Vol. 35, No. 3 (February 5, 1968), pp. 16–17.

Ben-Gurion, David.
Rebirth and Destiny of Israel. New York: Philosophical Library, 1954.

———.

"First Ones." In *Israel Government Yearbook 5723 (1962/63)*, edited by Reuben Alcalay. Israel: The Government Printer, 1963.

Ben-Moshe, Zvi.
"Reactions to the Shalit Case." *Congress Bi-Weekly*, Vol. 37, No. 4 (March 6, 1970), pp. 4–5.

Bentwich, Joseph S.
Education in Israel. Philadelphia: Jewish Publication Society of America, 1965.

Bentwich, Norman.
"Chief Rabbis—and An Office that Dates from Ottoman Times." *Jerusalem Post Weekly, Overseas Edition*, March 13, 1964.

Bentwich, Norman, and Helen Bentwich.
Mandate Memories: 1918–1948. New York: Shocken Books, 1965.

Berger, L., ed.
The Israel Yearbook 1963. Israel: Israel Yearbook Publications Ltd., 1963.

————.
The Israel Yearbook 1965. Israel: Israel Yearbook Publications Ltd., 1965.

————.
The Israel Yearbook 1967. Israel: Israel Yearbook Publications Ltd., 1967.

————.
The Israel Yearbook 1969. Israel: Israel Yearbook Publications Ltd., 1969.

————.
The Israel Yearbook 1971. Israel: Israel Yearbook Publications Ltd., 1971.

Binder, Leonard.
Religion and Politics in Pakistan. Berkeley and Los Angeles: University of California Press, 1961.

Birnbaum, Ervin.
"Old Problems in a New Guise." *Midstream,* Vol. 14, No. 5 (May 1968), pp. 23–31.

————.
The Politics of Compromise: State and Religion in Israel. Cranbury, New Jersey: Fairleigh Dickinson University Press, 1970.

Braham, Randolph L.
Israel: A Modern Education System. Washington: U.S. Government Printing Office, 1966.

Brilliant, Moshe.
"A Ticklish Question." *Israel Magazine,* Vol. 2, No. 9 (June 1970), pp. 36–42.

Cahn, Edmond.
"How Democracy Unites Us." *Congress Bi-Weekly,* Vol. 31, No. 14 (November 9, 1964), pp. 34–38.

Campbell, Robert D.
Pakistan: Emerging Democracy. Princeton: D. Van Nostrand Company, Inc., 1963.

Casper, Bernard M.
"Religious Life." *Israel Today,* No. 24. Jerusalem: Israel Digest, 1968.

Chigier, Moshe.
"The Rabbinical Courts in the State of Israel." *Israel Law Review,* Vol. 2, No. 2 (April 1967), pp. 147–181.

261

Cohn, Haim H.
"Secularization of Divine Law." In *Studies in Israel Legislative Problems, Scripta Hierosolymitana*, Vol. 16, edited by G. Tedeschi and U. Yadin. Jerusalem: The Hebrew University, 1966.

"Constitution of Israel: Proposed Text." *Jewish Frontier*, Vol. 16, No. 1 (January 1949), pp. 4–9.

Cowen, Ida G.
"Bene Israel and M'Dinat Israel." *Reconstructionist*, Vol. 30, No. 5 (April 17, 1964), pp. 12–20.

Czudnowski, Moshe M., and Jacob M. Landau.
The Israeli Communist Party and the Elections for the Fifth Knesset, 1961. Stanford: The Hoover Institute on War, Revolution, and Peace, Stanford University, 1965.

Dawidowicz, Lucy S.
The Golden Tradition: Jewish Life and Thought in Eastern Europe. New York: Holt, Rinehart & Winston, Inc., 1967.

Devlin, Kevin.
"Communism in Israel: Anatomy of a Split." *Survey*, No. 62 (January 1967), pp. 141–151.

Dunner, Joseph.
The Republic of Israel: Its History and Its Promise. New York: Mc-Graw-Hill Book Company, Inc., 1950.

Eisenstadt, S. N.
Israeli Society. New York: Basic Books, Inc., 1967.

Elman, Peter.
"Basic Law: The Government, 1968." *Israel Law Review*, Vol. 4, No. 2 (April 1969), pp. 242–259.

Elon, Menahem.
"The Sources and Nature of Jewish Law and Its Application in the State of Israel." *Israel Law Review*, Part I, Vol. 2, No. 4 (October 1967), 515–565; Part II, Vol. 3, No. 1 (January 1968), 88–126; Part III, Vol. 3, No. 3 (July 1968) 416–456; Part IV, Vol. 4, No. 1 (January 1969), 80–140.

Elston, D. R.
Israel: The Making of a Nation. London: Oxford University Press, 1963.

Englard, Izhak.
"The Problem of Jewish Law in a Jewish State." *Israel Law Review*,
Vol. 3, No. 2 (April 1968), pp. 254–278.

———.
"The Relationship Between Religion and State in Israel." In *Studies
in Israel Legislative Problems, Scripta Hierosolymitana*, Vol. 16, edited by G. Tedeschi and U. Yadin. Jerusalem: The Hebrew University, 1966.

Fein, Leonard J.
Politics in Israel. Boston: Little, Brown and Company, 1967.

Frank, M. Z.
"God of Abraham in the State of Israel." *Middle East Journal*, Vol.
5, No. 4 (Autumn 1951), pp. 407–423.

Freudenheim, Yehoshua.
Government in Israel. Dobbs Ferry, New York: Oceana Publications,
Inc., 1967.

Friedberg, Maurice.
"The Split in Israel's Communist Party." *Midstream*, Vol. 12, No. 2
(February 1966), pp. 19–28.

Ginossar, Shalev.
"Israel Law: Components and Trends." *Israel Law Review*, Vol. 1,
No. 3 (July 1966), pp. 380–395.

———.
"Who Is a Jew: A Better Law?" *Israel Law Review*, Vol. 5, No. 2
(April 1970), pp. 264–267.

Glasman, Naftaly S.
*Developments Toward a Secondary Education Act: The Case of Is-
rael*. Ann Arbor, Michigan: University Microfilms, Inc., 1969.

Goldman, Eliezer.
Religious Issues in Israel's Political Life. Jerusalem: Mador Dati,
1964.

Greenberg, Hayim.
"Notes on the Israeli Constitution." *Jewish Frontier*, Vol. 16, No. 5
(May 1949), pp. 31–38.

Halpern, Ben.
The Idea of the Jewish State. Cambridge: Harvard University Press,
1961.

Heiman, Leo.
"Religion in Israel's Army." *Jewish Frontier,* Vol. 22, No. 4 (April 1957), pp. 25–27.

Hertzberg, Arthur.
The Zionist Idea: A Historical Analysis and Reader. New York: Doubleday and Company, Inc., and Herzl Press, 1969.

Hurewitz, J. C.
The Struggle for Palestine. New York: W. W. Norton and Company, Inc., 1950.

Hyamson, Albert M.
Palestine Under the Mandate: 1920–1948. London: Methuen and Company, Ltd., 1950.

"Inside Israel." *New Outlook: Middle East Monthly,* Vol. 11, No. 9 (November-December 1968), p. 67.

Jakobovits, Immanuel.
"The Dissection of the Dead in Jewish Law." In *A Treasury of "Tradition,"* edited by Norman Lamm and Walter S. Wurzberger. New York: Hebrew Publishing Company, 1967.

Janowsky, Oscar I.
Foundations of Israel: Emergence of a Welfare State. Princeton: D. Van Nostrand Company, Inc., 1959.

Johnston, Scott D.
"The Multi-Party System of Israel: Some Aspects of Party Politics in the Parliament (Knesset)." *Studies on Asia,* Vol. 3 (1962), pp. 59–75.

————.
"Politics of the Right in Israel: The Herut Movement." *Social Science,* Vol. 40, No. 2 (April 1965), pp. 104–114.

————.
"A Comparative Study of Intra-Party Factionalism in Israel and Japan." *Western Political Quarterly,* Vol. 20, No. 2, Part I (June 1967), pp. 288–307.

Joseph, Bernard.
British Rule in Palestine. Washington: Public Affairs Press, 1948.

Katz, Jacob.
Tradition and Crisis: Jewish Society at the End of the Middle Ages. New York: The Free Press of Glencoe, Inc., 1961.

Katz, Shlomo.
"Mapam—A Case of Political Neurosis." *Jewish Frontier,* Vol. 17, No. 10 (October 1950), pp. 16–19.

Kimche, Jon.
"Succession and the Legacy in Israel." *Journal of International Affairs,* Vol. 18, No. 1 (January 1964), pp. 43–53.

————.
"A Mandate for Change." *Midstream,* Vol. 12, No. 1 (January 1966), pp. 51–66.

Kleinberger, Aharon F.
Society, Schools and Progress in Israel. London: Pergamon Press, 1969.

Koestler, Arthur.
Promise and Fulfillment: Palestine 1917–1949. New York: The Macmillan Company, 1949.

Kohansky, Mendel.
"Reform Judaism Meets in Israel." *Midstream,* Vol. 14, No. 9 (November 1968), pp. 54–61.

Kohn, Yehuda Leo.
"The Emerging Constitution of Israel." In *Israel: Its Role in Civilization,* edited by Moshe Davis. New York: Harper & Brothers, 1956.

Kraines, Oscar.
"Israel: The Emergence of a Polity." *Western Political Quarterly,* Vol. 6, No. 1 (September 1953), pp. 518–542.

————.
Government and Politics in Israel. Boston: Houghton Mifflin Company, 1961.

Krishnaswami, Arcot.
"The Status of Religions in Relation to the State." *Journal of Church and State,* Vol. 2, No. 1 (May 1960), pp. 44–60.

Landau, Jacob M.
The Arabs in Israel: A Political Study. London: Oxford University Press, 1969.

Laserson, Max M.
"On the Making of the Constitution of Israel." *Jewish Social Studies,* Vol. 14, No. 1 (January 1952), pp. 3–16.

265

League of Nations Association Research Committee.
The Palestine Mandate. Geneva: League of Nations Association, 1930.

Lehrman, Hal.
Israel: The Beginning and Tomorrow. New York: William Sloane Associates, 1951.

Leslie, S. Clement.
The Rift in Israel: Religious Authority and Secular Democracy. New York: Schocken Books, 1971.

Liebesny, Herbert J.
"Legal Processes: Stability and Change, Islamic Law." Unpublished paper delivered at the Annual Meeting of the American Political Science Association, Chicago, Illinois, September 9–12, 1964.

Likhovski, Eliahu.
"Can the Knesset Adopt a Constitution Which Will Be The 'Supreme Law of the Land'?" *Israel Law Review,* Vol. 4, No. 1 (January 1969), pp. 61–69.

Litvin, Baruch, comp. and Sidney B. Hoenig, ed.
Jewish Identity: Modern Responsa and Opinions on the Registration of Children of Mixed Marriages. New York: Philipp Feldheim, Inc., 1965.

Livneh, Eliezer.
"The Elections in Israel." *Midstream,* Vol. 12, No. 1 (January 1966), pp. 48–55.

Louvish, Misha, ed.
Facts About Israel: 1968. Jerusalem: Information Division, Ministry for Foreign Affairs, 1968.

———.
Facts About Israel: 1969. Jerusalem: Information Division, Ministry for Foreign Affairs, Keter Books, 1969.

Marmorstein, Emile.
Heaven at Bay: The Jewish Kulturkampf in the Holy Land. London: Oxford University Press, 1969.

Miller, Irving.
Israel: The Eternal Ideal. New York: Farrar, Straus and Cudahy, 1955.

Peretz, Don.
"Reflections on Israel's Fourth Parliamentary Elections." *Middle East Journal,* Vol. 14, No. 1 (November 1959), pp. 15–27.

266

Prittie, Terence.
Israel: Miracle in the Desert. New York: Frederick A. Praeger, Inc., 1967.

Rackman, Emanuel.
Israel's Emerging Constitution: 1948–51. New York: Columbia University Press, 1955.

Revusky, Abraham.
The Histadrut: A Labor Commonwealth in the Making. New York: New York League for Labor Palestine, 1938.

Rubinstein, Amnon.
"Israel's Piecemeal Constitution." In *Studies in Israel Legislative Problems, Scripta Hierosolymitana,* Vol. 16, edited by G. Tedeschi and U. Yadin. Jerusalem: The Hebrew University, 1966.

————.
"Law and Religion in Israel." *Israel Law Review,* Vol. 2, No. 3 (July 1967), pp. 380–414.

————.
"Hectic Aftermath to Dull Elections." *Hadassah Magazine,* Vol. 51, No. 4 (December 1969), pp. 15, 31.

Rubinstein, Aryeh.
"Israel's Integration Problem." *Midstream,* Vol. 9, No. 1 (March 1963), pp. 45–59.

Sachar, Howard Morley.
The Course of Modern Jewish History. New York: Dell Publishing Company, 1963.

Sacher, Harry.
Israel: The Establishment of a State. London: George Weidenfeld and Nicolson, 1952.

Sachs, Dan.
"Mapam Joins the Alignment." *Middle East Monthly,* Vol. 12, No. 1 (January 1969), pp. 38–40.

Safran, Nadav.
The United States and Israel. Cambridge: Harvard University Press, 1963.

————.
From War to War: The Arab-Israeli Confrontation, 1948–1967. New York: Pegasus, 1969.

Salpeter, Eliahu.
"Israel Knesset Elections." *Middle Eastern Affairs,* Vol. 12, No. 9 (November 1961), pp. 262–268.

Seligman, Lester G.
Leadership in a New Nation: Political Development in Israel. New York: Atherton Press, A Division of Prentice-Hall, Inc., 1964.

Shiloh, Isaac S.
"Marriage and Divorce in Israel." *Israel Law Review,* Vol. 5, No. 4 (October 1970), pp. 479–498.

Shulewitz, Malka Hillel.
"B'nei Israel versus The Rabbinate." *Jewish Frontier,* Vol. 30, No. 9 (October 1963), pp. 7–11.

Smith, Donald E.
India as a Secular State. Princeton: Princeton University Press, 1963.

———.
Religion and Politics in Burma. Princeton: Princeton University Press, 1965.

Smith, Herbert.
"Israel Elections, 1969." Mimeographed. New York: The Foreign Affairs Department, The American Jewish Committee, n.d.

Smith, Wilfred Cantwell.
Islam in Modern History. Princeton: Princeton University Press, 1957.

State of Israel, Central Bureau of Statistics.
Statistical Abstract of Israel 1965, No. 16. Israel: Jerusalem Academic Press Ltd., 1965.

———.
Statistical Abstract of Israel 1967, No. 18. Israel: The Government Press, 1967.

State of Israel, The Supreme Court.
Judgment: *High Court Application of Oswald Rufeison v. The Minister of the Interior* (Jerusalem: The Ministry of Justice, 1963).

Stein, Leonard.
The Balfour Declaration. New York: Simon and Schuster, 1961.

"Symposium: Can a Unified Code of Religious Customs be Introduced in Israel?" *Iggeret LaGolah,* No. 64 (September-October 1957), pp. 20–22.

von der Mehden, Fred R.
Religion and Nationalism in Southeast Asia: Burma, Indonesia, The Philippines. Madison: The University of Wisconsin Press, 1963.

Warhaftig, Zerah.
The Yeshivah in Israel. Jerusalem: Ministry of Religious Affairs, The Government Printer, n.d.

Weisbord, Robert G.
African Zion: The Attempt to Establish A Jewish Colony in the East African Protectorate, 1903–1905. Philadelphia: The Jewish Publication Society of America, 1968.

Weiss-Rosmarin, Trude.
"Comments and Opinions." *Jewish Spectator,* Vol. 28, No. 8 (October 1963), pp. 3–8.

Weizmann, Chaim.
Trial and Error: The Autobiography of Chaim Weizmann. New York: Harper & Brothers, 1949.

Werner, Alfred.
"Israel's Zealots in Gabardine: The Guardians of the City." *Commentary,* Vol. 11, No. 1 (January 1951), pp. 61–67.

Yadin, Uri.
"Reflections on a New Law of Succession." *Israel Law Review,* Vol. 1, No. 1 (January 1966), pp. 132–141.

Zander, Hannelore.
"The Israeli Draft Constitution." *Common Cause,* Vol. 3 (August 1949), pp. 44–47.

Zborowski, Mark, and Elizabeth Herzog.
Life Is With People: The Culture of the Shtetl. New York: Schocken Books, 1962.

Zidon, Asher.
Knesset: The Parliament of Israel. New York: Herzl Press, 1967.

Zinger, Zvi.
"Public Services on the Sabbath." In *A Treasury of "Tradition,"* edited by Norman Lamm and Walter S. Wurzburger. New York: Hebrew Publishing Company, 1967.

Zucker, Norman L.
"Israel's Multipartyism." *Jewish Spectator,* Vol. 27, No. 3 (March 1962), pp. 18–22.

————.
"Israel's Politics: Retrospect and Prospect." *Jewish Frontier,* Vol. 29, No. 4 (May 1962), pp. 12–16.

Zwergbaum, Aaron.
"The Civil Marriage Controversy in Israel." *Congress Bi-Weekly,* Vol. 30, No. 15 (November 4, 1963), pp. 18–20.

Encyclopedias

Encyclopedia of the Jewish Religion. Edited by R. J. Zwi Werblowsky and Geoffrey Wigoder. New York: Holt, Rinehart & Winston, Inc., 1966.

Jewish Encyclopedia. Edited by Isidor Singer. New York: Funk and Wagnalls Company, 1903.

Standard Jewish Encyclopedia. Edited by Cecil Roth. 3rd ed., rev. New York: Doubleday and Company, Inc., 1966.

Newspapers and Periodicals

Israel Digest

Jerusalem Post

Jerusalem Post Weekly, Overseas Edition

New York Times

Index

Academies, talmudic, 77–78, 138–139
Achad Ha-Am, 228
quoted in Brother Daniel ruling, 185, 187
Achdut ha-Avodah party
ideology and electoral history of, 44–45
and Jewish consciousness program, 142
and Pork Prohibition Law, 54–55
Agranat, Justice Shimon, and Shalit case, 192, 197
Agudat Israel party
on Bene Israelites, 117–118
and Chief Rabbinate, 77, 84
electoral history of, 46, 49
opposition to constitution, 65, 67, 69
philosophy of, 47–48, 50, 57, 214
schools of, 126, 128, 132–133, 134, 135–136, 136–137
and Shapira compromise, 201, 205–206
and status quo agreement, 51–52
Agunah, in Judaic law, 112–113
Al-ha-Mishmar, on Shapira compromise, 201
Alignment, 44–45
and Shapira compromise, 206
Aliyah
defined, 15–16
First, 15–17
Second, 21–22
Third, 26
Fourth, 26–27
Fifth, 28
Katzenelson on, 228–229
Alkalai, Rabbi Yehudah, 10, 11
American Committee for Safe-

guarding Human Dignity in Israel, 166–168, 168
American Council for Judaism, 188
Anatomy and Pathology Law, 165–169
Anglo-American Committee on Inquiry (1946), 33
Anti-Semitism, 12, 12–13, 14, 17, 19, 21, 28, 32–33
Arlosoroff, Chaim, 43
Associated Legislative Rabbinate of America, 155–156
Autopsies, 165–169
Avnery, Uri, expelled from Knesset, 202

Balfour Declaration, 23–24
Bangladesh, state and religion in, 212
Bar-Ilan, Rabbi Meir, 139, 228
Bar-Ilan University, 101, 139
Barkatt, Reuven, 202
Bar-Yehudah, Israel
and Brother Daniel question, 180–181
and "Who is a Jew?" question, 172–173, 173–174, 175, 176
Basic Laws, 70, 71
Basle Program, 18
Baths, ritual, 79
Bene Israel, 8–9
history of, 115–116
and "Who is a Jew?" question, 116–120
Ben-Gurion, David, 228
appointment of Toledano, 80–81, 82, 178
and constitution, 67–68
and education, 131, 132
on MacDonald White Paper, 31
and military, 148–149, 249
and political parties, 43, 45, 51

271

281

Weizmann, Chaim, 228
  on Churchill White Paper, 25
  and East Africa proposal, 20–21
  as president, 40
  Zionist activities of, 22
Who is a Jew Amendment, 215
Witkon, Justice Alfred, Shalit decision of, 193
Wizo, 70
Wolffsohn, David, 19, 21
Women
  conscription of, 65, 148–151
  equality of, 66, 69–70, 104
Women's Equal Rights Law, 104, 216
Woodhead Partition Commission, report of, 29
World Union for Progressive Judaism. *See* Judaism, Reform
World Zionist Organization, 17, 19, 19–20, 21, 22, 25, 125

Yemenites, education of children of, 129–131
Yeshivot, financing of, 78–79
Yishuv
  education in, 124–128
  history of, 15–17, 21–22, 22–23, 25–27, 28, 31–32
  Mapai in, 43
  political organization of, 38–39
Yosef, Rabbi Ovadia, elected Chief Rabbi, 86
Yoseph, Dov, 26, 43

Zeidman, Helen, 252–253
Zim Israel Navigation Company. *See* S.S. *Shalom*
Zionism
  Jewish opposition to, 19
  labor, 21–22, 26, 43

  political, 10, 13, 14, 15, 17, 18, 19–20, 24
  religious, 10
  Zionist Congresses, 18, 19–20, 20–21